George Kalendis

Partners for Peace

edited by George J. Lankevich

1. *The United Nations under Trygve Lie, 1945–1953* by Anthony Gaglione, 2001.
2. *The United Nations under Dag Hammarskjöld, 1953–1961* by Peter B. Heller, 2001.
3. *The United Nations under U Thant, 1961–1971* by Bernard J. Firestone, 2001.
4. *The United Nations under Kurt Waldheim, 1972–1981* by James Daniel Ryan, 2001.
5. *The United Nations under Javier Pérez de Cuéllar, 1982–1991* by George J. Lankevich, 2001.
6. *The United Nations under Boutros Boutros-Ghali, 1992–1997* by Stephen F. Burgess, 2001.

The United Nations under Boutros Boutros-Ghali, 1992–1997

Stephen F. Burgess

Partners for Peace, No. 6

The Scarecrow Press, Inc.
Lanham, Maryland, and London
2001

SCARECROW PRESS, INC.

Published in the United States of America
by Scarecrow Press, Inc.
4720 Boston Way, Lanham, Maryland 20706
www.scarecrowpress.com

4 Pleydell Gardens, Folkestone
Kent CT20 2DN, England

British Library Cataloguing in Publication Information Available

Library of Congress Cataloging-in-Publication Data

Burgess, F. Stephen, 1952–
    The United Nations under Boutros Boutros-Ghali, 1992–1997 / Stephen Burgess.
        p. cm. — (Partners for peace ; v. 6)
    Includes bibliographical references and index.
    ISBN 0-8108-3703-X (alk. paper)
        1. United Nations—History. 2. International police—History. 3. World politics—1989–
    I. Title. II. Series.

 JZ4984.5 .B87 2001
 341.23'09'049—dc21

                                                    2001049238

⊖™ The paper used in this publication meets the minimum requirements of
American National Standard for Information Sciences—Permanence of
Paper for Printed Library Materials, ANSI/NISO Z39.48-1992.
Manufactured in the United States of America.

Areas of Interest during Boutros Boutros-Ghali's Term

Contents

List of Abbreviations/Acronyms   ix

Preface   xv

1   An Agenda for Peace   1

2   Success in Complex Missions:
      Cambodia and Mozambique   19

3   Success at Restoring Democracy:
      Central America and Haiti   39

4   Failure: Angola and Somalia   59

5   Genocide: Bosnia and Rwanda   81

6   Sovereignty Eroded? Iraq, Arms Control, and
      Human Rights   117

7   The Mega-Conferences: Rio, Vienna, Cairo,
      Copenhagen, and Beijing   141

8   The United States Turns Away from the UN   173

9   Conclusion: The UN Redefined   195

Appendix A United Nations Members   211

Appendix B Excerpt from the Charter of the United Nations   213

viii   Contents

Chronology   215

Bibliography   245

Index   267

About the Author   279

List of Abbreviations/Acronyms

ANC	African National Congress of South Africa
ARENA	*Alianza Republica Nacionalista*
ASEAN	Association of Southeast Asian Nations
BADR-2000	medium-range ballistic missile
CEDAW	Convention for the Elimination of All Forms of Discrimination Against Women
CIS	Commonwealth of Independent States
COPAZ	National Commission for the Consolidation of Peace (El Salvador)
CSCE	Conference on Security and Cooperation in Europe
CSW	Commission on the Status of Women
CTBT	Comprehensive Nuclear Test Ban Treaty
CWC	Chemical Weapons Convention
DAW	Division for the Advancement of Women
DMZ	demilitarized zone
DPI	UN Department of Public Information
DPKO	UN Department of Peacekeeping Operations
DRC	Democratic Republic of the Congo (Congo-Kinshasa)
EC	European Community
ECLA	UN Economic Commission for Latin America
ECOMOG	ECOWAS Cease-Fire Monitoring Group in Liberia and Sierra Leone
ECOSOC	UN Economic and Social Council
ECOWAS	Economic Community of West African States
EU	European Union
FAA	Armed Forces of Angola
FADM	Armed Forces for the Defense of Mozambique
FAR	Rwandan Armed Forces (until 1994)

FLEC	Liberation Front of the Enclave of Cabinda
FMLN	*Frente Farabundo Marti para la Liberacion Nacionale* (El Salvador)
FNLA	National Liberation Front of Angola
FAO	Food and Agriculture Organization of the UN
FRELIMO	Front for the Liberation of Mozambique
FRODEBU	Democratic Front of Burundi
FUNCINPEC	Front for an Independent, Neutral, Peaceful, and Cooperative Cambodia
FYROM	Former Yugoslav Republic of Macedonia
G-7	Group of Seven
G-77	Group of 77
GA	General Assembly
GAO	U.S. General Accounting Office
GATT	General Agreement on Tariffs and Trade
GEF	Global Environmental Facility
GFLS	Group of Frontline States (southern Africa)
IAEA	International Atomic Energy Agency
ICBL	International Campaign to Ban Land Mines
ICFY	International Conference on the Former Yugoslavia
ICITAP	International Criminal Investigative Training Assistance Program (Haiti)
ICJ	International Court of Justice
ICPD	International Conference on Population and Development
ICRC	International Committee of the Red Cross
IFOR	NATO Implementation Force in Bosnia
IGO	International Governmental Organization
ILO	International Labor Organization
IMF	International Monetary Fund
INSTRAW	International Research and Training Institute for the Advancement of Women
JDF	Japanese Defense Force
JNA	Yugoslav National Army
KFOR	Kosovo Implementation Force
MICIVIH	Human Rights Monitoring Mission in Haiti
MINUGUA	UN Verification Mission in Guatemala
MINURSO	UN Mission for the Referendum in Western Sahara

MIPONUH	Civilian Police Mission in Haiti
MNF	multinational force (Haiti)
MONUA	UN Observer Mission in Angola
MONUC	UN Organization Mission in the Democratic Republic of the Congo
MPLA	Popular Movement for the Liberation of Angola
NAM	Non-aligned Movement
NATO	North Atlantic Treaty Organization
NGO	non-governmental organization
NIEO	New International Economic Order
NPT	Nuclear Non-proliferation Treaty
NRA	National Resistance Army of Uganda
OAS	Organization of American States
OAU	Organization of African Unity
OCHA	UN Office for the Coordination of Humanitarian Affairs
OECD	Organization for Economic Cooperation and Development
ONUC	UN Operation in the Congo
ONUCA	UN Observer Group in Central America
ONUMOZ	UN Peacekeeping Mission, Mozambique
ONUSAL	UN Observer Mission in El Salvador
OSCE	Organization for Security and Cooperation in Europe
PDD-25	U.S. Presidential Defense Directive 25
PLO	Palestine Liberation Organization
POLISARIO	Popular Front for the Liberation of Western Sahara
RENAMO	Mozambique National Resistance Movement
RPA	Rwandan Patriotic Army
RPF	Rwandan Patriotic Front
RUF	Revolutionary United Front (Sierra Leone)
SADCC	Southern African Development Coordination Conference
SADC	Southern African Development Community
SNC	Supreme National Council (Cambodia)
SOC	State of Cambodia
SRSG	Special Representative of the Secretary-General
TNC	transnational corporation
TRC	South African Truth and Reconciliation

	Commission
UNAMIC	UN Advance Mission in Cambodia
UNAMIR	UN Assistance Mission for Rwanda
UNAVEM I, II, III	UN Verification Missions in Angola
UNCED	UN Conference on the Environment and Development, 1992
UNCRO	UN Confidence Restoration Operation (Croatia)
UNCTAD	UN Conference on Trade and Development
UNDOF	UN Disengagement Observer Force (Israel-Syria)
UNDP	UN Development Programme
UNEF I, II	UN Emergency Force (Israel-Egypt)
UNEP	UN Environment Programme
UNESCO	UN Educational, Scientific, and Cultural Organization
UNFICYP	UN Peacekeeping Force in Cyprus
UNFPA	UN Fund for Population Activities
UNGOMAP	UN Good Office Mission in Afghanistan and Pakistan
UNCHR	UN Commission for Refugees
UNHCR	UN High Commission for Refugees
UNICEF	UN Children's Fund
UNIFEM	Voluntary Fund for the UN Decade for Women
UNIFIL	UN Interim Force in Lebanon
UNIKOM	UN Iraq-Kuwait Observer Mission
UNIIMOG	UN Iran-Iraq Military Observer Group
UNITA	Union for the Total Independence of Angola
UNITAF	Unified Task Force on Somalia (Operation Restore Hope)
UNMIC	UN Advance Mission in Cambodia
UNMOGIP	UN Military Observer Group in India and Pakistan
UNMOT	UN Observer Mission in Tajikistan
UNOMIG	UN Observer Mission in Georgia
UNMIH	UN Mission in Haiti
UNOMIL	UN Observer Mission in Liberia
UNOMSA	UN Observer Mission in South Africa
UNOMUR	UN Observer Mission in Uganda and Rwanda
UNOSOM I, II	UN Operation in Somalia
UNOVEN	UN Observer Mission to Verify the Electoral

	Process in Nicaragua
UNPREDEP	UN Preventive Deployment Force (Macedonia)
UNPROFOR	UN Protection Force in the former Yugoslavia
UNSCOM	UN Special Commission for the Disarmament of Iraq
UNSMIH	UN Support Mission in Haiti
UNTAC	UN Transitional Assistance Authority in Cambodia
UNTAG	UN Transitional Assistance Group (Namibia)
UNTSO	UN Truce Supervision Organization (Palestine)
UNPRONA	Unity for National Progress (Burundi)
URNG	Guatemalan National Revolutionary Unity
WFP	World Food Programme
WHO	World Health Organization
WTO	World Trade Organization
ZNG	Croatian National Guard

Preface

The period from 1992 to 1997 was one of the most momentous in the twentieth century. The global system was in the midst of a tectonic shift, from a bipolar to a unipolar world. The previous systemic transformation had occurred during an even more cataclysmic period, the Second World War, and had given birth to the United Nations. With the collapse of the Soviet Union at the end of 1991, the world featured only one dominant power for the first time in centuries. With unipolarity, the United States grasped the opportunity to lead smaller powers and the United Nations toward the U.S. vision of global concord. U.S. leadership during the 1991 Gulf War led many to think that the UN could fulfill the original promise of the 1945 Charter and function as a collective security body. A strong sense of optimism emerged in President George Bush's January 1991 declaration of a "New World Order" on the eve of the war with Iraq. A new sprit of humanitarianism was evident in "Operation Restore Hope," the December 1992 intervention to aid the people of Somalia.

This book concerns the UN during the transformative period of the 1990s. During this period, states employed the UN with the aim of accomplishing a wide variety of demanding and complex tasks. Consequently, a time of trial-and-error began. By 1997, it had become clear which tasks the UN was capable of performing and those that were beyond its capabilities. Secondarily, the book is about UN Secretary-General Boutros Boutros-Ghali and the imprint that he attempted to make on the UN. Of the seven secretaries-general, Boutros-Ghali was the most determined to guide the UN toward greater autonomy and power. Initially, his efforts bore fruit, especially as he received support from the United States in a number of different operations. However, after the October 1993 killings of eighteen U.S. Army Rangers in a UN operation in Somalia and subsequent widespread recriminations in the United States against the UN, American political leaders turned against Boutros-

Ghali and the UN. Antagonism toward the secretary-general and the UN was reinforced by the 1994 "Republican revolution" in the U.S. Congress. Subsequently, the United States rejected Boutros-Ghali and his ambitious vision and distanced itself from the UN.

Given the contemporary nature of the topic, an historical narrative is inappropriate in the writing of such a book. Instead, political analysis is employed, which focuses on identifying and explaining UN success and failure, particularly in the area of peace and security. By describing and explaining success and failure, the book arrives at predictions of what the UN is capable of doing in the future and its limitations.

The starting point for the book is *An Agenda for Peace*, the 1992 blueprint for expanded UN activity in the area of peace and security. Presented by Secretary-General Boutros-Ghali and endorsed by the United States and other nations, *An Agenda for Peace* was a seminal document. It outlined ambitious aims and intentions, as well as the modus operandi, for the UN in preventing and resolving conflict and in keeping and building peace. *An Agenda for Peace* provided an intellectual basis for multi-dimensional peacekeeping operations in Cambodia and Mozambique and for the failure of "armed peacemaking" in Somalia.

The remainder of the first chapter introduces the other agenda of the UN, specifically in promoting "global regimes." Environmental protection and human rights regimes had attained widespread acceptance by the 1990s and became manifest in the UN "mega-conferences" of 1992-95. At these conferences, disputes erupted over the content of the regimes and the obligations of states. In particular, countries of the South focused on development, as opposed to the ecological concerns of the North. Furthermore, some leaders in the South even objected to *An Agenda for Peace* in that it detracted attention and resources away from national development efforts.

The second and third chapters proceed to examine successful cases of UN peacekeeping. Operations in Cambodia, Mozambique, Central America, and Haiti demonstrate what the UN can achieve, especially in the areas of "multi-dimensional" peacekeeping and peace building. These successes and others in the 1990s turned out to be more significant than many had thought possible beforehand. The fourth chapter turns to cases of failure, specifically in Angola and Somalia, and explains why the UN was not successful. Chapter 5 deals with two cases, Bosnia and Rwanda, where failure and its tragic consequences were more egregious than in Somalia and Angola. These two cases of ethnic cleansing and genocide have come to haunt the UN and will continue to do so well into the twenty-first century. The chapter also deals with the establishment of the international criminal tribunals for the former Yugoslavia and Rwanda and the related initiative to create an International Criminal Court.

The first five chapters, which focus on conflict management and peacekeeping lead logically to chapter 6 and an analysis of UN efforts to compel Iraq to surrender its weapons of mass destruction and to develop respect for human rights. UN intervention in the internal affairs of Iraq is used as a case with which to analyze more broadly the impact which the UN and global regimes have made on the erosion of state sovereignty. Included in the analysis are other examples of interventions in the name of human rights, humanitarianism, and arms control. The book then turns to issues of globalism and development. Chapter 7 deals with the "mega-conferences" of the 1992-95 period. These conferences, including Rio on the environment, Vienna on human rights, Cairo on population, Copenhagen on social development, and Beijing on women, defined the UN during the mid-1990s as much as its major peace operations. A theme of chapters 6 and 7 concerns the development of international regimes pertaining to global issues.

Chapter 8 focuses on the UN's decline and redefinition during the 1994-97 period, when U.S. antagonism toward Boutros-Ghali and the UN was strong. The chapter covers the 1994 Republican revolution and the momentum toward unilateralism, which helped push the Clinton administration into confrontation with Boutros-Ghali. Also covered in this chapter are moves away from conflict management by the UN and toward "regionalization," particularly embodied by U.S. reliance on NATO (and Croatia) to impose peace in Bosnia in 1995. In spite of the setbacks during the 1994-97 period, the book concludes that the UN passed through a trial by fire and arrived in a stronger position in 1997 than before 1992. Now, the UN is grounded in a more solid foundation and possesses a clearer vision of its role in the world.

Acknowledgments

The seeds for this book were planted several years ago, when I was involved in the planning and execution of a conference on "The United Nations at Fifty," at Hofstra University, New York, as well as in mounting a photographic exhibit. At the conference, I agreed to a request to write a book about the UN under Boutros-Ghali, as part of a planned "Partners for Peace Series." I acknowledge the assistance of series editor, George Lankevich, and conference co-convenor, Bernard Firestone.

I was chosen to write the book because of my association with the UN during the 1990s. Each January, from 1993 until 1998, I led a workshop, "The United States and the United Nations." During the workshop, personnel from the UN Secretariat, non-governmental organizations (NGOs), and various missions to the UN gave briefings to students on a wide range of issues, which provided considerable material for this book. The years in which I led the workshop were especially exciting, as the UN was engaged in an array of activities, including major peacekeeping operations and the "mega-conferences." I acknowledge the assistance of the UN Department of Public Information in arranging briefings that provided material for the book. In addition, I thank personnel from the UN Secretariat, ambassadors and their assistants to the UN, and NGO officials for their generosity in providing briefings.

From 1992 to 1998, my spouse, Janet Beilstein, worked for the UN Secretariat and, from 1994 to 1998, she was employed as a Social Affairs Officer in the Division for the Advancement of Women, which provided me with the opportunity to collaborate with her on a number of projects. The subjects included women in political decision making, women in peacekeeping, and the problems of rural women. In addition, I provided assistance and occasional advice, especially through much of 1995, in preparation for the Fourth World Conference on Women in Beijing. Furthermore, I assisted her during annual meetings of the Commission on the Status of Women and the Convention for the Elimination of All Forms of Discrimination Against Women (CEDAW). Therefore, I am grateful for the conduit that Janet Beilstein provided to the UN and the considerable assistance that she gave me in the writing and rewriting of this book.

I thank Paul Diehl, a principal scholar in the field of international politics, for reading a preliminary draft of the manuscript and providing helpful suggestions. I am grateful to Barbara Crossette, UN Bureau Chief of *The New York Times,* for examining a later draft and providing encouraging comments. I thank Roger Coate, a leading scholar in the study of the UN and international organization, for reading a draft and for providing encouragement. I appreciate the guidance and encouragement in my research and scholarship provided to me by Karen Mingst, Jeffrey Herbst, John Harbeson, Donald Rothchild, David Sorenson, Scott Gates, and Jacek Kugler. A special note of thanks goes to Michael Lucivero, who supported me as a research assistant in the initial stages of this project. Also of assistance were Chris Burlingame, Jaime van Dyke, and Katharine Dubin.

Disclaimer

After review for security and policy, it has been found that this book does not discuss or include classified material and does not discuss current United States Air Force or United States Department of Defense policy. Therefore, the book has been cleared for security and policy.

1

An Agenda for Peace

In 1993, the United Nations was engaged in massive and complex operations to bring peace and reconstruction to Somalia, as well as to Cambodia, Mozambique, and El Salvador. Then, on October 3, 1993, eighteen U.S. Army Rangers died at the hands of warlord forces in Mogadishu, Somalia. Immediately, American politicians publicly denounced the UN Somalia mission and questioned U.S. involvement in UN operations. Suddenly, U.S. policymakers developed an aversion to foreign interventions, especially those that aimed at peace enforcement and rebuilding shattered states. Six months later, in April 1994, the UN did not intervene but, instead, withdrew as the genocidal killings of more than 800,000 Rwandans continued for three agonizing months. As the genocide unfolded, the United States and other states on the UN Security Council resisted acknowledging that genocide was occurring.

In September 1995, the Beijing Conference on Women marked the culmination of a series of five "mega-conferences," from 1992 to 1995, involving thousands of participants from all parts of the world, which dealt with five different sets of major global issues. By the following year, 1996, the UN was nearly bankrupt, with limited resources to help implement the "platforms for action" of the mega-conferences or to launch major projects and with few prospects for any further mega-conferences.

During the secretary-generalship of Boutros Boutros-Ghali, the UN reached a high water mark where it appeared that the world body would fulfill its ambitious 1945 founding goals. In 1992-93, the UN appeared to be capable of maintaining peace through collective security, assisting the development of poorer, conflict-prone states, and promoting human rights. However, after the Mogadishu killings, the United States reduced its support for the UN, and the organization declined in importance. By 1997, the UN appeared capable of performing many tasks, but less than was envisaged in 1992-93.

This chapter introduces the UN under Boutros-Ghali by examining the ambitious visions for the UN in 1992-93 of the principal actors, including the secretary-general and the United States. It traces the origins of those visions and considers the ramifications for the UN. Of particular concern are the changes that occurred, particularly as the United States and other nations came to realize the limitations of the world body.

The UN before the End of the Cold War

The dynamics of the UN were dramatically different during the Cold War. Due to the U.S.-Soviet confrontation, the Security Council was largely ineffectual, and the collective security function of the UN lay dormant. Instead, UN blue-helmeted peacekeepers or observers were occasionally dispatched by the Security Council to maintain cease-fires. Because of the Cold War, there were many conflicts in which the UN was not allowed to intervene. In the conflicts in which it became involved, the UN could do little or nothing to resolve them.

Before the end of the Cold War, most of the conflicts occurred in the South (Africa, Asia, and Latin America). Often, surrogates fought "proxy" wars, with pro-Soviet guerrilla forces (self-proclaimed "revolutionary" movements) confronting pro-U.S. regimes and with pro-U.S. forces (self-styled "freedom fighters") fighting pro-Soviet states. In these conflicts, it was almost impossible for the UN Security Council to become involved. In the communist world, totalitarian dictatorships managed to suppress rival nationalisms and prevented the outbreak of conflicts.

Because of the Cold War stalemate in the Security Council, the General Assembly became the more active and visible branch of the UN. As an emerging majority in the General Assembly, the South's "Group of 77" and Non-Aligned Movement (NAM) pursued their interests. The Group of 77 sought to increase the flow of development resources and create a New International Economic Order. The NAM allied with Communist states in campaigns to end apartheid, which led to the suspension of South Africa from the General Assembly from 1974-94, and to achieve self-determination for the Palestinians, leading to the General

Assembly's "Zionism is racism" resolution. Therefore, the United States and the West, which had championed the creation of the UN, steadily lost influence in the world body. In the early 1980s, relations between the United States and the UN reached a low point, as President Ronald Reagan and his administration launched a counterattack against the increasing influence of the South and communist states.

A second major trend was the rise of what can be termed "globalism" during the 1970s. Driven by non-governmental organizations (NGOs) and progressive West and North European states (which had achieved high levels of material prosperity), globalists promoted universal application of human rights and women's rights, as well as environmental conservation and management of resources and population growth. The movement gave rise to a series of UN conferences in the 1970s and to the strengthening or creation of UN agencies to deal with global issues. The Group of 77 countries came to support the conferences, attracted especially by the lure of greater development resources. As conferences convened and as globalism gathered momentum, the two superpowers pushed their respective agendas. In particular, the United States insisted on the acceptance of civil and political rights as paramount, while the communist states and the Group of 77 promoted economic and social rights.

The End of the Cold War and the UN in Transition

In 1985, Mikhail Gorbachev became premier of the Soviet Union and began to reach out to the West in order to gain assistance to halt his country's decline. In response, the Reagan administration became less confrontational and more moderate. In 1986, the administration allowed pro-U.S. dictators to be overthrown in the Philippines and Haiti, and Congress reversed Reagan's policies toward South Africa and Nicaragua. By 1987, the Soviet Union was cooperating with the United States in resolving protracted conflicts and reducing the number of weapons of mass destruction.

In 1987, Gorbachev reversed long-standing Soviet policy and openly called for an expanded role for the Security Council and the secretary-general in conflict management in order to make the UN an effective peacemaking body.[1] Gorbachev signaled to the United States that the council could be reactivated and that the secretary-general could be called upon to assist in the resolution of long-standing Cold War conflicts. Suddenly, U.S.-Soviet cooperation elevated the council to its intended place as the most active and visible UN body. Forty years of ideological

stalemate in the council ended, and a burst of activity commenced to end
long-standing conflicts. Vetoes became outmoded and were replaced by
consensus-building and long council meetings. Also, the secretary-
general's role changed, as he became a more active servant of the council, instead of an autonomous peacemaker. From 1986, the council
increased the peacekeeping budget each year, and, by the time Boutros-
Ghali arrived as secretary-general in 1992, the peacekeeping budget had
out-stripped the regular UN budget.

When Javier Pérez de Cuéllar assumed the office of secretary-general
in 1982, he became the ineffectual figurehead of a body that was in
serious danger of disintegration. Less than five years later, the United
States, Soviet Union, and other states on the Security Council were
calling upon him to increase his role in conflict-management activities.
Besides helping to organize a wave of new peacekeeping missions, he
became a more energetic peacemaker, by using his "good offices" and
fact-finding missions and by engaging in mediation. The secretary-
general's success in negotiating, especially in 1987 and 1988, an end to
the Iran-Iraq War was a tribute to his diplomatic skill and, particularly,
his ability to gain Iran's trust by creating an aura of impartiality and
autonomy from the United States. Subsequently, the notion grew that the
secretary-general could become an effective peacemaker if he was
autonomous from the United States and other council members. Autonomy and leadership in peacemaking were fundamental concepts for
Boutros-Ghali and were embodied in *An Agenda for Peace.*

While Pérez de Cuéllar's care in distancing himself from the United
States helped bring success in negotiations with Iran, the conditions for a
settlement were based upon U.S. power. At the time of the negotiations,
the U.S. Navy headed a coalition of forces and constrained Iran from
escalating the war against oil tankers in the Persian Gulf. The United
States had helped to maintain a balance of power between Iran and Iraq,
which had led the two belligerents to fight to a state of mutual exhaustion. Furthermore, U.S.-Soviet cooperation in the Security Council
provided the secretary-general with powerful backing in his mediation
efforts. Subsequently, the secretary-general was also successful in
negotiating the Soviet exit from Afghanistan, after Gorbachev had
signaled the Soviet desire to withdraw without losing face.

In December 1988, the Nobel Peace Prize was awarded to the UN
"blue helmets," mainly for their performance in observing the cease-fires
that ended the Iran-Iraq War (UNIIMOG) and the Afghan War
(UNGOMAP). The award was timely, because it presaged a much-
expanded UN role in peacekeeping operations. In 1989, the UN began

overseeing the withdrawal of Cuban troops from Angola (UNAVEM I) and the transition to independence in Namibia (UNTAG). The Angola-Namibia agreement had been negotiated by U.S. Assistant Secretary of State for African Affairs, Chester Crocker, and was implemented by UNAVEM I and UNTAG. The UNTAG operation paved the way for similarly ambitious multi-dimensional missions, involving peacekeeping and peace building and, occasionally, peace enforcement.

As a result of a rising number of new and complex missions, the work of the UN Secretariat expanded exponentially and led to the establishment of the Department of Peacekeeping Operations to manage them. The UN became involved in implementing peace agreements and keeping the parties committed to peace, as well as demilitarizing warring groups, observing human rights, and monitoring elections. Two essential indicators of the UN's rapidly increasing role in conflict management were annual increases in the peacekeeping budget, which grew from $230 million in 1988 to $3.61 billion in 1993 and the number of peacekeepers, which rose to a peak of more than 80,000 in 1993.[2]

Because of the Soviet about-face, the United States suddenly regained control over the UN through the Security Council. With a reinvigorated council, the United States forged cooperative links with the secretary-general and reversed its previous position of withholding resources from the UN. In 1989, the Bush administration began negotiations to resolve the UN budget deficit caused by the Kassebaum Amendment. Also, the Bush administration did not object as it continued to pay over 30 percent of an expanding peacekeeping budget.

As the Security Council revived, the influence of the South through the General Assembly diminished. The General Assembly and other UN agencies, such as UNESCO and ILO, ceased passing controversial resolutions (mainly aimed against Israel), as the Soviet Union moved away from supporting the NAM and began cooperating with the United States. In addition, the flow of resources to the South, including those from UN agencies diminished. UN operations in the South were constricted, as U.S. payments arrears began to impinge from the late 1980s onwards. Perversely, American arrears provided the United States with greater leverage over UN budget and staffing decisions. However, U.S. austerity efforts did not stop plans for several "mega-conferences" in various world capitals in the early 1990s.

The Gulf War, the UN, and the "New World Order"

The reassertion of U.S. dominance at the UN and the restoration of a UN-based peace and security regime reached an apogee with the Security Council's compliance with U.S. strategic objectives during the Gulf War (1990-91). Saddam Hussein's decision to send Iraqi forces into Kuwait in August 1990 provided the Bush administration with the opportunity to lead the council in employing UN Charter Chapter VII to endorse a U.S.-led collective security operation. Also, President Bush was able to use the UN as a forum to build a coalition to liberate Kuwait and ratchet up concerted pressure against Iraq. The council invoked Chapter VII first to impose sanctions on Iraq, then to authorize the use of force in what became a highly militarized collective security operation, and then to dictate post-war conditions to Iraq.

Between the launching of Operation Desert Shield in August 1990 and Operation Desert Storm in January 1991, the Soviet Union and China did little to stand in the way of the United States, as the Security Council passed resolution-after-resolution against Iraq. The secretary-general obligingly assumed a subsidiary role and observed strict guidelines set by the United States and the council in dealing with Iraq. UN cooperation during the Gulf crisis, the multilateral Operation Desert Shield, and the building of a coalition led President Bush to formulate his vision of a "new world order" and to proclaim it on the eve of Operation Desert Storm on January 16, 1991. In doing so, he expressed the determination to utilize the UN as much as possible in the maintenance of peace and security. President Bush envisaged the UN as a major vehicle for defending international law and order and democratic regimes and for mounting humanitarian operations to alleviate suffering from man-made and natural disasters. Subsequently, the Bush administration involved the UN in resolving crises in the Middle East, the former Yugoslavia, and Haiti.

The Bush administration began to deploy U.S. forces in UN missions, well beyond their traditional role of preparing to fight the USSR. U.S. contingents were deployed to help start UN operations in Western Sahara and in the former Yugoslavia (including the preventive deployment operation in the Former Yugoslav Republic of Macedonia). Most significant was the employment of U.S. air power and troops for humanitarian missions. The first was Operation Provide Comfort to rescue and relieve Kurdish refugees in April-June 1991 in the wake of the Gulf War. The operation produced dramatic results, with relatively little cost in men and materiel. Air power and troops were also involved in flood relief for

Bangladesh and the rescue of Filipinos from a volcanic eruption. The U.S. military mounted Operation Provide Hope, which airlifted needed food supplies to the newly independent Russian Federation in the volatile winter of 1992.

The Election of Boutros Boutros-Ghali

In 1991, Javier Pérez de Cuéllar left his post as secretary-general after ten years of change. When he assumed the post in 1982, some observers were writing the UN's obituary. By the time he left, there was renewed hope for the world body and for its role in promoting world peace. However, the UN still faced imposing problems. With the disintegration of the Soviet Union in December 1991, the spotlight turned away from nuclear confrontation and toward a more complex set of problems. One problem were so-called "rogue states," such as North Korea, Iran, Iraq, and Serbia, and leaders, such as Saddam Hussein and Slobodan Milosevic, that sought to challenge principles of the UN Charter and President Bush's new world order. Another was the collapse of states, including the USSR and Yugoslavia, as well as Liberia, Somalia, and Zaire, and the rise of ethnic cleansing and warlords.

As 1991 drew to a close and with the UN basking in the euphoria of the Gulf War triumph, the surprisingly successful second term of Secretary-General Pérez de Cuéllar came to an end. The UN faced the task of choosing a new secretary-general as skilled diplomatically as the departing one. One criterion limited the search. Since three Europeans, an Asian and a Latin American had already served in the position, most states, especially those from the Group of 77, accepted that it was now "Africa's turn." In the autumn of 1991, Boutros Boutros-Ghali of Egypt and Bernard Chidzero of Zimbabwe emerged as the two African candidates.

As stipulated in the UN Charter, the Security Council began the search and selection process. With the end of the Cold War, the council did not have to weed out the candidates who were objectionable to the United States and the USSR. Instead, France stepped in and promoted the candidacy of Boutros-Ghali, especially since he was a francophone and francophile. The USSR also supported him, partly because he had served as head of the Egypt-USSR Friendship Association.[3]

The United States and Britain pursued other plausible candidates but did not oppose Boutros-Ghali. China had no objections. Once the Security Council decided in favor, the nomination passed to the General Assembly, where most members of the Group of 77, and, particularly, most Arab and African states, supported Boutros-Ghali. With widespread support, the General Assembly elected him as the sixth secretary-general on December 3, 1991.

The personality of Boutros-Ghali was to be central to the UN's fortunes during the mid-1990s. He arrived at the UN at age sixty-nine, with decades of service to Egypt as a diplomat and foreign policy official. His main claim to fame was his role in negotiations between 1977 and 1979, which led to Camp David Accords between Egypt and Israel. Boutros-Ghali achieved success as a diplomat, in spite of a character that, according to many reports, was "iconoclastic" and not well suited to the world of negotiations and compromise. He began his career as an academic and, to some observers, he became known as the "professor." Based upon his own research and experience in international affairs, Boutros-Ghali arrived at the UN with a well-developed vision and with the determination to proceed as he saw fit. He found it difficult to accept advice at variance with his own ideas and to change course when the necessity arose. Subsequently, Boutros-Ghali's personality made it difficult for him to sustain a cooperative working relationship with the United States and with other actors at the UN. He lacked the flexibility to change course when the need arose. In particular, the secretary-general's insistence on confronting Somalia's warlords helped to lead the UN and the United States down the road to disaster in 1993.

While Boutros-Ghali's long experience was an asset, it also meant that he carried a considerable amount of baggage. For example, from 1978 to 1991, he was responsible for maintaining good diplomatic relations for Egypt with Somalia's dictator, Siad Barre. A year after Siad Barre's overthrow, Boutros-Ghali became secretary-general and began to play the role of peacemaker with the warlord groups who had superseded Siad Barre. Remembering Boutros-Ghali's close relations with the deposed dictator led the Somali warlords to treat UN peacemaking efforts with suspicion and to greet his peacemaking trip to Mogadishu in January 1993 with violence.

Boutros-Ghali and *An Agenda for Peace*

On January 1, 1992, Boutros-Ghali began working as secretary-general and immediately faced several major tasks. Foremost was fulfilling the request by the Security Council, made at the end of January 1992, for a report on the present state and future direction of UN activities in maintaining international peace and security. The request came from an extraordinary meeting (the first ever held) of heads of state and government whose states held seats on the Security Council. The leaders gathered included U.S. President Bush, French President Mitterand, and British Prime Minister Major (who chaired), as well as the new President of Russia, Boris Yeltsin. The meeting was convened in order to consider new ways of using the Security Council and the UN to further international peace and security in the wake of the Gulf War and the Cold War. The leaders asked the secretary-general to produce a blueprint for preventing and ending conflicts, as well as for restoring and building peace.

The secretary-general assembled a task force to deliberate on the Security Council's request and produce an outline of the report. In May 1992, the report was drafted. In both the deliberative and drafting processes, the new secretary-general played an active and central role, pushing for a bold and controversial document. With *An Agenda for Peace* drafted, on June 17, 1992, he delivered the report to the Security Council, and, on September 15, 1992, Boutros-Ghali presented it to the General Assembly. The report sparked considerable debate, and the new secretary-general took center stage in those discussions.[4]

An Agenda for Peace went well beyond traditional conceptions of post-conflict peacekeeping, which had been the UN's major peace and security activity since 1948. It dealt with the entire conflict process, introducing the concepts of early warning, preventive deployment, and armed peacemaking (peace enforcement), as well as post-conflict peace building, to the UN lexicon. The proposal for an early warning system to assess threats to peace was revolutionary. The Secretariat's Department of Political Affairs and Department of Humanitarian Affairs, UNHCR, and other specialized agencies, and even ECOSOC were to be charged with monitoring inter-state frictions and the spillover of refugees and guerrillas from one country to another. Even more controversial was the idea of monitoring the internal situation within states to provide early warning of massive human rights abuses and impending civil war. States from the South strongly objected to early warning systems and preventive deployment, fearing the violation of their sovereignty by the UN and by other states.

The adoption and development of an early warning system would lead logically to preventive measures. *An Agenda for Peace* called for preventive diplomacy in which the UN and regional security organizations would be involved to help defuse crises. Even more controversial was the proposal for preventive deployment of UN forces to stop the outbreak of conflict and spillover to neighboring states. States from the South objected to the proposal, envisioning UN-endorsed intervention in their internal affairs.

An Agenda for Peace then considered peacemaking, including armed peacemaking (or peace enforcement), which was intended to stop wars that were beginning or already raging or breaking out again. This was both the most revolutionary and problematic part of the secretary-general's report. In considering the diplomatic process, the report proposed that authority devolve from the Security Council to the secretary-general who could mediate autonomously and to the General Assembly, which could initiate peace missions. Turning to diplomacy, Boutros-Ghali stated that "the good offices of the secretary-general may at times be employed most effectively when conducted independently of the deliberative bodies."[5]

Even more controversial was the proposal for the deployment of armed peacemaking (or peace enforcement) missions when implementation of a negotiated cease-fire agreement proved impossible. More specifically, the Military Staff Committee, called for in Article 47 of the UN Charter, was to be revived and strengthened, and given Chapter VII enforcement powers. To respond to emergencies, the UN would establish a rapid deployment force in order to enforce peace. By recommending peace enforcement and centralized control of units, the secretary-general expected to be granted unprecedented command authority to intervene and stop conflicts. This expectation is made clear in *An Agenda for Peace,* which states that, the deployment and operation of "on-call" peace-enforcement units "would, as in the case of peacekeeping forces, be under the command of the secretary-general."[6]

The proposal for peace enforcement authority and for a UN rapid reaction force provoked controversy and skepticism. Many states, especially those in the South, envisioned the scenario of UN forces, led by the secretary-general, taking sides and intervening against them. Subsequently, the UN did take sides, after prodding from Boutros-Ghali, in attempting to enforce peace in Somalia.

While the Bush administration tentatively accepted the proposal for UN-led peace enforcement, there were many strong unilateralists, who believed that the UN was seeking to command U.S. troops and supersede American sovereignty. The Nordic states, Canada, and other UN peacekeeping stalwarts feared that calls for peace enforcement would drown out demands for measured changes in traditional peacekeeping.[7]

Not as contentious, but still controversial, was the post-conflict peacekeeping section of *An Agenda for Peace.* The report dealt with the financial and material resources of peacekeeping. In order to expedite the dispatching of "blue helmets" to the field, the report called for states to designate forces that they would be willing to commit to traditional peacekeeping missions. In regard to financing, the report proposed various ways to bring greater stability and reliability. At the same time, the secretary-general acknowledged acceptance of the U.S. demand for financial restraint. Accordingly, the authorization and funding of peacekeeping missions would be more restrictive. A consequence of this bargain was the U.S. ability to constrain the UNAMIR mission to Rwanda and to block any mission to Burundi, while genocidal activities proceeded in both countries.

Post-conflict "peace building" appeared to be universally acceptable, involving disarmament and demobilization of fighters, mine clearance, and strengthening of administrative, political, and police structures. However, peace building also provoked controversy. Member states from the South feared that an emphasis on peace building would channel aid to post-conflict situations and divert it from long-term projects for fostering sustained socio-economic development. Another objection from the South focused on the emphasis in *An Agenda for Peace* on Western-style competitive electoral democracy in the building of peace. Some leaders in the South rejected the imposition of Western ideas and institutions in regions of the world that they asserted were culturally distinct.

Another innovative proposal in *An Agenda for Peace* was to increase cooperation between the Security Council and regional organizations in the area of peace and security. With the end of the Cold War and re-newed effectiveness of the council, it had become easier to implement Chapter VIII of the UN Charter, in which the council would provide approval for regional initiatives, as well as assistance. "Regionalization" would assist the UN goal of reducing the burden and expense of peacekeeping. The danger was that regional organizations would direct operations in a direction that would not be supported by the entire council. Such an eventuality occurred in Kosovo in March 1999, as NATO forged ahead to use force against Serbia without seeking approval from the council, thereby violating Chapter VIII, Article 53.

Both the Security Council and General Assembly spent many months considering and debating the proposals in *An Agenda for Peace*. Starting in October 1992, the council issued a series of statements that supported some, but not all of the proposals. The council supported and facilitated improved communications between the Secretariat and troop-contributing countries, so that the appropriate forces could be sent quickly where they were needed. In addition, the capacity in the Secretariat to plan and coordinate missions was improved, with an operations center and in-creased military staffing. The council issued statements supporting strengthened "fact-finding" for peacemaking; increased cooperation with regional organizations in conflict prevention and resolution; use of the Department of Humanitarian Affairs for prevention; and enhanced safety of peacekeeping personnel. The council voiced concerns about the use of sanctions, which harmed civilians and did not alter the behavior of leaders, and called for more effective targeting. In April 1993, the council issued a general statement on the various components of peace building. However, the council provided no specific proposals for strengthening the UN's capacity to build (and finance) peace. In regard to peacekeeping, the Security Council went well beyond previous statements and, particularly supported the right of peacekeepers to self-defense.[8]

The Security Council did not comment on the more controversial proposals for preventive deployment, peace enforcement, and command of peacekeeping and enforcement units by the secretary-general, and the right to take sides to preserve peacekeeping operations. The silence of the council on these issues reflected uncertainty and ambiguity, as well as the potential veto of China as a staunch supporter of sovereignty and opponent of UN intervention. While the Bush administration paid lip service to a "new world order" and Operation Desert Storm-style peace enforcement, the United States and its allies did not take any serious action to stop Bosnian Serb aggression and ethnic cleansing, starting in April 1992 and extending for more than three years. Furthermore, some defenders of traditional peacekeeping saw the proposals for enforcement as a threat to a vital function that the UN had performed very well for decades.

Regardless of Security Council reservations or other criticism, Boutros-Ghali forged ahead to implement controversial proposals for preventive deployment, peacemaking, and peace enforcement in *An Agenda for Peace*. In regard to peacemaking, he followed through on his claim that the secretary-general could be effective if he were more autonomous from the United States and the Security Council. Starting in mid-1992, Boutros-Ghali (and his Special Representatives) became involved in managing conflicts with limited reference back to the Security Council and the United States. As will be demonstrated in greater detail in chapter 4, Boutros-Ghali's personal efforts at mediation in Somalia proved counter-productive, as did his sudden announcement, in August 1992, that additional peacekeeping forces would deployed. He compromised the impartiality of his Special Representative, Mohamed Sahnoun, and imperiled the UN peacekeeping mission, UNOSOM I. When Boutros-Ghali visited Mogadishu in January 1993 to make peace, warlord groups launched violent demonstrations and personal attacks against him. Throughout 1993, Boutros-Ghali boldly pressed for peace enforcement in

Somalia, which resulted in defeat for the UN and jeopardized his position as secretary-general.

In regard to preventive deployment, both Boutros-Ghali and the United States pushed for the first UN mission (UNPREDEP) in Macedonia. In December 1992, forces from the United States and other member states arrived to forestall a predicted Serbian invasion, in the wake of Serb aggression in Croatia and Bosnia. In arranging for implementation of the mission, the secretary-general acquired considerable freedom of maneuver from the council.

In line with the peace building and peacekeeping proposals in *An Agenda for Peace*, Boutros-Ghali and the Security Council cooperated in mounting complex, multi-dimensional peacekeeping missions. The multi-dimensional approach first succeeded in Namibia in 1989-90 and achieved further successes under Boutros-Ghali in Mozambique, El Salvador, Cambodia, and Haiti. As will be demonstrated in chapters 2 and 3, these operations combined elements of cease-fire monitoring, disarmament and demobilization of warring forces, and administration, as well as the holding of elections, refugee repatriation, reconstruction, and development assistance.

With the Somalia defeat, the Clinton administration woke up to the unacceptable costs of UN peace enforcement and U.S. involvement, as well as the problematic policy of "assertive multilateralism." The May 1994 U.S. Presidential Defense Directive 25 (PDD-25) forbade American involvement in Somalia-style peace enforcement missions and provided a sharply different vision for the UN in maintaining peace and security. As will be demonstrated in chapter 5, PDD-25 came in the midst of American denial that genocide was occurring in Rwanda and refusal to authorize a mission to stop the killing. U.S. withdrawal from peace enforcement created friction with the secretary-general, as did renewed U.S. concerns over resource utilization, namely the mushrooming peacekeeping budget.[9]

With growing ambivalence of the United States toward committing resources to the UN, the United States promoted two countries that were increasing their contributions, Japan and Germany, for permanent membership on the Security Council. However, expansion of the council became bogged down in the General Assembly. The U.S.-UN relationship deteriorated further from 1993 to 1995 over policy toward Bosnia. Weak leadership of UNPROFOR by the secretary-general and UN Special Representative Yasushi Akashi provoked American political leaders to denounce the UN as Bosnian Serb "appeasers," as Serb forces continued to devastate Sarajevo and the Bosnian Muslims.[10]

In the wake of the Somalia reversal and Rwandan genocide and in the midst of the Bosnia quagmire, Giandomenico Picco, lieutenant to Secretary-General Javier Pérez de Cuéllar, wrote a seminal article in *Foreign Affairs*. In the article, he stated that "the assumption of powers by the secretary-general to manage the use of force might well be a suicidal embrace."[11] The argument that developed between the UN and NATO in Bosnia over the use of force exemplified the problems that occurred when the secretary-general assumes command of military forces. Picco argued that the Security Council alone should authorize the use of force and that leading states, such as the United States or the United Kingdom, or regional organizations, such as NATO, should lead forces in conflict-filled situations. Instead of commanding forces, the secretary-general should play a supportive role to the Security Council in arranging for the use of force for both armed peacemaking and peacekeeping.

In January 1995, the secretary-general issued an update of *An Agenda for Peace*, which re-emphasized the 1992 proposals, especially the need for a rapid reaction force under UN command. In addition, he called for expanded resources and greater powers for the secretary-general in mediation and peacekeeping. He noted that insufficient resources were available to hire skilled diplomats for mediation and observers for preventive diplomacy. He criticized the Security Council and the United States for micro-managing conflicts, a responsibility that, he believed, should be reserved for the secretary-general.[12]

Boutros-Ghali's proposals were not warmly received, especially in the United States after the "Republican revolution" and a sharp rightward shift in Congress. In attempting to fulfill his goals of expanded power and autonomy, Boutros-Ghali had turned to the "good citizens" of the UN, such as the Nordic states, Canada, and The Netherlands. These states had supported traditional peacekeeping, rather than peace enforcement in 1992, but they were anxious to prevent the erosion of power from the UN. In particular, The Netherlands supported the concept of a rapid reaction force, commanded by UN headquarters.

The secretary-general also attempted to bolster support for his position by linking *An Agenda for Peace* with *An Agenda for Development*, thereby appealing to the Group of 77. In response to a request from the General Assembly, the secretary-general produced *An Agenda for Development* in 1995, and, subsequently, the two *Agendas* appeared together in one volume. Boutros-Ghali had come to recognize, as early as the 1992 debate over *An Agenda for Peace*, that the newfound focus on peace and security had detracted from the UN's traditional orientation toward socio-economic development in the South.

Boutros-Ghali's efforts to recoup the UN's position proved to be fruitless. By 1995, the UN had plunged deeper into financial crisis, especially as the United States failed to make back payments of more than one billion dollars in dues. The Republican-controlled Congress and, especially Senator Jesse Helms, exhibited hostility toward the UN and the secretary-general. On the ground in Bosnia, it became painfully clear that the UN lacked the salience and force to resolve the conflict. Therefore, the United States turned to NATO air power and the Croatian army to drive the Bosnian Serbs and Slobodan Milosevic to the bargaining table. The United States led the way in replacing UNPROFOR with a much stronger NATO force that implemented the Dayton Accords. Thus, it appeared that regional organizations, such as NATO and the ECOWAS Military Observer Group in Liberia and Sierra Leone, might eclipse the UN, especially in the area of enforcing peace and security.

The Mega-Conferences and *An Agenda for Development*

In the late 1980s, momentum was building for the UN to be the focal point in a "quantum leap" in the addressing of global problems. These included global warming, population explosion, poverty, and resource depletion, as well as political and civil rights, women's rights, and quality of life issues. The impetus came from the growing movements in each of these areas, all of which espoused a global approach to the issues, and from the Group of 77. Globalist NGOs, such as Greenpeace and Amnesty International, and progressive European states had succeeded in promoting international conventions, especially those dealing with human rights and the environment in the 1970s and 1980s. The globalists believed that a new wave of international conferences in the 1990s could strengthen "regimes" in the various issue areas and raise them to a new level of acceptance and compliance.

In contrast, the G-77 countries focused more on their own socio-economic development and supported solutions to global problems that might benefit them. In the 1970s, the G-77 had used their majority in the General Assembly and UNCTAD to promote the "New International Economic Order," which would be financed by the North. However, the global economic slowdown, starting in the mid-1970s, helped to short-circuit the NIEO and led the G-77 to look to alternative strategies. In the 1980s, the G-77 joined forces with the globalists in pushing for UN leadership to highlight a number of problems, including those related to socio-economic development. In expressing a willingness to join with the globalists in solving global problems, the G-77 made it clear that they would not sacrifice their own national development.

As a consequence of pressure from globalists and the G-77, seven major conferences convened from 1990-96. They covered children, human rights, and the environment, as well as social development, population, women, and cities. Before each of the conferences, NGO forums convened, which enabled pressure groups to adopt common positions and influence member states. All of the conferences had a development orientation. In particular, the period from 1992 to 1995 was a period of notable activity and expense for the UN. Globalists made considerable progress in highlighting a range of issues and in broadening and deepening global regimes. However, the 1995 Women's Conference in Beijing proved to be the last mega-conference (the 1996 Habitat Conference in Istanbul was more modest). Budget constraints and U.S. opposition ended prospects for any further mega-conferences. In the future, meetings dealing with global issues would convene outside at UN headquarters in New York or Geneva. More modest review conferences would convene every five years to assess implementation of agreements made at the mega-conferences and monitor compliance with international conventions.

In regard to the Group of 77, they obtained pledges of assistance at the mega-conferences to deal with sustainable development, social development, and the management of population growth and family planning. At the same time, the South was losing the battle to prevent resources flowing away from development and toward peace and security. Throughout the 1990s, the Group of 77 struggled to keep development at the top of the agenda. When the South used the General Assembly to request Boutros-Ghali to prepare a report, which became *An Agenda for Development*, it was a pyrrhic victory. When the secretary-general issued *An Agenda for Development,* complementing *An Agenda for Peace,* budget shortfalls had depleted resources for both development and peace and security.

Conclusion

This chapter portrayed the elevated status the UN enjoyed in 1992 and the vision of Secretary-General Boutros-Ghali and those of world leaders. It focused on the commitment that was made to peace enforcement that would precipitate the organization's decline. More specifically, Boutros-Ghali's determination to expand the UN's role beyond traditional peacekeeping, as manifested in *An Agenda for Peace,* culminated in a backlash against the UN after the failure of UNOSOM II. Another ingredient in the UN's decline was the ambivalent position of the United States toward the world body. On the one hand, both the Bush administration, with the new world order and the Gulf War, and the Clinton administration, with its initial commitment to "assertive multilateralism," subscribed to an active UN role in peace and security, including peace enforcement. On the other hand, the United States was unwilling to allocate additional resources, either financial or human, to strengthen the UN. With the killing of the U.S. Rangers in Mogadishu, the commitment to peace enforcement eroded, and engagement with the UN declined. The 1994-95 Republican Revolution, like the Reagan administration from 1981-86, estranged the United States from the UN and escalated the dues arrears problem into a crisis.

By 1992, the UN had developed an inflated, unrealistic vision of what it would be able to accomplish in the wake of the Cold War and the Gulf War. On the one hand, this vision contributed to failure, to declining relations with the United States, and to near-bankruptcy of the UN. On the other hand, the UN was able to achieve as much, if not more, from 1992-97 than in any other five-year period since 1945. The UN mounted several difficult and complex peacekeeping missions during the period and proved that it could put an end to civil strife by building peace, repatriating refugees and holding elections. The UN's first foray into preventive deployment proved successful. Through the efforts of the globalists, the UN was able to highlight a range of problems that would continue to confront the world well into the twenty-first century and to elicit positive responses and promises of action from states.

Notes

1. Mikhail Gorbachev, "The Realities and Guarantees of a Security World," (New York: USSR Mission to the United Nations Press Release No. 119, September 17, 1987).

2. "A Note on the Financial Crisis," <www.un.org/Depts/dpko/dpko/intro/finance.htm> United Nations Web site.

3. Dennis C. Jett, *Why Peacekeeping Fails* (New York: St. Martin's Press, 1999), 27-30. See also, Boutros Boutros-Ghali, *Unvanquished: A U.S.-UN Saga* (New York: Random House, 1999), 8-11.

4. David Cox, *Exploring* An Agenda for Peace: *Issues Arising from the Report of the Secretary-General* (Ottawa: Canadian Centre for Global Security, 1993), 10.

5. Boutros Boutros-Ghali, *An Agenda for Peace: Preventive Diplomacy,*

Peacemaking and Peacekeeping (New York: United Nations, 1992), 22.

6. Boutros-Ghali, *An Agenda for Peace*, 26.

7. Cox, *Exploring*, 5.

8. Cox, *Exploring*, 24.

9. Stephen J. Cimbala, *Collective Insecurity: U.S. Defense Policy and the New World Disorder* (Westport, Conn.: Greenwood Press, 1995), 186-87.

10. Brian Hall, "World's Cops, Kicked Around," *New York Times,* January 2, 1994, Section 6, 23-24.

11. Giandomenico Picco, "The UN and the Use of Force," *Foreign Affairs* 73, no. 5 (October 1994), 15.

12. Barbara Crossette, "UN Chief Chides Security Council on Military Missions," *New York Times,* January 6, 1995, 3. Boutros-Ghali reasserted the importance of the secretary-general's command over UN "blue helmets" and criticized "micro-management" by the Security Council in his report of January 3, 1995. See "Supplement to An Agenda for Peace: Position Paper of the Secretary-General on the Occasion of the Fiftieth Anniversary of the United Nations," A/50/60, S/1995/1.

2

Success in Complex Missions: Cambodia and Mozambique

In the 1990s, the UN succeeded in carrying out several complex peacekeeping operations, expanding the scope of UN capabilities in the area of peace and security. Until 1989, UN peacekeeping was relatively simple, usually involving a cease-fire agreement, separation of warring forces, and the insertion of "blue helmets" as monitors. The main location of operations was in the Middle East, as well as nearby Cyprus and Kashmir. The major exception to the peacekeeping norm was ONUC in the Congo, 1960-64, where the UN played a role in African nation building. In 1989, the UN Transitional Assistance Group in Namibia mounted the first multi-dimensional operation, which marked the beginning of a second generation of peacekeeping missions. UNTAG, like many of the operations that followed, involved peacekeeping and peace building, including troop demobilization, refugee repatriation, and election supervision.

The end of the Cold War rendered a substantial number of internal conflicts ripe for resolution and brought calls for the UN to oversee the transition from civil war to domestic peace and tranquility. By 1992, the UN was involved in the process of managing almost a dozen significant conflicts, most of them internal. A chronological account of UN operations from 1992-97 would illustrate the stress that the Secretariat and Security Council experienced during this period. (Please see the chronology at the end of this volume). However, such an approach would lack analytical clarity. Instead, the initial successes of the UN under Boutros-Ghali are examined, followed by the failures that ended his hopes for a second term as secretary-general. Therefore, the focus in the next two chapters is on successful peacekeeping operations, which occurred mainly between 1992 and 1994. Four operations, those in Mozambique, Cambodia, El Salvador, and Haiti, stand out as major successes. The conflicts in Mozambique, Cambodia, and El Salvador, were especially intractable and vicious. Civilians were killed, mutilated, and displaced in large numbers. The conflict in Haiti involved the widespread persecution of pro-democratic forces by a military regime and paramilitary gangs. All four operations were unprecedented in the degree to which they intruded into the internal affairs of sovereign states and, consequently, in the size and diversity of the UN contingents that were dispatched. At the same time, all four of the successes contained negative elements, which are examined in the next two chapters.

The four successful operations amounted to one of the greatest advances in the area of peace and security made by the UN since 1945. Accordingly, the focus of this chapter is on *major* successes in the area of peace and security. In addition, the UN achieved a number of successes from 1992-97, which were not as path breaking as the four cases considered here. For example, the United Nations Observer Mission in South Africa (UNOMSA) played a significant, though secondary role, in the transition from apartheid to democracy. The UN entered South Africa in August 1992, when political violence was at a peak and negotiations to move toward full-fledged democracy were at a standstill. UNOMSA helped to dampen the violence and create the necessary conditions where negotiations could resume and elections could take place. Similarly, in the former Soviet republics of Georgia and Tajikistan, the UN played a role in stopping conflicts from spiraling out of control, although full-fledged peace was not consolidated.

Cambodia and UNTAC

Cambodia witnessed one of the largest and most complex UN missions, as well as the resolution of one of the most intractable conflicts that the UN has ever faced. A low intensity war in Cambodia became a conflagration in 1970, ending in genocide by the Khmer Rouge regime from 1975-78 and provoking a Vietnamese invasion at the end of 1978. From 1979-91, a Soviet and Vietnamese-backed government fought three guerrilla movements, backed by the China, Thailand, and the

United States. The winding down of the Cold War led to the diminution of Soviet support for Vietnam and the Hun Sen regime in Phnom
Penh. In turn, Vietnam and ASEAN countries began diplomatic overtures to end the Cambodian conflict, including the arrangement of
meetings between Hun Sen and Prince Norodom Sihanouk. As Vietnam sought to end its isolation from the West, the regime announced in
April 1989 that it would withdraw its forces from Cambodia in September 1989. The Vietnamese declaration left Hun Sen with little
choice but to agree to talks in Paris, which started in July 1989.

As the peace talks in Paris unfolded, distrust became the main
obstacle. The three guerrilla movements lacked any incentive to stop
fighting, especially due to their belief that Hun Sen would never share
power. They called for the establishment of an interim administration
and a power-sharing arrangement before demobilization. In turn, Hun
Sen distrusted the guerrilla movements, especially the Khmer Rouge,
believing that any power-sharing arrangement would lead to the return
of a reign of terror and to his own demise. He wanted guarantees that
he would still possess power under any sharing agreement. In January
1990, Australia sought to break the impasse and presented detailed
proposals for UN involvement as an interim administration and as the
guarantor of the power-sharing arrangement, which would pave the
road to peace.

In September 1990, in Jakarta, the four factions accepted an agreement in principle. It immediately established a quadripartite Supreme
National Council (SNC) that would represent the "State of Cambodia"
(SOC) internationally. The agreement also stipulated an interim UN
administration that would govern Cambodia until elections could be
held and a new government established. However, Hun Sen continued
to object to any power-sharing arrangement that included the Khmer
Rouge. In addition, the Khmer Rouge rejected any concession that
allowed Hun Sen's administration to remain intact, contending that
power would not really be shared. Consequently, an agreement was
concluded only on October 23, 1991. In the final analysis, the promise
of unprecedented UN involvement and foreign assistance helped to
bring the four parties together. Nineteen states signed the agreement,
led by six ASEAN states, and the five permanent members of the
Security Council.[1]

With the signing of the agreement, the Security Council established
the United Nations Advance Mission in Cambodia (UNAMIC), which
arrived in Phnom Penh in November 1991 to pave the way for the

United Nations Transition Authority in Cambodia (UNTAC). However, Secretary-General Pérez de Cuéllar failed to appoint a Special
Representative, which left the UN rudderless in Cambodia for more
than two months. Finally, in January 1992, the new secretary-general
asked Yasushi Akashi, the undersecretary-general for disarmament and
a Japanese, to head UNTAC. In appointing Akashi on January 9, 1992,
Boutros-Ghali bypassed the UN's Cambodia expert, Rafeeuddin
Ahmed, for someone who had no Southeast Asia experience. The
secretary-general appointed Akashi primarily so that he could abolish
the latter's position at the UN.[2]

In addition, Boutros-Ghali was seeking greater Japanese participation in and leadership of UN peacekeeping missions, especially since
Japan had become the second largest contributor to the UN budget.
Japanese Defense Force (JDF) troops would be dispatched, for the first
time, to serve in a peacekeeping operation, though with very strict rules
of engagement. However, Boutros-Ghali was taking a risk by encouraging Japanese leadership in a region where hatreds from the Second
World War still lingered.

On February 28, 1992, the UN Security Council created UNTAC, at
a cost of more than $1.7 billion, three times more than the entire 1986
peacekeeping budget.[3] In addition, UNTAC received an unusually long
mandate of eighteen months and was authorized to consist of 16,000
peacekeeping troops, 3,600 police, and 1,000 international civilian
staff.[4] The civilians would be responsible for administering the country,
repatriating refugees, monitoring human rights, and conducting elections. The first troops arrived on March 11 and Akashi on March 15.
UNTAC deployment slowly took place over the next six months, with
the civilian contingent the last to reach full strength.

The country that the UN was entering had been ravaged by more
than twenty years of war and by the Khmer Rouge genocide from 1975
to 1978. Civil society had been decimated, the people coerced and
intimidated, and the social basis for democracy undermined. Land
mines, which were everywhere in the rural areas, had produced tens of
thousands of disabled people and caused the neglect of large parts of
Cambodia that should have been under cultivation. The country had
become one of the poorest in the world, with an annual per capita
income of less than $200.[5] Given the appalling situation and the deep
distrust among the four factions, it was difficult to predict success for
UNTAC and establishment of a peaceful and democratic Cambodia.

As UNTAC slowly deployed, the two main antagonists, Hun Sen and the Khmer Rouge, continued to violate the Paris Accords and launch attacks, absent a significant body of UN blue helmets to deter them. On March 29, 1992, Hun Sen ordered an army offensive against the Khmer Rouge. By May, the Khmer Rogue was claiming UN bias in favor of Hun Sen and was refusing to implement Phase II of the Paris Accords, which required cantonment and demobilization of forces. Along with the slow arrival of peacekeepers, another problem was that Akashi and UNTAC were not assuming control of Cambodia, as stipulated in the Paris Accords. Government ministries remained in the hands of the Hun Sen regime (the SOC), and UN administrators (mainly French) chose to collaborate with SOC officials, rather than exercise authority over them. Furthermore, Akashi did not utilize his extraordinary powers to guarantee the Paris Accords by overruling Hun Sen or the leaders of the other three factions. Instead, the Special Representative chose to negotiate continually with the four factions in order to keep the peace process moving toward the goal of elections. The approach taken by Akashi and his UNTAC colleagues can be explained by their background as career international civil servants who were accustomed to settling, rather than confronting, differences with the representatives of states.[6]

In April 1992, Boutros-Ghali traveled to Cambodia to assist the peace process. He believed that the key to success and especially to holding Hun Sen and the Khmer Rouge to the Paris Accords was by cultivating Prince Norodom Sihanouk. Among the methods Boutros-Ghali employed, was his focus on their shared backgrounds as francophiles. At their first meeting, Sihanouk expressed grave concerns about the viability of the Paris Accords. Consequently, he asked the secretary-general to maintain an UNTAC presence at least three months after the elections and a permanent UN presence to deter Hun Sen or other leaders from a possible coup. While Boutros-Ghali wanted to raise Sihanouk's spirits, he knew that the United States, in particular, was concerned about the cost of UNTAC and wanted prompt withdrawal.[7]

As events unfolded, Prince Sihanouk failed to take control of the situation, due to his cancer treatments in North Korea and his erratic personality. In his absence and given Akashi's low-key management style, Hun Sen continued to exercise control of the Cambodian state. He intimidated opposition parties, including the royalist party, the United Front for an Independent, Neutral, Peaceful, and Cooperative

Cambodia (FUNCINPEC), led by Prince Norodom Ranariddh. Furthermore, Hun Sen alienated the Khmer Rouge, which compelled the movement to retreat into the bush, thereby hampering UNTAC's access to large parts of the Cambodian-Thai borderland.

By July 1992, Khmer Rouge noncompliance was affecting the other three factions. Only 7 percent of fighters had been demobilized and UNTAC was in danger of failing. Diplomatic efforts by Japan, ASEAN, and France were unable to convince the Khmer Rouge to cooperate. Akashi was faced with the choice of either abandoning the mission or isolating the Khmer Rouge, minimizing Hun Sen's dominance, and holding elections. He chose the latter, imposing economic sanctions against the Khmer Rouge, while striving to reach an outcome that would be supported by the Cambodian people and by the international community. Akashi dismissed the Deputy Commander of UNTAC, General Michel Loridon of France, for strongly advocating enforcement measures against the Khmer Rouge.[8]

The Security Council provided limited help for Akashi, passing resolutions but providing virtually no enforcement mechanisms. The only coercive measure was the limited embargo against the Khmer Rouge. China, erstwhile ally of the Khmer Rouge, supported the sanctions, while Thailand disobeyed them. However, the Security Council took no action against the Thai army's complicity with the Khmer Rouge.

.The UN had been placed in an untenable position of implementing a flawed and tenuous agreement, maintaining the trust of four antagonistic factions, and avoiding moves leading to the resumption of fighting and mission collapse. Although UNTAC did not have an explicit enforcement mandate, Akashi had been given guarantor powers, which permitted him to act against any or all of the four factions. On the ground, UNTAC suffered from poor logistics and weak command, control, and communication. In addition, some peacekeeping contingents, as well as the civilian police, were poorly trained and unprepared for such a complex operation. Among civilian staff, there was a split. On the one side were the francophones, who were responsible primarily for administration and who leaned toward the SOC and against the Khmer Rouge. On the other, were anglophones, who were responsible for, among other things, human rights monitoring and who opposed the SOC, with its widespread human rights abuses. As a result, UNTAC did not always speak with one voice or act in unison. The problems that UNTAC faced demonstrated that the UN was not prepared for such a large and complex multi-functional mission and that it was still in the transition process from the traditional peacekeeping mode.

In spite of the fundamental problems, UNTAC began to make progress. Although peacekeepers were deployed slowly and when 1,700 troops failed to arrive at all, the Force Commander, Australian Lt. General John Sanderson, skillfully coordinated military contingents from thirty-four different nations into a fairly effective peacekeeping force. Eventually, UNTAC peacekeepers covered most of Cambodia and helped to end most of the hostilities, despite their failure to demobilize the warring sides. The operation was able to extricate, in the face of Khmer Rouge intimidation, 360,000 refugees from camps along the Thai-Cambodia border and resettle them in time for the election campaign in April 1993. UNTAC stepped up demining operations and the demobilization of guerrillas and regular army soldiers. These and other measures lessened the level of fear among ordinary Cambodians and created the conditions for political campaign and electoral activities to occur.

UNTAC civilian staff began the political process by securing the release of political prisoners and by encouraging Cambodians to create and join political parties. In spite of the reluctance of Secretary-General Boutros-Ghali, Akashi approved the establishment of Radio UNTAC, which provided people with objective news and electoral guidance. UNTAC became the electoral commission for Cambodia, striving to ensure a free and fair process. UNTAC also worked to guarantee the development of a free press. In order to offset the built-in advantages of Hun Sen and the SOC, the UN and Japan began to fund other political parties. In particular, assistance flowed to FUNCINPEC, which emerged as the primary opposition to Hun Sen.[9]

On October 13, 1992, a year after the signing of the Paris Accords, the Security Council maintained that elections should proceed in spite of Khmer Rouge opposition.[10] In November, elections were set for no later than May 1993. In December, the Khmer Rouge launched a wave of violence to disrupt the peace process. Nevertheless, Akashi and UNTAC persevered. On March 8, the council confirmed the dates of Cambodian elections as May 23-27.[11] The Khmer Rouge reacted with another wave of violence, with the aim of disrupting or forcing the postponement of the elections. On March 11, the Khmer Rouge killed thirty-three Vietnamese civilians in the worst atrocity during UNTAC's mission. In April and May, the Khmer Rouge launched a new wave of attacks on civilians and UNTAC peacekeepers and officials, as the date of the elections approached. On April 13, Khmer Rouge officials withdrew from Phnom Penh, severing all links with UNTAC and the peace process.[12]

The withdrawal of the Khmer Rouge from Phnom Penh and attacks on the peace implementation process provoked more crises for UNTAC. Again, when the mission confronted failure, Akashi and the UNTAC leadership decided to press on with the process. They had calculated that the Khmer Rouge was too weak in most of Cambodia to disrupt the elections and that the Khmer Rouge could be excluded from a government of national unity, with minimal disruption.

By April 1993, UNTAC had succeeded in registering five million potential voters, which constituted close to all of the projected voting age population. Khmer Rouge attacks in the countryside failed to derail the voter registration process. In particular, aid to FUNCINPEC had created the grounds for robust political competition. The election campaign began on time on April 7. Nine hundred supervisors from forty-four countries and more than 50,000 Cambodian election officers helped to guide the process. Radio UNTAC broadcasts stressed that the balloting would be secret and that the people should not fear reprisals. At the end of April, after the Khmer Rouge withdrawal from Phnom Penh, some advisors urged Boutros-Ghali to abandon the peace process and evacuate the UN from Cambodia. The secretary-general rejected their advice. Instead, he sent Akashi to Beijing for an extraordinary meeting of the Supreme National Council, with the mission of ensuring Sihanouk's return to Cambodia, which would provide reassurance for potential voters. In spite of a pre-election Khmer Rouge attack on a UN unit, in which two Chinese engineers were killed and seven wounded, Sihanouk returned on May 22, and the elections began the following day.

From May 23 through 28, UNTAC managed the voting process in Cambodia. Due to the protection and reassurance that had been provided by UNTAC, 90 percent of eligible voters turned out. Such a high turnout in the face of a Khmer Rouge boycott and threats of violence indicated that Cambodians had an overwhelming desire for peace. Subsequently, a range of international observers deemed the elections "free and fair." On June 10, UNTAC declared Prince Ranariddh's party, FUNCINPEC, the winner of the elections with 45.5 percent of the vote. Hun Sen's Cambodian People's Party won 32.2 percent. Besides defying the Khmer Rouge, more than two-thirds of voters rejected Hun Sen and SOC, and almost half of them called for renewal of the monarchy. Soon afterwards, the constituent assembly met to draft a new constitution. The two major issues were whether or not a constitutional monarchy and a government of national unity should be established.

UNTAC was able to stay on more than four months after the elections. In September 1993, the leaders of the two major parties met with Prince Sihanouk and agreed to the establishment of a constitutional monarchy and to a government of national unity, in which the two major parties would share power. Subsequently, the Constituent Assembly ratified the constitution on September 21, and Sihanouk declared a "National Government of Cambodia," with himself as king and prime minister. Prince Ranarridh was named first deputy prime minister and Hun Sen was made second deputy prime minister. Government ministries and governorships were divided between the two major parties. Once the governmental arrangements were settled and the constitution was ratified, UNTAC transferred sovereignty to King Sihanouk and began to withdraw.

As UNTAC withdrew, King Sihanouk continued to request that the UN remain in Cambodia for an extended period of time. He felt that the power-sharing arrangement was fragile and feared that it would not last. However, the UN had other commitments to fulfill and lacked the resources to remain. As the king feared, the power-sharing arrangement came to an end. In July 1997, Hun Sen violently ended the government of national unity, accusing Prince Ranarridh of making overtures to the Khmer Rouge. However, Hun Sen moved quickly to reestablish a semblance of cooperation in time for elections in July 1998, which were judged to be "free and fair." As a result, Hun Sen had grabbed the upper hand, with the royalists playing a subordinate role. On a positive note, the Khmer Rouge disintegrated following the elections. The collapse led to the revival of plans for a war crimes tribunal. Unfortunately, the leader of the Khmer Rouge, Pol Pot, died before the tribunal could try him.

In conclusion, UNTAC took on a formidable task and performed above expectations. While the end result was by no means perfect, it was far better than the pre-existing condition of war and intimidation. Peace prevailed in most of the country, the Khmer Rouge disintegrated, and the two main parties continued to work together to govern Cambodia. The country had not become a full-fledged democracy but had become freer and more democratic than before. With regard to UNTAC, it was a most ambitious mission that achieved more than could be expected, given the UN's lack of experience at multi-dimensional peacekeeping. The UN partially took over an entire country and attempted to perform a large number of tasks, many of which the mission completed successfully. Akashi and UNTAC attempted to perform a balancing act between using its authority and mediating disputes. While Akashi can be criticized for not using his authority under the Paris Accords assertively enough, he must be credited for not taking sides and destroying the process altogether by attempting to enforce peace, as occurred in Somalia in 1993. In addition, the Security Council proved just as averse as Akashi to peace enforcement and passed resolutions with little teeth to them.

Mozambique and ONUMOZ

War in Mozambique lasted even longer than in Cambodia. From 1964, the Front for the Liberation of Mozambique (FRELIMO) fought Portuguese colonial forces in a guerrilla independence war and swept to power in 1974. By 1976, the FRELIMO government was fighting against the Mozambique National Resistance Movement (RENAMO) and the white minority regime in Rhodesia. In 1980, RENAMO escalated its attacks, with backing from apartheid South Africa. The Mozambican civil war of the 1980s became a most intractable and vicious conflict, highlighted by the brutality of RENAMO forces against the civilian population and by millions of displaced people. By 1984, the RENAMO-South African onslaught against Mozambique had borne fruit. The Nkomati Accord (a non-aggression pact) signaled the submission of Mozambique to South Africa and the end of African National Congress of South Africa (ANC) guerrilla operations from Mozambican soil. In spite of a string of concessions made by the government, RENAMO attacks on Mozambique continued from 1984 until 1992. In 1986, Foreign Minister Joaquim Chissano assumed power after President Samora Machel's death in a plane crash and intensified peacemaking efforts and moved Mozambique closer to the West.

The winding down of the Cold War and the Soviet policy shift toward cooperation with the West brought withdrawal from Southern Africa and the phasing out of commitments to Angola and Mozambique. The apartheid regime responded by making peace overtures to its adversaries, including the imprisoned ANC leader, Nelson Mandela. The first breakthrough came in 1988, as the Soviets and Cubans agreed to withdraw from Angola in exchange for a South African withdrawal from Namibia. In the same year, South Africa agreed to resurrect Mozambique's Cabora Bassa Dam. Improving relations with Mozambique and negotiations to end the conflict with the ANC diminished the apartheid regime's motive for supporting RENAMO. Subsequently, in June 1989, RENAMO's First Party Congress agreed to peace talks. In July, FRELIMO's Fifth Congress renounced Marxism-Leninism. In August 1989, the first peace talks took place in Nairobi, Kenya. With the ending of Soviet support and FRELIMO's renunciation of socialism, the government moved closer to the United States and the West and began to work with the IMF and World Bank in attempting to resurrect the economy, after more than twenty-five years of almost continual conflict. In February 1990, the new South African president, F. W. de Klerk, released Nelson Mandela and lifted the ban on the ANC, thereby minimizing any residual motive for aiding RENAMO guerrilla activities. With the ending of external sources of support, the Mozambican conflict had become ripe for resolution.

In July 1990, negotiations began in Rome between the government and RENAMO, who were still two bitter enemies and required mediators to conduct the talks. A breakthrough came at the end of July, when President Chissano announced FRELIMO's decision to scrap the fifteen-year-old one-party system and to introduce a multi-party political system, which would include RENAMO. The commitment to multi-partyism was ratified when, on November 2, the Mozambique Assembly approved a new constitution. The constitution also included universal suffrage, an independent judiciary, the right to strike, freedom of the press, and a market economy.

With the political groundwork laid, the government and RENAMO agreed to a partial cease-fire on December 1, 1990. The agreement called for the opening of essential transport routes and the withdrawal of foreign forces from Mozambique. An international Joint Verification Commission was set up to monitor the agreement. The most important strategic points of the war had been railways and pipelines that ran from Southern African Development Coordination Conference (SADCC) countries through to Mozambican ports. The cease-fire agreement opened those routes with the goal of reviving the war-ravaged economy. Zimbabwean forces, which were guarding the transport routes, were to be withdrawn, and a dialogue was to be started between Zimbabwe and RENAMO. The promised withdrawal of

Zimbabwean forces would remove outside distractions from Mozambican negotiations between the FRELIMO government and RENAMO.[13]

Negotiations proceeded throughout 1991. In February and March, cease-fire violations occurred; otherwise, most of 1991 was peaceful. On October 18, 1991, the government and RENAMO signed the first protocol of the General Peace Agreement. It covered the basic principles, asserting the legitimacy of the Mozambican government and agreeing on the establishment of a commission to supervise and monitor compliance with the General Peace Agreement. On November 13, the parties concluded a second protocol, which permitted the formation of political parties. Most importantly, the agreement legalized the main opposition movement, RENAMO. In spite of the agreement, Mozambique was still a long way from successful implementation of the peace accords.

Until 1992, peacemaking for Mozambique took place without UN involvement. However, it became clear to the mediators and to both parties that a prominent UN role would be necessary in operationalizing and implementing the peace agreement. On June 10, 1992, the mediators and parties invited the UN, as well as countries that both sides accepted, France, Portugal, the United Kingdom, and the United States, to act as observers at the talks. With assurances that Mozambique was on the way to a full cease-fire, Boutros-Ghali offered the services of the UN to Mozambique. RENAMO's leader, Alfonso Dhlakama declared that he was ready for a UN-supervised cease-fire and for the conversion of RENAMO from a guerrilla organization to a political party. On July 9, the government requested UN electoral assistance in the process of converting to a multiparty democracy. On July 16, the government and RENAMO signed the Declaration on Guiding Principles for Humanitarian Assistance, which stipulated non-discrimination in the delivery of aid.[14]

During the 1980s, Mozambique had experienced a humanitarian catastrophe, and there was a need to return home almost six million displaced people and refugees, more than a quarter of the population. Much of rural Mozambique was infested with millions of landmines. RENAMO-controlled areas were some of the worst affected, and RENAMO did not trust the government to allow aid shipments into those areas. Negotiations eventually broke down over the government's claims of sovereignty over those areas.

On October 4, 1992, the government and the RENAMO rebels concluded the Rome Accord for a complete and formal cease-fire, and, on October 15, the formal cease-fire began. At the same time, the UN Special Representative for Mozambique, Aldo Ajello of Italy, arrived in the country. In spite of the cease-fire agreement, violations began almost immediately and escalated in subsequent months. In response, the secretary-general reported to the Security Council on the urgent need for peacekeepers to be sent to monitor the cease-fire. On November 17, the secretary-general appealed to Italy for advance deployment of troops to help protect the Beira Corridor that linked Zimbabwe to the sea, as well as other major transport routes, pending the withdrawal of Zimbabwean and Malawian forces. Government forces also began to break the cease-fire. Resolving the crisis, Dhlakama and RENAMO agreed to allow Zimbabwean troops to remain until the Italians arrived.[15]

On December 16, 1992, the Security Council formally authorized ONUMOZ, with a mandate that would last until October 1993, when elections were due to be held.[16] In organizing ONUMOZ, the council and UN Secretariat sought to learn from the mistakes of UNAVEM II in Angola in 1992 and the successes and shortcomings of UNTAC in 1992-93. In contrast to UNAVEM II, the UN provided a stronger mandate and a larger contingent of peacekeepers for ONUMOZ. The Supervisory and Monitoring Commission, the Cease-fire Commission, and the National Elections Commission became effective institutions, bringing together major donors, such as the United States, and the political parties. In addition, with $19 million in aid, RENAMO eventually converted from a guerrilla movement into a political party and proved to be much more cooperative than either the Union for the Total Independence of Angola (UNITA) or the Khmer Rouge in Cambodia.[17]

On January 7, 1993, Dhlakama informed the secretary-general that the cantonment and demobilization of RENAMO forces could not begin until 65 percent of UN troops were deployed. On January 22, the secretary-general replied and informed Dhlakama that 100 observers would arrive within a week to verify the first phase of cantonment and demobilization. More than three months after the Rome Accords and the secretary-general's appeal, ONUMOZ forces began to arrive. In February, the Italians, the first contingent of ONUMOZ, began to arrive, and the Brazilian Force Commander arrived. Full deployment of more than 6,000 blue helmets was achieved by May 1993, which included battalions from Bangladesh, Botswana, Italy, Uruguay, and Zambia. In addition, the UN dispatched support units from six other countries.

Despite the arrival of UN troops, both sides continued to be suspicious of each other and stalled in demobilizing their forces, as had been the case in Cambodia and Angola. From March to June 1993, RENAMO withdrew from the Supervisory and Monitoring Commission and from the Cease-fire Commission. Dhlakama continued to spend much of his time in the former guerrilla base at Maringue in central Mozambique, rather than in the capital, Maputo. On August 23, the process of RENAMO's transformation took a major step forward, when Dhlakama occupied a residence in Maputo and met with President Chissano. Subsequently, direct talks began about the integration of RENAMO-controlled areas into the rest of Mozambique, the establishment of assembly points for the cantonment of troops, and the expansion of UN police activities. This breakthrough opened the way to peacekeeping forces, humanitarian assistance, and the process of aiding RENAMO to transform itself from a guerrilla movement into a political party.

In spite of the positive steps forward, demobilization of the opposing forces was not on schedule and threatened to create another Cambodia-type crisis. On September 13, 1993, the Security Council expressed concern about the delays.[18] In October, Boutros-Ghali visited Mozambique and obtained the agreement of both sides to a revised timetable, in which demobilization would begin in January 1994. The parties also reached agreement on police matters and the composition of the National Elections Commission. Because of the secretary-general's efforts, the peace process was placed back on track. In response, a previously skeptical council renewed the ONUMOZ mandate on November 5, for six months and authorized the deployment of more than a thousand civilian police observers.[19]

In January 1994, demobilization began and proceeded tentatively, starting with paramilitary forces. By February, all of the forty-nine assembly areas were open, ready to receive government and RENAMO troops, and the electoral process began, with the establishment of the National Elections Commission and a UN Trust Fund to provide assistance to registered political parties in Mozambique. An appeal was made to Italy and other states to provide increased funding for the conversion of RENAMO into a political party, and on March 4, Italy agreed to make a further contribution.

On March 10, the demobilization of forces began and gradually accelerated. By April 28, according to the secretary-general, more than 49,000 soldiers from government forces and RENAMO had reported to assembly areas; however, ONUMOZ had demobilized only 13,000 troops.[20] The integration of forces began with the appointment on April 6, of joint high commanders of the new Armed Forces for the Defense of Mozambique (FADM) from the government and RENAMO. On April 11, President Chissano announced that elections would take place on October 27 and 28, 1994. Subsequently, the electoral process began, as 1,500 voter-registration teams began travelling around Mozambique. In spite of the dangers, the teams began slowly, but methodically, to register millions of potential voters. On May 5, the Security Council renewed the ONUMOZ mandate again and extended the mission until November 15, 1994, when it was projected that the security situation would be under control after the elections.[21]

By July 1994, ONUMOZ was about a year behind schedule but was still on track. However, as the elections approached, a series of problems arose. Foremost among them were delays in the demobilization of forces, as well as in the formation of the new armed forces (FADM). The delays led to violent demonstrations by RENAMO troops. The government protested to the Cease-fire Commission that RENAMO was continuing to violate the cease-fire and that ONUMOZ was allowing such violations to go unchecked. In response, the secretary-general and Security Council intervened, urging both sides to meet the August 15 deadline for demobilization and dispatching a mission to discuss full implementation of the peace agreement with both parties. Due to UN intervention, both sides resumed the demobilization process in dramatic fashion.   On August 16, the old Armed Forces of Mozambique high command demobilized. Authority, equipment and infrastructure transferred to the new FADM. Three days later, RENAMO military leaders demobilized. By the end of August, demobilization was declared completed, and the process of verification began. In less than a month, almost 30,000 government troops and more than 12,000 RENAMO guerrillas were demobilized.[22]

The verification process confirmed that the demobilization, though difficult to complete, was highly successful. More than 67,000 government troops and almost 25,000 RENAMO guerillas reported to assembly camps, then more than 57,000 troops and more than 20,000 guerrillas were demobilized.[23] Less than 10,000 soldiers remained, and they underwent training for the new unified FADM. As a result of demobilization, the FADM was top-heavy, with too many officers and too few enlisted men. However, the massive demobilization was fortuitous in that Mozambique was one of the poorest countries in the world and could ill afford a large standing army.

ONUMOZ faced other tasks that were just as challenging as demobilization, including the repatriation of refugees, resettlement of displaced persons, and removal of land mines. The UNHCR organized refugee repatriation programs for hundreds of thousands of refugees and assisted in their resettlement. By August 1994, 73 percent of 1.7 million refugees had been repatriated, and, by the end of 1994, the UN had helped to resettle four million out of a total of five million internally displaced persons.[24] The UN, as part of peace building, aided in the reconstruction of rural villages and in regenerating agricultural activity. One crucial task that the UN was tardy in undertaking, due to bureaucratic wrangling, was the removal of as many as two million land mines. Without land-mine removal, rural dwellers were faced with considerable danger in resettling and resuming agricultural activities and in participating in voter registration, campaigns, and elections. Finally, in August 1994, a campaign began to remove land mines began, which was to continue for several years.

In spite of the dangers and the logistical difficulties, the voter registration campaign successfully concluded after four months. On September 2, it was announced that 6.4 million people or 81 percent of those eligible, had registered to vote. On September 7, the election campaign began, with twelve presidential candidates, led by Chissano and Dhlakama and fourteen political parties, headed by FRELIMO and RENAMO.[25]

The election campaign lasted seven weeks, resulting in lively competition, but relatively little violence. On October 21, the secretary-general reported to the Security Council that conditions existed for the holding of free and fair elections, and he deployed UN electoral observers to Mozambique. On October 24, the campaign ended, and the nation prepared to vote.

The election process seemed to be going smoothly, when a major crisis commenced. On the eve of the elections, October 26, Dhlakama announced that RENAMO was boycotting the elections. RENAMO leaders felt that the electoral process had favored FRELIMO, especially with government control of the media. In response to the crisis, an emergency meeting of the Group of Front Line States (GFLS) of Southern Africa was convened. At the meeting, the GFLS called on the major foreign powers to back the peace process and compel RENAMO to participate in the elections. As in Cambodia, the secretary-general was faced with a choice to proceed or postpone the elections; again he did not waiver. On October 27, the elections proceeded as planned. High voter turnout on the first day of over 50 percent of those registered indicated that the RENAMO boycott was not working.[26]

As the boycott fizzled, Dhlakama met with the UN Special Representative, international members of the Supervisory and Monitoring Commission, the U.S. ambassador, and senior officials of neighboring countries. Especially prominent in efforts to end the impasse was the new South African President, Nelson Mandela. Quickly, Dhlakama abandoned the boycott and announced that RENAMO would participate in the elections after all. On October 28, RENAMO rejoined the process in time for the second day of voting, and the secretary-general decided to add a third day. After polling ended on October 29, the elections were declared to be "free and fair."[27]

Three weeks after the conclusion of voting, on November 19, the UN declared the election results. President Chissano had won the presidential elections. FRELIMO won a majority of seats, 129, in the new National Assembly, while RENAMO claimed 112 and a coalition of three smaller parties took nine seats.

On December 8, the new national Assembly convened and the next day, Chissano was inaugurated. FRELIMO maintained power at the national level, with RENAMO as the opposition and gaining control of several provinces. With the political order established, ONUMOZ lost little time in withdrawing from Mozambique. On December 23, ONUMOZ began to withdrawal, and, by January 1995, the process was complete. While the withdrawal of UN peacekeepers appeared premature, the UN and several UN specialized agencies stayed involved in Mozambique in peace building, reconstruction, and development activities. In the forthcoming years, peace prevailed in Mozambique, and the UN could concentrate on improving the Mozambican economy and social infrastructure.

Conclusion

UNTAC must be evaluated as a success, while ONUMOZ was even more successful than UNTAC. While UNTAC failed to keep the Khmer Rouge in the peace process, ONUMOZ persevered and bridged the enormous gap of distrust between FRELIMO and RENAMO. ONUMOZ was able to secure a cease-fire, as well as comprehensive cantonment and demobilization, while UNTAC failed and placed the peace process in jeopardy. ONUMOZ reached out to RENAMO and was able to influence Dhlakama to take successive steps from guerrilla movement to opposition political party. The nineteen million dollars given to RENAMO proved to be a good investment for peace. The Special Representative, Aldo Ajello, was patient, extending deadlines and allowing the peace process to take a year longer than planned. Also, the Security Council was willing to extend the mandate and fund it. Thus, when Dhlakama balked during the elections in October 1994, it was too late. Most guerrilla fighters had been demobilized, and Mozambicans no longer feared going to the polls. In contrast, Akashi was unable to reach out and influence the Khmer Rouge and allowed Hun Sen to continue to control the state apparatus for his own benefit. The maintenance of strict deadlines led to the failure of demobilization in Cambodia and to an on-time election, which FUNCINPEC won but was forced to share power with Hun Sen. More comparisons among the success stories and conclusions are to be found in the next chapter.

Notes

1. Michael W. Doyle, *UN Peacekeeping: UNTAC's Civil Mandate* (Boulder, Colo.: Lynne Rienner, 1995), 22-24.

2. Boutros Boutros-Ghali, *Unvanquished: A U.S.-UN Saga*, (New York: Random House, 1999), 30.

3. UN Security Council Resolution 745, February 28, 1992.

4. James A. Schear, "Riding the Tiger: The United Nations and Cambodia's Struggle for Peace," in *UN Peacekeeping, American Policy, and the Uncivil Wars of the 1990s,* William J. Durch, ed. (New York: St. Martin's Press, 1996), 151.

5. Doyle, *UN Peacekeeping*, 50-51.

6. Steven R. Ratner, *The New UN Peacekeeping: Building Peace in Lands of Conflict after the Cold War* (New York: St. Martin's Press, 1996), 169-71.

7. Boutros-Ghali, *Unvanquished*, 31-33.

8. Trevor Findlay, *Cambodia: The Legacy and Lessons of UNTAC* (Oxford: Oxford University Press, 1995), 37-38.

9. Boutros-Ghali, *Unvanquished*, 79-80.

10. UN Security Council Resolution 783, October 13, 1992.

11. UN Security Council Resolution 810, March 8, 1993.

11. Schear, "Riding the Tiger," 154.

12. Cameron Hume, *Ending Mozambique's War: The Role of Mediation and Good Offices* (Washington, D.C.: United States Institute of Peace, 1994), 43-46.

13. Pamela L. Reed, "The Politics of Reconciliation: The United Nations Operation in Mozambique," in *UN Peacekeeping, American Policy, and the Uncivil Wars of the 1990s,* William J. Durch, ed. (New York: St. Martin's Press, 1996), 281.

15. Reed, "The Politics of Reconciliation," 285-86.

16. UN Security Council Resolution 797, December 16, 1992.

17. Richard Synge, *Mozambique: UN Peacekeeping in Action, 1992-1994* (Washington, D.C.: United States Institute of Peace, 1997), 50-52.

18. UN Security Council Resolution 863, September 13, 1993.

19. UN Security Council Resolution 882, November 5, 1993.

20. Report of the Secretary-General on Mozambique, S/1994/511, April 28, 1994.

21. UN Security Council Resolution 916, May 5, 1994.

22. Dennis C. Jett, *Why Peacekeeping Fails* (New York: St. Martin's Press, 1999), 105.

23. Reed, "The Politics of Reconciliation," 294.

24. Reed, "The Politics of Reconciliation," 296-98.

25. *The United Nations and Mozambique, 1992-1995,* UN Blue Book Series, Vol.V (United Nations: Department of Public Information, 1995), 61.

26. Reed, "The Politics of Reconciliation," 300.

27. Jett, *Why Peacekeeping Fails,* 111.

3

Success at Restoring Democracy: Central America and Haiti

As in Cambodia and Mozambique, the UN succeeded in bringing peace to El Salvador and Haiti. As in Southern Africa and Southeast Asia, the UN became involved in Central America and the Caribbean in the 1990s because of the end of the Cold War. Even more than in Cambodia and Mozambique, the primary goals of UN missions in El Salvador and Haiti were to establish human rights and democracy, as well as peace. The two missions in the Caribbean and Central America best illustrated the shift of the UN, since the end of the Cold War, toward the adoption of human rights and democracy as fundamental principles of the UN in practice, as well as in rhetoric.

In the 1980s, Central America, especially, was a battleground between revolutionary forces, backed by Cuba and the Soviet Union, and hard-line conservatives, supported by the United States. In 1979, the Sandinistas had fought their way to power in Nicaragua and had begun a process of social transformation and the centralization of power. In 1980, revolutionary guerrillas in nearby El Salvador escalated their attacks on the government. In Guatemala, long-running warfare between the government and guerrillas escalated and resulted in waves of massacres of the majority Mayan population by government forces. The United States responded, especially after the Reagan administration took office in 1981, with strong support for counterinsurgency, especially in El Salvador, and by arming and training the contra (counterrevolutionary) rebels to overthrow the Sandinistas in Nicaragua.

The end of the Cold War brought the termination of aid for the allies of the Soviet Union and Cuba and a corresponding diminution of anti-communist paranoia by the right in Central America. In 1987, five Central American states reached a peace agreement, which would end insurgencies and bring guerrillas into the political process. They agreed to invite the UN and the Organization of American States (OAS) to observe the peace process. The first breakthrough came in Nicaragua in 1989, when the Sandinistas agreed to elections, with the firm belief that they would win. The UN sent an electoral observer mission, UNOVEN, to the country in August 1989 and a military observer group (ONUCA) to the region in November. UNOVEN and the OAS helped to ensure that political competition developed and that Nicaraguans gained faith in the electoral process. ONUCA monitored demobilization by guer-rilla movements and paramilitary groups, which helped to reassure people, especially in Nicaragua, so that they could resume normal activities. In February 1990, UNOVEN and the OAS observed the elections, which the Sandinistas lost, as well as the handover of power to the new president, Violetta Chamorro. In Nicaragua, as in Namibia, the UN broke with Cold War policy that discouraged electoral obser-vation and commenced UN endorsement of electoral democracy and active involvement in election monitoring and training throughout the world.

The resolution of the conflict in El Salvador was not as easy to conclude as that in Nicaragua. The war in El Salvador had been more vicious and had been fought primarily inside of the country, in contrast to Nicaragua where the contras conducted cross-border raids. Conse-quently, peacemaking took place in stages over a span of more than five years. In July 1990, the government and the *Frente Farabundo Marti para la Liberacion Nacionale* (FMLN) guerrillas reached agree-ment on human rights standards and requested that the UN monitor the human rights situation. After some deliberation, the UN created the UN Observer Mission in El Salvador (ONUSAL) in May 1991, the first UN mission with human rights monitoring as its top priority.[1]

In September, the ONUSAL Human Rights Division issued its first report. It claimed that the situation was improving despite continued fighting and that a good faith effort was being made to implement the agreement. In order to rectify the human rights abuses of the 1980s, a Truth Commission was created, and, in December, Secretary-General

Pérez de Cuéllar appointed three eminent persons from Latin America as its members. In February 1992, the Human Rights Division reported that violations of fundamental human rights were still prevalent. In June, its fourth report focused on due process of law, as well as the right to life and the integrity and security of person. In July, the Truth Commission arrived in El Salvador and began collecting testimonies. In August, the Human Rights Division reported that, in spite of serious concerns relating to summary executions, violent death and threats, the overall human rights situation in El Salvador had improved from 1991 to 1992.

With ONUSAL, the UN broke new ground by endorsing civil and political rights, as well as electoral democracy. In addition, Secretary-General Pérez de Cuéllar became intensely involved in the negotiations at an early stage, in contrast to Cambodia and Mozambique where the UN only became involved in the implementation talks.[2]

In August 1991, U.S. Secretary of State James Baker, and the Soviet Foreign Minister asked Pérez de Cuéllar to take personal leadership of the negotiating process in El Salvador. They requested that he press both sides to reach rapid agreement on remaining political issues and on a cease-fire. The secretary-general agreed and invited President Cristiani and the High Command of the FMLN to come to UN Headquarters for talks.[3]

In September, the government, FMLN, and secretary-general, made progress toward a final peace settlement.[4] They agreed on a "compressed" agenda for negotiations and on a series of measures. These included reducing the size of the armed forces and purging the ranks of human rights abusers, as well as the creation of a new National Civilian Police force. Agreement was reached on the institution of a land-transfer program, which was a central FMLN demand. A National Commission for the Consolidation of Peace (COPAZ) would be established to oversee implementation of all political agreements, which would become the most important institution for building peace between the government and the FMLN.

Pérez de Cuéllar was determined to conclude the negotiations before he left office on December 31, 1991. The day after Christmas, he invited the parties to UN Headquarters. On the last day of the year, the government and the FMLN signed the Act of New York, which complemented previous agreements and completed the negotiations on all substantive issues of the peace process. On January 10, 1992, the new secretary-general, Boutros Boutros-Ghali, conveyed to the Security

Council his recommendations regarding how ONUSAL should implement the Act of New York. After the government and the FMLN reached agreement on all outstanding issues and signed the act, the council broadened and extended the ONUSAL mandate through October 31 and added military and police divisions to the mission.[5]

On January 16, the peace agreement was signed at Chapultepec Castle in Mexico City in a ceremony attended by Boutros-Ghali. At the end of January, the cease-fire took hold, the deployment of 373 ONUSAL military personnel from ten countries, largely from Spain, commenced. Also, 631 ONUSAL police observers began to arrive. Police deployment proceeded more slowly than military deployment, due to resistance from Salvadoran authorities.[6]

As in the case of Mozambique, the Salvadoran peace process unfolded much more slowly than the UN had anticipated. In May 1992, Boutros-Ghali informed the Security Council that it would be necessary to maintain, rather than reduce, the strength of the ONUSAL Military Division. In fact, ONUSAL military strength was maintained for seven months and ended only in 1994. The secretary-general and council expressed concern about delays in the demobilization process, new police force formation, and land-transfer program. In response to UN concerns, the government and the FMLN worked out a timetable for implementation of the peace agreement. However, following further setbacks in the summer of 1992 in carrying out provisions of the agreement, the government and the FMLN again adjusted backwards the implementation timetable. At the end of September, the FMLN lost patience and informed the UN that it would suspend destruction of its weapons and demobilization of its forces. The guerrilla movement would not resume cooperation until new dates were set for the start of the land transfer and other aspects of the agreement that had fallen behind schedule. In mid-October, the secretary-general proposed a compromise solution to the land issue. After obtaining clarifications, the government and the FMLN accepted the compromise.[7]

Besides the land reform delays, the government was slow in purging the armed forces of serious human rights abusers. In September 1992, the Ad Hoc Commission on Purification of the Armed Forces of El Salvador finished its review of individual officers' professional competence and human rights records and submitted its report to the secretary-general and to President Cristiani. At the end of October, with the government delaying the purging process, UN representatives went to El Salvador for consultations. In early November, agreement was reached on purging the armed forces, as well as the demobilization of the FMLN and destruction of its weaponry. In response to the agreement, the secretary-general proposed a new target date of December 15 for the complete dismantling of the FMLN military structure and the formal cessation of the armed conflict. At the beginning of December, President Cristiani informed the UN that administrative decisions had been adopted to begin purification of the armed forces. In response, the FMLN resumed demobilization of its combatants and began the destruction of weapons.

With the final demobilization of FMLN combatants and the movement's legalization as a political party, the armed conflict between the government and the FMLN came to a formal end. Eleven months after the final peace agreement was signed in Chapultepec Palace, Boutros-Ghali, President Cristiani, the FMLN's General Command, and other dignitaries attended a ceremony in San Salvador. Subsequently, the ONUSAL Military Division was reduced in number. However, serious problems remained. In January 1993, the secretary-general reported that the government was not in compliance with the recommendations of the Commission on Purification of the Armed Forces and that the FMLN had not completed the destruction of its remaining arms and equipment. In response, the Security Council expressed concern about continued delays by the government and the FMLN.

In the first half of 1993, the civilian components of ONUSAL continued to make progress on the electoral and human rights fronts. The secretary-general recommended that the UN verify elections, scheduled for March 1994, in response to a request by the Salvadoran government. On March 15, the Truth Commission report was made public, containing the results of the investigation into human rights violations committed during the civil war and recommendations for punishment and for preventing a repetition of such acts. The Security Council welcomed the report and called on all parties to comply with its recommendations and with all other obligations. On March 20, El Salvador's Legislative Assembly passed a broad amnesty law. In response, Boutros-Ghali and other international observers expressed concern at the haste of the amnesty. Concern existed that major human rights abusers may have escaped punishment. In contrast, President Cristiani expressed reservations, especially because the report singled out some of his political associates. In its periodic report, the Human Rights Division found that, although some disturbing practices persisted, there had been a continuing trend toward an overall improvement in the human rights situation. On May 20, the secretary-general transmitted to the government, the FMLN, and COPAZ an analysis of the Truth Commission's recommendations, identified the actions required, and emphasized that implementation be completed before the elections. In addition, Boutros-Ghali proposed expansion of the ONUSAL mandate to include an electoral division and, on May 27, the council concurred, paving the way for the commencement of the process of preparing for voter registration and elections.[8]

Just as the peace process seemed to be gathering momentum, a crisis occurred. On May 23, 1993, an explosion at an automobile repair shop in Managua, Nicaragua, led to the discovery of an FMLN weapons cache. Subsequent investigations by ONUSAL with the cooperation of the FMLN revealed the existence of 114 weapons caches in El Salvador, Nicaragua and Honduras. In reaction, the secretary-general wrote to the FMLN that the discovery raised "very serious questions of confidence and trust," and the Security Council described the FMLN's actions as "the most serious violation to date" of the peace accords.[9]

In response to the discovery, the Nicaraguan and Honduran governments sought to remove all secret arms caches belonging to the FMLN. By mid-August, ONUSAL announced that it had verified the destruction of all of the FMLN's weapons and equipment. The episode demonstrated that the peace process still was far from completion. On the one hand, the government could not trust the FMLN to be fully compliant with the peace accords. On the other hand, the FMLN was still fearful of death squads and right-wing leaders and dissatisfied with the land transfer program and the reform of the armed forces and police.

In July, the secretary-general reported that the government had removed from active service all army officers identified for dismissal, in line with recommendations of the Commission on Purification of the Armed Forces. A week later, President Cristiani wrote to Boutros-Ghali and stated that the government was moving toward full compliance with the recommendations of the Truth Commission. However, three months later, the secretary-general found that the process was moving too slowly and urged the government, the FMLN, and others involved to speed up the implementation of the recommendations of the Truth Commission before the election campaign began.

In September 1993, the Human Rights Division reported that the ambiguous situation of the previous two years had persisted, with signs of improvement amidst continuing violence. However, another crisis occurred at the end of October, when two leaders of the FMLN were murdered, death-squad style, within the space of a week. In response, the secretary-general and Security Council recommended a vigorous investigation into the apparent pattern of politically motivated murders, as recommended in the Truth Commission report. A joint group for the investigation of politically motivated illegal armed groups was formed. In January 1994, the Human Rights Division reported that the situation had taken a serious turn for the worse, starting in August 1993. The deterioration had occurred as preparations for elections were gathering momentum.

On November 20, 1993, the election campaign commenced. At the same time, problems in voter registration, death-squad activity, and delays in land transfer were undermining previous achievements. On January 19, 1994, voter registration ended, and legislative elections took place the next day. Municipal elections followed on February 20. As presidential elections approached, difficulties persisted with the voter roll, and concerns grew about the maintenance of internal order, the land-transfer program and the reintegration of former combatants and displaced persons. On March 16, the secretary-general reported that, despite the remaining difficulties and the mistrust among the political contenders, the conditions for the holding of free and fair elections were "generally adequate." After the first round of elections in March, he noted that flaws were evident and that election supervisors were experiencing mixed results in trying to correct them.[10]

On March 20, the elections began. In the presidential contest, the candidate for the *Alianza Republicana Nacionalista* (ARENA), Armando Calderon Sol, won 49.26 percent of the vote, and the *Coalition Convergencia Democratica/FMLN/Movimiento Nacional Revolucionario* candidate, Ruben Zamora, received 25.29 percent.[11]

With no candidate obtaining more than 50 percent of the vote, a run-off was scheduled for late April between the candidates with the most votes. On April 24, Armando Calderon Sol was declared the winner of the presidential election and was inaugurated as president of El Salvador on June 1. While election observers found some irregularities and shortcomings, ONUSAL proclaimed that the elections, in general, were free and fair, and the Security Council congratulated El Salvador on the "peaceful and historic" elections and called for implementation of measures to fulfill the peace accords.[12]

On May 11, Boutros-Ghali recommended that ONUSAL's mandate be extended until the end of November to verify implementation by the parties of the peace accord provisions. The government and the FMLN reached accord on a "timetable for the implementation of the most important outstanding agreements." While expressing concern that important elements of the peace plan remained only partially implemented, the Security Council welcomed the progress that had been made and extended the ONUSAL mandate until the end of November.[13]

At the end of July, the Joint Group for the Investigation of Politically Motivated Illegal Armed Groups issued its report and concluded that such groups appeared to be pursuing the destabilization of the peace process. Concerns remained about public security, the reintegration of former combatants and the constitutional reforms recommended by the Truth Commission. On a positive note, the Human Rights Division reported an improvement in the situation, owing to the formation of the joint investigative group and other steps, taken by the government, the FMLN, civil society actors, and the international community. However, it noted that the existence of organized crime networks, coupled with the inadequate functioning of the justice system, were the greatest obstacles to the effective exercise of human rights in El Salvador. In October, the division reported that, in preparation for its withdrawal, it had gradually shifted its focus to reforming and strengthening El Salvador's permanent human rights institutions.[14]

In September 1994, the secretary-general reported that the government and the FMLN had made progress in carrying out the May 19 timetable, and the Security Council welcomed the steps taken by the new president to ensure full compliance with the peace accords. On October 4, the government and the FMLN signed a joint declaration reflecting their determination to see the peace accords fully and urgently implemented for the benefit of all Salvadorians. At the end of October, the secretary-general recommended that the ONUSAL mandate be extended, at much reduced strength, to ensure that unfinished commitments, particularly those concerning security were implemented. On November 23, the council urged the government and the FMLN to intensify their efforts to comply with the May 19 timetable and extended ONUSAL until the end of April 1995.[15]

On December 19, the General Assembly called upon the government and all political forces involved in the peace process to fulfill their commitments and commended the efforts of the Central American peoples and governments to consolidate peace. On February 6, 1995, the secretary-general proposed the establishment of a small team of UN officials to continue the verification responsibilities and the "good offices" functions carried out by ONUSAL, and the Security Council agreed, and on April 30, the ONUSAL mandate ended, after more than three years of operation.

The UN mission in El Salvador must be judged as a success. In El Salvador, the UN played a leading role in making, keeping, and building peace, helping to bring about a cease-fire, a demobilization of forces, and the integration of guerrillas into society. In that regard, ONUSAL was just as successful as ONUMOZ in Mozambique and more successful than UNTAC in Cambodia, though on a smaller and less dangerous scale. After considerable effort, ONUSAL also created the conditions for left-of-center forces to operate with diminished fear of death squads. However, ONUSAL was not successful in ensuring the full implementation of peace agreement reforms, including land transfer and restructuring of the police and army.

As the UN achieved success in El Salvador, another Central American mission was launched in Guatemala. In September 1994, the UN General Assembly, rather than the Security Council, established the UN Verification Mission in Guatemala (MINUGUA) to verify human rights agreements reached by the government and the guerrilla movement, the Guatemalan National Revolutionary Unity (URNG). Soon after, more than 250 human rights monitors, legal experts, police, and specialists on the Mayan people arrived in Guatemala, and many were posted to remote areas. Their presence helped to improve a human rights situation that had improved from horrendous (worse than El Salvador's) to merely tenuous. In 1996, elections were held. Agreement was reached on a cease-fire, reconstituting the army, and reintegrating the URNG into society. Agreement was also concluded on land reform, as well as constitutional and electoral reforms. On December 29, a final peace agreement was signed.[16]

The outgoing secretary-general, Boutros Boutros-Ghali, and the new one, Kofi Annan, recommended sending military observers to verify the agreements, and, on January 20, 1997, the Security Council authorized them. In February, 132 military observers deployed, the URNG submitted a list of 3,750 guerrillas to be demobilized, and the army provided lists of units that had been redeployed to bases.[17] Eight assembly points were established, and, on March 3, the United Nations Verification Mission in Guatemala took control of the demobilization process. Two days later, URNG guerrillas reported to the assembly points and surrendered their weaponry. MINUGUA also became involved in removing hundreds of land mines and other explosive devices. By May, URNG had turned in all its weapons for destruction and demobilized its guerrillas. On May 17, the military observer group began to withdraw. As in Nicaragua and El Salvador, the UN had helped to bring about a peace in Guatemala that was, at once, stable and tenuous.

Haiti

The case of Haiti diverges from the other three success stories. In Haiti, there were no guerrilla movements and no armed conflicts of either high or low intensity. Paramilitary gangs, who were intimidating the local population, were using the only appreciable violence. What made Haiti a major success was the fact that the UN intervened for the first time in its history to restore human rights and a democratically elected government, against the will of a military dictatorship.[18]

UN involvement in Haiti began in December 1990, when the UN sent election monitors to supervise the first democratic presidential elections by universal suffrage in 185 years of independence. During the campaign, Jean-Bertrand Aristide and his party, *Lavalas* ("wash clean" in Haitian Creole), mobilized the poor with the promise of a better life and reduced privileges for the elite. Consequently, large numbers of Haitians, 85 percent of those registered, turned out to vote and elected Aristide president, with an overwhelming two-thirds of the vote. Aristide took office on February 7, 1991. In office, he continued to mobilize the poor and verbally attack the Haitian elite.[19]

On June 15, 1991, the Organization of American States (OAS), including Haiti, concluded the Santiago Commitment to Democracy and Renewal of the Inter-American System. The commitment bound OAS member states to act upon any "sudden or irregular interruption of the democratic institutional process" within any state in the Western Hemisphere.[20] This was a revolutionary agreement for a hemisphere where military dictatorships had been the norm, and it committed OAS states to intervene in the sovereign affairs of fellow states to restore democracy. The Santiago commitment coincided with a rising commitment by many states in the UN to democracy and human rights. Some delegations to the UN began to speak of the right to intervene in cases of massive human rights abuses and the abrogation of democracy.

As the confrontation between *Lavalas* and the elite intensified, the army decided to act, and, in September 1991, overthrew President

Aristide. Instead of arresting Aristide, the army allowed him to leave for exile in Venezuela where he began to work for his return. In line with the Santiago Agreement, the OAS imposed a trade embargo on Haiti shortly after the coup. After hesitating to implement the OAS embargo, the United States, the remaining superpower, ordered a halt on all exports to and imports from Haiti, except for the delivery of humanitarian aid. At the same time, the Bush administration began maneuvers to impede the return of Aristide and *Lavalas* to power, as well as to stop the flow of Haitian refugees to the United States. In November, the U.S. Ambassador to Haiti called on Aristide to replace his prime minister, Rene Preval, and to delay any plans to return for at least six months. The Bush administration criticized Aristide as "intransigent" for objecting to Haitian parliamentarians' veto of his choice for prime minister and to their proposition to allow his return at an unspecified date in exchange for lifting the OAS embargo.

In early 1992, Aristide arrived in Washington, D.C., where he began two years of lobbying efforts for action by the United States, the OAS, and the UN to facilitate his return to Haiti. He joined efforts to stop repatriation of asylum seekers to Haiti by the United States and to strengthen the trade embargo against the military regime of Raoul Cedras. Despite its verbal commitments, the Bush administration failed to enforce the embargo, allowing the delivery of oil and other supplies, particularly via the Dominican Republic. The administration also failed to implement its threat to freeze the assets of pro-coup leaders and cancel their U.S. visas. In June, after first denouncing the installation by the military and parliament of ex-presidential candidate Marc Bazin as acting prime minister, the United States called on Aristide to negotiate with him. In response, Aristide formed his own presidential commission, led by Father Antoine Adrien and composed of parliamentarians, business people, and professionals. Aristide authorized the commission to represent his government in Haiti and liaise with the army and with Haitian society.

In September, Aristide spoke, as Haiti's head of state, at the opening of the UN General Assembly. In his address, Aristide called on the United States and OAS to tighten the embargo against the military regime and its supporters and for the European Union (EU) and the UN to join in the effort. Aristide, a defrocked priest, was particularly critical of the Vatican for recognizing the Bazin government and sending a representative to Haiti. Subsequently, the UN joined the OAS in the embargo, acting, for the first time, to support the restoration of democracy in a sovereign state. In December, Boutros-Ghali appointed the Argentinean diplomat, Dante Caputo, as Special Envoy to Haiti, and the OAS also made him their envoy.[21]

In January 1993, the new U.S. President, Bill Clinton, reneged on a campaign promise and declared that he would continue the Bush administration's policy of repatriating Haitian refugees. The Clinton administration succeeded in enlisting Aristide's support by promising a tougher stance against the military regime. Fulfilling his pledge, Aristide, in a radio broadcast, urged Haitians not to flee by boat. In the meantime, the regime held parliamentary elections, which the Clinton administration denounced as illegal, and fourteen new pro-military senators and deputies took their seats in the legislature.

In March 1993, after considerable diplomatic activity, Lawrence Pezzullo, President Clinton's special envoy, joined with UN-OAS envoy Caputo in presenting a peace plan. It called for a multinational force to go to Haiti, the resignation of the army high command, a broad amnesty for the army, and the formation of a new consensus government. While endorsing the plan, Aristide reluctantly accepted the principle of an armed multi-national peacekeeping force in Haiti. Also in March, after gaining approval from the regime, the OAS International Civilian Mission (MICIVIH) deployed to Haiti to verify respect for human rights and to report abuses. In April, the General Assembly authorized UN participation in MICIVIH.

In June 1993, the Haitian junta rejected the Caputo-Pezzullo plan, and acting Prime Minister Bazin resigned in protest against the junta's action. In response, President Clinton urged the UN to adopt tougher sanctions against Haiti, including a worldwide fuel and arms embargo and a targeting and freezing of assets of pro-coup Haitians and state enterprises. After the UN imposed an oil and arms embargo, the regime leader, General Raul Cedras, capitulated and traveled to the United States in July where he and President Aristide signed the Governors Island Accord. The ten points of the accord included Aristide naming a new prime minister, the UN suspending the embargo, and reconstituting parliament. They also included reform of the army and police, amnesty for coup leaders and supporters, and General Cedras' resignation in preparation for Aristide's return to Haiti on October 30. In keeping with the accord, the illegally elected members of parliament resigned, the parliament approved Aristide's new prime minister, Robert Malval, and the Security Council suspended the embargo. On September 23, the United Nations Mission in Haiti (UNMIH), with

Dante Caputo as Chief of Mission, was established to modernize the army and create a new police force. However, at the same time, murders and human rights violations by the military and paramilitary death squads increased.

On October 11, 1993, lightly armed members of the anti-Aristide Revolutionary Front for the Advancement and Progress of Haiti (FRAPH) appeared on the Port-au-Prince docks and stopped the U.S.S. *Harlan County* from docking. They prevented the disembarkation of about 200 U.S. and Canadian soldiers, who had been sent as UNMIH trainers to begin professionalizing the Haitian Army, as called for by the Governors Island Accord. In the wake of the killing of eighteen U.S. Rangers in Mogadishu, Somalia, President Clinton backed down and ordered the *Harlan County* to return to the U.S. Naval Base at Guantanamo, Cuba. In response, the Security Council voted to reinstate sanctions if Cedras did not comply with the Governors Island Accord and resign. After Cedras refused, the UN re-imposed the oil and arms embargo.[22]

Emboldened by the *Harlan County* success, FRAPH and the military unleashed a new wave of repression and murder, including the assassination of Guy Malary, the Minister of Justice. The junta forced MICIVIH to withdraw. Aristide then called for a total blockade of Haiti, and, on October 28, he addressed the General Assembly and demanded UN intervention to restore him to power.

In the wake of the *Harlan County* setback, the U.S. State Department, the CIA, and Pezzullo stepped up efforts to persuade Aristide to abandon plans to return to power. The U.S. Ambassador pressed prime minister Malval to broaden his cabinet to include pro-military ministers. The CIA held a special briefing for members of the U.S. Congress on Aristide's alleged "mental instability." Soon afterwards, it was revealed that the CIA had on its payroll the high-ranking officers involved in the coup against Aristide in 1991.

In December 1993, Prime Minister Malval resigned after he failed to convene a national reconciliation conference between the pro-democratic camp and pro-coup supporters. Aristide and nine of ten ministers in Malval's cabinet rejected the conference. In January 1994, Aristide organized a conference of his own in Miami where his supporters, including members of the Congressional Black Caucus and Jesse Jackson, criticized the Clinton administration's refugee policies and its failure to take a stronger stance toward the coup leaders.[23]

Canada, France, the United States, and Venezuela announced that they would strengthen sanctions, if the junta failed to resume the Governors Island process by January 15. However, the deadline passed without further action. In a token gesture, the United States canceled the visas of 500 Haitian army personnel. On January 26, MICIVIH returned to Haiti to resume monitoring the worsening human rights situation.

In February, Pezzullo made a final effort to compel Aristide to capitulate and prodded him to accept a new plan supposedly drafted by Haitian parliamentarians. The plan called for a broad coalition government, an amnesty law for the coup-makers, the retirement of Cedras, the transfer of Police Chief Michel Francois, and the lifting of the embargo. However, it failed to propose a date for Aristide's return. Aristide flatly rejected the plan. In congressional testimony in March 1994, Pezzullo admitted that the plan had originated in the State Department and that he and the U.S. Ambassador had handpicked the parliamentary delegation that was flown to Washington to present the plan.

Aristide countered the Pezzullo plan with his own eight-point plan. It called for a total trade embargo against Haiti until Cedras and other coup leaders submitted, as well as a parliamentary vote on a general amnesty law, a law to separate the army and the police, and the initiation of UNMIH. According to the plan, Aristide would then name a new prime minister and return to Haiti within ten days. In March, the Congressional Black Caucus and liberal Democratic members of Congress introduced a bill calling for tougher U.S. sanctions against the junta. They also demanded Pezzullo's resignation. In April, Randall Robinson, Director of TransAfrica, a Washington, D.C.-based NGO, began a hunger strike and called on President Clinton to fire Pezzullo and change his policies toward the Haitian military and the refugees.

In May, the Security Council adopted new resolutions calling for the departure of Cedras and the other coup leaders, imposed a comprehensive set of sanctions against the coup leaders and supporters, and threatened to further tighten the embargo.[24] U.S. Embassy officials in Port-au-Prince leaked a memorandum accusing the Haitian left and Aristide supporters of manipulating and fabricating human right abuses in Haiti. President Clinton ignored the memo and fired Pezzullo, appointing former Congressman William Gray III as his new special envoy to Haiti. The Clinton administration announced a change in refugee policy, which would allow them to apply for political asylum at sea or in a third country. Robinson ended his hunger strike.

In an effort to more effectively target sanctions toward the Haitian elite, Canada, the Dominican Republic, France, the Netherlands, and the United States suspended commercial flights to Haiti. The Clinton administration froze the bank accounts of the coup leaders and their supporters and ordered a ban on international transactions. In July, as the flow of refugees increased, the Clinton administration announced that they would no longer be eligible for asylum in the United States. On July 20, as the flood of refugees continued, the United States announced that it was placing new refugees in the Guantanamo Naval Base in Cuba, as well as in other countries.

On July 31, the Security Council adopted Resolution 940, authorizing, under Chapter VII of the UN Charter, a U.S.-led multinational force (MNF) to use "all means necessary" to remove the coup leaders from power.[25] In addition, the resolution expanded the mandate of the UN Mission (UNMIH), so that it could take over from the MNF in assisting the Aristide government in sustaining a secure and stable environment in preparation for presidential elections, scheduled for December 1995. A new UN Special Representative and UNMIH Chief of Mission, Lakhdar Brahimi, replaced Dante Caputo. The Haitian junta responded to the tougher measures by increasing their repression. A group of "attaches" (a death squad) assassinated Father Jean-Marie Vincente, a close friend of Aristide's. Father Vincente was the first priest to be killed by the regime. Once again, the junta expelled MICIVIH human rights observers.

In September 1994, President Clinton appeared on national television to announce and explain an impending military intervention to oust the Haitian military regime and return President Aristide to office. Clinton dispatched former President Jimmy Carter, retired General Colin Powell, and Senator Sam Nunn of Georgia to negotiate the terms of the junta's departure and the mode of entry of a 20,000-strong U.S.-led MNF. As the MNF threatened to storm Haitian ports, General Cedras gave permission for the force to land. On September 19, the MNF landed in Haiti unopposed. As the MNF took control of Haiti and seized weapons caches, Police Chief Francois fled to the Dominican Republic. The legitimate parliament reconvened and passed a limited amnesty law covering political crimes but not other criminal acts. Cedras announced that he might not resign as agreed, but the ranking U.S. Army general was able to change the coup leader's mind. Cedras and General Biamby, the other high-ranking member of the regime, left Haiti for exile in Panama.[26]

On October 15, President Aristide returned to Haiti, and thousands of joyous Haitians welcomed him. Entering Haiti in the wake of the MNF, MICIVIH returned to human rights monitoring. UNMIH began the process of creating a new police force. MICIVIH worked closely with UNMIH, particularly with civilian police monitors. The mission paid special attention to individual civil and political rights and to freedom of association and freedom of the press. By 1995, MICIVIH had 200 international staff, including 102 UN human rights observers, in the field.[27]

On March 31, 1995, the MNF handed over responsibility for Haiti to UN Special Representative and Chief of Mission Brahimi. UNMIH fully deployed over 6,000 military personnel and almost 800 civilian police. On April 28, President Aristide disbanded the armed forces, which placed much greater responsibility for security on the new Haitian National Police with the U.S.-led International Criminal Investigative Training Assistance Program (ICITAP). Five thousand new Haitian police officers received training and were deployed throughout the country. At the same time, UNMIH provided much needed security throughout Haiti, especially to humanitarian aid convoys, airports, storage locations, and seaports, as well as in preparations for legislative and presidential elections. The government, the Friends of the Secretary-General for Haiti (Argentina, Canada, France, the United States, Venezuela, and Chile), MICIVIH, and UNMIH formed working groups to deal with disarmament, urban disorders, and fire-fighting, as well as justice, prisons, and human rights matters. UNMIH also paved the way for development projects to begin in the Western Hemisphere's poorest country.

In 1995, the biggest question was whether President Aristide would observe the constitutional requirement that he step aside after one five year term at the beginning of 1996. Later, elections for parliament, local government, and president were held. On December 17, 1995, Rene Preval was elected president with 88 percent of the vote.[28]

Complying with the constitution, President Aristide stepped down on February 7, 1996, and President Preval was inaugurated. Soon afterwards, Aristide began to prepare for the next presidential elections in December 2000 and challenged his old ally, Preval. Since Aristide supporters controlled Parliament, Preval was unable to enact policies and programs, some of which were crucial to receiving international assistance. For much of his term, Preval was even unable to appoint his own prime minister, and was compelled to bypass Parliament, which stopped functioning. The UN had helped to restore the democratically elected government of Haiti, but it could not guarantee successful democratic governance.[29]

On June 28, 1996, the Security Council established the UN Support Mission in Haiti (UNSMIH) to replace UNMIH. The number of troops would be reduced from more than 6,000 to 600 plus 700 voluntarily funded personnel, and the civilian police from almost 800 to 300.[30] Because of Haiti's diplomatic recognition of Taiwan, China had imposed obstacles in the Security Council to renewing UNMIH. In addition, the United States, in particular, wanted to reduce its deployment. UNSMIH was necessary, because the Haitian National Police was not yet in a position to ensure a secure environment and because a number of armed groups threatened the regime and the development of democracy. After several extensions, UNSMIH came to an end on July 31, 1997, and the Council replaced it with the UN Transition Mission in Haiti (UNTMIH), which remained until November.[31] The final UN operation was the Civilian Police Mission in Haiti (MIPONUH), which replaced UNTMIH and remained until 1999.[32]

Conclusion

The successes of the UN in the 1990s under Boutros Boutros-Ghali were path breaking and demonstrated how some of the proposals in *An Agenda for Peace* could be implemented. The UN intervened with multi-dimensional peacekeeping missions in four countries, which had been experiencing major civil strife. In all four cases, peacekeepers first had to make peace, compelling opposing forces to abide by peace agreements sufficiently so that peace could be established and maintained. The UN assumed a role in the administration of all four countries. Most significantly, the UN demonstrated, for the first time, a commitment to civil and political rights by deploying human rights monitors and to multiparty democracy by preparing for elections and then helping to run and monitor them. The UN remained in the countries to help build the peace and to lay the groundwork for socio-economic and political development.

The four missions were also different. UNTAC was the most complex in terms of functions and the number of factions, particularly the intractable Khmer Rouge, as well as the largest in scale. Partly due to the Khmer Rouge, UNTAC leaders decided to stick to a pre-determined timetable. In contrast, the other three missions showed greater flexibility and achieved a higher degree of demobilization and democratic stability. ONUMOZ was almost as large and complex as UNTAC and was able to secure the largest demobilization of soldiers of the four missions and the establishment of a stable, multi-party democracy in a country that was deemed too poor and too divided to do so. The UN, particularly the secretary-general, became involved in peacemaking in El Salvador at an earlier stage than in Cambodia and Mozambique. Early UN involvement in El Salvador facilitated the implementation of the agreement by ONUSAL, which was able to bring peace and democracy to a society that had been bitterly divided and terrorized by death squads. In Haiti, the UN became involved at an early stage in attempting to compel a military dictatorship to surrender power in favor of a democratic regime. Eventually, the Security Council authorized the use of force, under Chapter VII of the UN Charter, to intervene in a sovereign state to restore democracy. None of the other three missions possessed or exerted such authority.

The next two chapters will analyze four major failures by the UN. At first glance, the four successes featured peace agreements that all of the parties had signed and sufficient forces and mandate to deter potential defectors, except for the Khmer Rouge. However, upon closer analysis of the success stories, all could have failed if the UN had been less attentive or had exerted less political will. Peace agreements and cease-fires, by themselves, guarantee little. As will be demonstrated in the next chapter, both parties in Angola signed two major agreements, which they subsequently broke. In conclusion, the successes of the UN were not as easily achievable as they might first appear.

Notes

1. UN Security Council Resolution 693, May 20, 1991.

2. Mark LeVine, "Peacemaking in El Salvador," in *Keeping the Peace: Multidimensional UN Operations in Cambodia and El Salvador,* Michael W. Doyle, Ian Johnstone, and Robert C. Orr, eds. (Cambridge: Cambridge University Press, 1997), 241-43.

3. *The United Nations and El Salvador,* UN Blue Book Series, Volume IV (New York: Department of Public Information, 1995), 68-75. See the chronology.

4. *The United Nations and El Salvador,* 68.

5. UN Security Council Resolution 729, January 14, 1992.

6. Kimbra L. Fishel and Edwin G. Corr, "UN Peace Operations in El Salvador: The Manwaring Paradigm in a Traditional Setting," in *The Savage Wars of Peace: Toward a New Paradigm of Peace Operations,* John T. Fishel, ed. (Boulder, Colo.: Westview Press), 51. The Spanish contingent helped to reassure the Salvadoran government of ONUSAL's neutrality.

7. Fen Osler Hampson, "The Pursuit of Human Rights: The United Nations in El Salvador," in *UN Peacekeeping, American Policy, and the Uncivil Wars of the 1990s,* William J. Durch, ed. (New York: St. Martin's Press, 1996), 86-88.

8. UN Security Council Resolution 832, May 27, 1993.

9. *The United Nations and El Salvador,* 72.

10. Reports of the Secretary-General on the United Nations Observer Mission to El Salvador, S/1994/179, February 16, 1994, S/1994/304, March 16, 1994, S/1994/375, March 31, 1994.

11. Hampson, "The Pursuit of Human Rights," 93-94.

12. UN Security Council Resolution 920, May 26, 1994.

13. UN Security Council Resolution 920, May 26, 1994.

14. Hampson, "The Pursuit of Human Rights," 98.

15. UN Security Council Resolution 961, November 23, 1994.

16. *Basic Facts about the United Nations* (United Nations: Department of Public Information, 1998), 92.

17. *Basic Facts,* 92-93.

18. David Malone, "Haiti and the International Community: A Case Study." *Survival.* Vol. 39, No. 2 (Summer 1997), 126-46.

19. Alex Dupuy, *Haiti in the New World Order: The Limits of the Democratic Revolution* (Boulder, Colo.: Westview Press, 1997), 175-83. See the book's chronology.

20. Thomas Weiss, *Military-Civilian Interventions* (Lanham, Md.: Rowman & Littlefield, 1999), 175.

21. Chetan Kumar, *Building Peace in Haiti* (Boulder, Colo.: Lynne Rienner, 1998), 41.

22. UN Security Council Resolution 875, October 16, 1993.

23. William Booth, "Aristide at Meeting, Renews Appeal for Haitian Democracy," *Washington Post,* January 16, 1994, A20.

24. UN Security Council Resolution 917, May 6, 1994.

25. UN Security Council Resolution 940, July 31, 1994.

26. Douglas Farah, "Unity of Haitian Leaders Cracks under U.S. Pressure." *Washington Post,* September 25, 1994, A42.

27. *Basic Facts,* 92-93.

28. "Preval is Declared Winner in Haiti," *Washington Post,* December 24,

1995, A16.
29. Kumar, *Building Peace*, 44.
30. UN Security Council Resolution 1063, June 28, 1996.
31. UN Security Council Resolution 1123, July 30, 1997.
32. Kumar, *Building Peace*, 44-45.

4

Failure: Angola and Somalia

The success stories in Cambodia, Mozambique, El Salvador, and Haiti demonstrated that the UN could accomplish far more than it had been able to during the Cold War. UNTAC, ONUMOZ, ONUSAL, and UNMIH were large and complex missions, which fulfilled a number of tasks that the UN had not previously undertaken. In all four missions, the UN was involved in peacemaking and peace enforcement, even before peace could be kept. The missions demonstrated that the UN could fulfill the ambitious objectives outlined in *An Agenda for Peace*. The prerequisites for success in all four cases included authorization by *de jure* governments to enter their countries to help implement peace agreements and a sufficiently strong mandate to deal with threats, which undermined the agreements.

In spite of its successes, the UN under Boutros Boutros-Ghali will be remembered more for its failures. Before 1992, UN objectives were modest, and, therefore, peacekeeping missions did not anticipate nor experience failure. Before 1992, when the UN was unsuccessful, it was because the organization was unable to become involved in the resolution of many conflicts, due to the Cold War, and because it was unable to make peace in intractable conflicts where blue helmets were stationed, such as Cyprus, Kashmir, and the Middle East. Already, in 1992 alone, two UN missions were in the process of failing to achieve their objectives. In Angola, UNAVEM II was unable to stop the resumption of civil war, and, in Somalia, UNOSOM I was totally incapable of ensuring the delivery of relief supplies to starving Somalis. In both cases, the secretary-general and the Security Council failed to correctly assess the threats to peace and authorize missions with sufficient mandates to deal with those threats. In the case of Angola, the problem was that the peace agreement, which had not involved UN participation, called for a limited role for the UN. Another problem was the volume of missions that the UN was undertaking. In 1992, the UN placed six major missions in the field at once and had difficulties managing all of them.

After 1992, the problem was a failure to adjust to prevailing realities. In 1993, UNOSOM II was given Chapter VII enforcement powers and intervened against one of the warring sides in Somalia and with too much force. In 1992, the UN failed to respond to ethnic cleansing and genocide in Bosnia, and UNPROFOR entered with an insufficient mandate to stop the conflict. In Rwanda, the UN failed to adjust when genocide erupted in 1994, and it withdrew. In 1995, UNAVEM III was given a greater mandate and more peacekeeping troops, but was unable to compel Jonas Savimbi to fully demobilize UNITA forces in Angola and abide by peace agreements.

Angola and UNAVEM

Failure in Angola took place at two different stages, UNAVEM II in 1992 and UNAVEM III in 1996-97. When UNAVEM II failed, it was thought that an insufficient mandate and inability to demobilize forces were responsible. This impression seemed to be confirmed, when ONUMOZ was given an enhanced mandate and a larger force and succeeded in demobilizing forces and bringing peace in Mozambique. Subsequently, when UNAVEM III was created in 1995, it was designed along the same lines as ONUMOZ, with the belief that an enhanced mandate and thousands of blue helmets would bring demobilization and success. However, UNAVEM III failed as well, shifting the focus of analysis from the UN's mandate to the behavior of Jonas Savimbi and UNITA. After 1997, Savimbi's unwillingness to subordinate himself to President Eduardo dos Santos in sharing power and to relinquish control of diamond areas became the most important explanation for UN failure.

The conflict in Angola has been one of the longest lasting, starting in the early 1960s with the struggle of African national liberation movements against Portuguese colonialism. While three movements, the Popular Movement for the Liberation of Angola (MPLA), the Front for the National Liberation of Angola (FNLA), and UNITA, began fighting against the Portuguese, they also occasionally attacked each other. With the winding down of colonial rule in 1974 and 1975, the three movements reached a unity agreement and then reneged and began fighting each other. South African and Cuban intervention in 1975 escalated the fighting into a fully-fledged civil war. From 1975 until 1988, civil war raged in Angola as the MPLA government, backed by thousands of Cuban troops and the Soviet bloc fought against UNITA, supported by South Africa and, covertly, by the United States. In the 1980s, UNITA gained international stature among conservatives in the West and was able to maintain a presence in its ethnic Ovimbundu region of central Angola and wrest control of the diamond region of northeast Angola. Consequently, UNITA became a self-reliant and substantial movement. In contrast, RENAMO did not attain international stature and remained largely dependent on South African support.

In 1986, the United States began to finance UNITA, after the repeal of the Clark Amendment. At the same time, Mikhail Gorbachev sought to reduce Soviet support and begin the withdrawal of 50,000 Cuban troops.[1] In 1988, the winding down of the Cold War and a South African setback in the battle of Cuito Cuanavale in southeastern Angola set the stage for negotiations to withdraw Cuban troops from Angola in return for South Africa granting Namibia independence. Under the direction of Chester Crocker, U.S. Assistant Secretary of State for Africa, an agreement was signed in New York in December 1988. Shortly thereafter, the Security Council authorized both UNAVEM I in Angola and UNTAG in Namibia. From 1989 to 1991, seventy military observers monitored Cuban withdrawal from Angola.[2]

While the Cuban troops withdrew under UNAVEM supervision, the MPLA government and UNITA forces continued to fight. By March 1990, the fighting had reached stalemate and, in April, the two sides agreed to negotiations in Portugal, with U.S. and Soviet observers. After a year of talks, the parties signed the Bicesse Peace Accords. The accords called on both sides to cease fire and canton their forces at fifty assembly points where they would demobilize. The MPLA government and UNITA were to establish a Joint Political-Military Commission of the MPLA government and UNITA to monitor the cease-fire and a Joint Verification and Monitoring Commission to supervise the demobilization of forces. Both commissions would have international observers from Portugal, the Soviet Union, and the United States, and the UN was called upon to verify demobilization activities and the creation of a neutral police force. UNITA was to be given assistance and security assurances in converting from a guerrilla movement into a political party. Presidential and parliamentary elections would be held and monitored by international observers. The parties did not specifically request that the UN assume control of or even become involved in election monitoring.

With the Bicesse Accords and the withdrawal of the last Cuban troops in May 1991, the Security Council authorized UNAVEM II to supersede UNAVEM I.[3] The new budget and mandate were modest and allowed for the monitoring of demobilization and the creation of a new police force. Already in 1991, missions had been created on the Kuwait-Iraq border, in El Salvador, and Western Sahara, and the council did not feel that UNAVEM II was important enough to warrant a larger budget. Therefore, the budget of UNAVEM II was just over $100 million.[4]

On June 1, 1991, the first of an authorized 350 military and ninety police observers deployed for UNAVEM II. In spite of tremendous logistical difficulties, all had arrived by September 30. From June through October, the military observers deployed to the assembly points. While some soldiers began to report and surrender their weapons before the deadline in July, the observers found that insufficient progress was being made. Both sides distrusted each other so much that they balked at implementing perhaps the most important provisions of the Bicesse Accords. In spite of widespread non-compliance, the mandate of UNAVEM II did not include any provisions for enforcement. By October, less than 60 percent of soldiers had reported to assembly camps. This was three months after the deadline for demobilization. In addition, the presence of thousands upon thousands of land mines and badly deteriorated roads made travel difficult, if not dangerous, for UNAVEM II units and for guerrillas and MPLA government forces reporting to assembly points. In a major setback for UNAVEM II, 36,000 MPLA government troops quit the assembly points at the end of 1991.[5]

At the end of 1991, the MPLA government recognized that only the UN had the authority and neutrality to ensure that the upcoming elections would be free and fair. After the Angolan government requested UN electoral supervision, the new secretary-general, Boutros Boutros-Ghali, went to the Security Council and asked for an expansion of the mandate. On March 24, 1992, the council expanded UNAVEM II's mandate to include verifying the impartiality of electoral officials, the freedom of parties to form, operate, and articulate their positions, fair access to the media, and the freedom and fairness of the elections themselves.[6]

While the mandate of UNAVEM II was significantly expanded, the budget was increased only marginally. Again, other missions, such as UNTAC, seemed to be more important and dangerous than UNAVEM II.

Even so, thousands of armed soldiers continued to remain outside of the assembly points and were prepared to resume hostilities.

In March 1992, Boutros-Ghali contacted Margaret Joan Anstee and, with no notice, asked her to become Special Representative of the Secretary-General (SRSG) and Chief of Mission in Angola, the first woman to hold those positions. After agreeing, Boutros-Ghali asked her to report as soon as possible to Luanda. She arrived in Luanda on March 18, 1992 and was almost immediately confronted with numerous problems and obstacles. As a woman SRSG and Chief of Mission, Anstee was faced with male chauvinist attitudes from Angolan leaders and UN personnel alike. After observing the paltry resources and mandate given to UNAVEM II, she commented that the task of completing the mission was like "trying to make bricks without straw."[7]

Besides the problem of demobilization of forces, another impediment was the slow progress in creating a neutral police force. The two sides failed to establish neutral monitoring teams. UNAVEM II civilian police were left with no trainees. Subsequently, the MPLA-dominated civilian police played a major role in the resumption of hostilities in October 1992. In an attempt to speed up troop demobilization, the U.S. Air Force sent C-130s to Angola in July 1992 for a three-month period to transport primarily Angolan government soldiers from assembly points to their home areas. However, as elections approached at the end of September, it was clear that less than half of all soldiers and guerrillas had been demobilized.

The formation of the National Election Commission and the start of voter registration in May 1992 prompted Anstee and UNAVEM II to switch focus and protect the electoral process. Anstee's decision was comparable to that of UNTAC Special Representative Akashi, who decided to shift emphasis from troop demobilization and police retraining to assist with the protection, organization, implementation, and supervision of the elections. However, UNAVEM II had less than 500 troops to accomplish the task, whereas UNTAC had 15,000.[8]

The registration of voters took place from May 20 to August 10. UNAVEM II attempted to ensure that registration was comprehensive and uniform throughout Angola. However, in the oil-rich Cabinda enclave, the separatist movement, the Liberation Front for the Enclave of Cabinda (FLEC), was able to intimidate much of the populace from registering. Anstee and other UNAVEM II officials appealed to the National Election Commission to extend the registration period to allow Cabindans to vote.[9] However, the commission refused, wanting to press on with the electoral process before a crisis occurred. In August, a high number of people had registered to vote for a country that had been racked with war and millions of land mines. It was estimated that 92 percent of the eligible population had registered to vote.[10]

The elections took place on September 29 and 30, 1992. The voter turnout was very high, approximately 92 percent of 4.8 million registered voters.[11] The UN and other international observers reported relatively few problems during the elections. However, as soon as the elections were over, the MPLA and UNITA began to declare that they had won the elections. The process of vote counting and ensuring that the elections were "free and fair" took over two weeks. Finally, on October 17, 1992, the UN certified the elections and called for a run-off election for president. In the presidential elections, President dos Santos won 49.57 percent of the vote, while UNITA leader, Jonas Savimbi, had 40.07 percent. According to the new constitution, a run-off election for president was necessary. For parliament, the ruling party, MPLA, won 53.74 percent of the vote and 129 seats, winning an absolute majority. UNITA received 34.1 percent and 70 seats. Ten other parties shared the remaining 21 seats.[12]

When the results were announced, Savimbi and UNITA refused to accept them, arguing that the Angolan government had exercised undue influence over the electoral process. Savimbi's failure to abide by the results touched off violent incidents between Angolan government and UNITA forces, which soon intensified. On October 31, Angolan government police units launched a major attack in Luanda on UNITA officials and forces that had been stationed there under the Bicesse Accords. The attack ignited fighting throughout Angola, which soon became as bloody or even bloodier as before the Accords.

In spite of the collapse of the peace process, the UN Security Council renewed the UNAVEM II mandate on several occasions in 1992, 1993, and 1994 hoping that the process could be revived. During that time, southern and central African states became involved in negotiations with the Angolan government and UNITA. Finally, in October 1994, these African states managed to persuade the two parties to agree to the Lusaka Protocol to the Bicesse Accords, which was signed on November 20. The protocol was designed to build upon the Bicesse Accords and the results of the 1992 elections, by establishing a government of national unity in Luanda and implementing out the comprehensive demobilization of forces. The protocol called upon the UN to establish a greater presence and to wield a stronger mandate than that of UNAVEM II.

UNAVEM III and Withdrawal

On February 8, 1995, the Security Council created UNAVEM III to implement the Lusaka Protocol. In accordance with the requests of African states and the protocol, the council designed UNAVEM III along the lines of ONUMOZ and UNTAC, with more than 7,000 peacekeepers and observers and a broad mandate. The mandate included verifying the cease-fire, demobilization and disarmament of forces, and the creation of a neutral police force. The mandate also included assisting in the extension of central administration to all parts of the country, guaranteeing the free movement of people and goods and security for UNITA, and monitoring of a second round of elections.[13]

The Angolan government eased UNAVEM III's burden by postponing elections until the year 2000. Thus, UNAVEM III's mandate went beyond the monitoring and verifying that had been the responsibility of UNAVEM II. UNAVEM III was charged with overseeing each stage of the process, from peacemaking to peace building. The UN was to receive, guard, and transport all weapons. Finally, the SRSG was given complete authority over the operation.

In February 1995, UNAVEM III began to deploy 6770 military peacekeepers, 350 military observers, and 260 police monitors. For the 1995-96 period, the cost of UNAVEM III was $383 million and, factoring in government in-kind services and facilities, actually was $500 million.[14] The SRSG and Chief of Mission was Alioune Blondin Beye, a highly respected diplomat from Senegal who began to work impressively to make peace in Angola. Significantly, UNAVEM III was given a deadline of February 1997, which provided it with two years to complete the mission and then withdraw. The deadline was intended to put pressure on the parties to complete the peace process.

The most important task of UNAVEM III was to successfully oversee the demobilization of Angolan government and UNITA forces. Subsequently, UNAVEM III oversaw the demobilization of more troops than UNAVEM II. However, as in 1992, both sides held in reserve their best troops and did not send them to assembly points, in preparation for a possible resumption of hostilities. In 1995, there were even worse logistical problems than in 1992. More than three million people were displaced, almost half of the population, and Angola possessed millions of land mines. UNAVEM III tried a number of measures to move forward the peace process. Boutros-Ghali visited Angola in July 1995 to bolster UNAVEM III and encourage the two parties to continue the process.

UNAVEM III leaders were determined to inform all Angolans about purpose of the mission and set up a radio station that attempted to counter the partisanship of MPLA and UNITA broadcasts. UNAVEM III also introduced a human rights component to monitor and report the abusive practices of both the Angolan government and UNITA.

By 1996, Savimbi and UNITA were balking at total demobilization and a power-sharing arrangement with the MPLA government. The best UNITA troops still had not been sent to the assembly points. UNITA officials in Luanda broke with Savimbi and sought to win over the rest of the movement in order to implement the Lusaka Protocol. As 1996 proceeded, it became apparent that Savimbi had triumphed and that the Lusaka Protocol would not be fulfilled. On October 11, 1996, the Security Council emphasized that continuing delays and unfulfilled promises, particularly by UNITA, in implementing successive timetables for the completion of key military and political issues were no longer acceptable.[15]

In response, UNITA submitted a list of tasks that it had to fulfill by November 15. In response, UNAVEM III prepared a revised timetable for implementation. However, UNITA did not fulfill it. By the end of 1996, UNAVEM III had reached an impasse, achieving only partial demobilization.

In December 1996, UNAVEM III began to withdraw, in line with the deadline of February 1997. In the meantime, the UN considered what to do after UNAVEM III had departed. The Security Council's answer was the UN Observer Mission in Angola (MONUA), which was established on June 30, 1997. The mandate of MONUA was to assist the parties in consolidating peace and national reconciliation, enhance confidence building, and create an environment conducive to long-term stability. MONUA was also charged with the completion of the demobilization process and the incorporation of UNITA forces into the Armed Forces of Angola (FAA). Civilian police were to stay behind to continue to create a neutral police force and disarm the population.[16]

MONUA's mandate proved to be a façade, as UN personnel were gradually withdrawn and the Angolan government and UNITA returned to full-scale fighting. Within two years, on February 26, 1999, MONUA was terminated. The peace process lay in ruins. Although UNITA had split, the division of Angola and the balance of power between Savimbi's forces and the Angolan government's remained. However, the UN hoped that, with sanctions and other pressures, UNITA would soon decline and disintegrate, much like the Khmer Rouge did in Cambodia.

In conclusion, both UNAVEM II and UNAVEM III failed. The primary reason was the unwillingness of Savimbi and UNITA to surrender their power and wealth that came from controlling half of Angola. In contrast to Mozambique, Angola was richer in resources, so there was more at stake for both sides. In the face of both sides' intransigence, there appears to be little more that the UN could have done. Perhaps if UNAVEM II had been given a greater mandate and more troops, they could have built trust between the Angolan government and UNITA, especially over demobilization. However, 1992 was a very active time for the UN, and the parties to the Bicesse Accords did not insist on UN leadership. By 1995, UNAVEM III was forced to try to overcome even greater distrust than existed during 1992, so the task was even more complex and difficult to complete.

Somalia and UNOSOM

In January 1991, the collapse of the Mohamed Siad Barre dictatorship in Somalia led to anarchy and clan warfare that became particularly intense in the capital city, Mogadishu. From 1978 to 1990, the United States and Egypt had supported the Siad Barre regime as an ally in the Cold War against pro-Soviet Ethiopia. In 1990, Siad Barre actually sent troops to the Persian Gulf in support of Operation Desert Shield and hoped that the United States would reciprocate by continuing support for his regime. However, with the end of the Cold War and growing U.S. support for democratization, the Bush administration quickly phased out support to the Barre dictatorship. Within months, Siad Barre and his regime could no longer resist rebel attacks and fled Mogadishu. The rebels installed an interim president, Ali Mahdi Mohamed, but he was unable to consolidate power in the face of clan-based "warlord" forces. The Somali state collapsed, and the country descended into anarchy. With attention centered on the Gulf, the United States, Egypt, and other countries failed to step in to mediate and impose a peace plan.

Throughout 1991 and 1992, forces of clan-based warlords attacked peasant farmers, stealing their food and crops. Also, warlord forces stole relief supplies from international aid agencies. Consequently, the warlords contributed to expanding food shortages and a growing famine. In 1991 and 1992 anarchy reigned, and warlords seized pieces of Somalia, roughly according to their clan bases. The capital city, Mogadishu, became a war zone. With no force in Somalia, including Interim President Mohamed, able to unite the country and with the inability of the

Organization of African Unity (OAU) to involve itself, Somali non-combatants and leaders of neighboring states turned to the UN to deal with a growing catastrophe. Subsequently, the Security Council took the lead in dispatching envoys to make peace between the warring factions, and the World Food Program and other UN agencies, as well as NGOs, were tasked with coordinating the delivery of humanitarian relief to a growing population of starving and sick people.

In January 1992, the Security Council imposed an arms embargo on Somalia.[17] Under-Secretary-General James Jonah negotiated a cease-fire. However, the agreement broke down, as the warlords resumed fighting and blocking and plundering relief supplies. UN agencies were slow to respond to the growing humanitarian disaster.

After months of debate and inaction, in July 1992, the Security Council authorized the UN Operation in Somalia and the deployment of more than 3,000 peacekeepers.[18] Boutros-Ghali appointed Mohamed Sahnoun as the Special Representative of the Secretary-General (SRSG) to Somalia. Sahnoun negotiated agreements with the warlords to cease firing and to allow the delivery of humanitarian relief supplies. An advance force of 500 Pakistani troops were dispatched to stop the looting of food supplies and to ensure the delivery of food in order to halt the growing famine, which threatened hundreds of thousands, if not millions, of Somalis. However, UNOSOM I forces were immediately pinned down in the Mogadishu harbor district when they arrived in Somalia, and they were never reinforced. As the weeks passed, it became increasingly apparent that the deployment of UNOSOM I was insufficient to stop the looting of supplies and the growing famine.[19]

Boutros Boutros-Ghali, who had been partly in charge of Egypt's foreign affairs and established close relations in the 1980s with the dictator, Siad Barre, caused problems for UN peacemaking and peacekeeping efforts in Somalia. The chief warlord, Mohamed Farah Aideed, and several other warlords believed that Boutros-Ghali was biased against them, and the secretary-general's assertive diplomacy in Somalia helped to confirm their impressions. Boutros-Ghali undermined his own SRSG, as Sahnoun began to make progress in his mediation efforts. At the end of August 1992, without consulting Sahnoun or the warlords, Boutros-Ghali unilaterally announced the deployment of 3,000 additional troops to reinforce the 500 blue helmets in Mogadishu harbor.[20] This action infuriated the warlords and angered Sahnoun, who had reached an agreement that no further peacekeepers were to be deployed. In September, Boutros-Ghali reprimanded Sahnoun and then precipitated his resignation, after Sahnoun organized a peace conference among the warlords and Somali elites in the Seychelles.

The United States and Operation Restore Hope

President Bush's decision in November 1992 to send more than 24,000 troops to Somalia in Operation Restore Hope, with UN endorsement, ranks as one of the most intriguing decisions that any world leader has made. The Somalia mission was not in the U.S. national interest. Somalia contained no significant natural resources, and the Cold War rivalry with the Soviet Union over the Horn of Africa had ended by 1992. Operation Restore Hope represented a substantial commitment of U.S. power and was solely intended to put an end to a humanitarian catastrophe. Consequently, President Bush's decision was an act of humanitarian idealism and a demonstration of his commitment to his self-proclaimed "new world order."[21] After President Bush's defeat in the November 1992 presidential elections, he felt the need to "do something" before he left office and wished to shore up his place in history. An even more important key factor that led to the intervention was that the views of President Bush and UN Secretary-General Boutros-Ghali converged over the need for U.S. intervention.

U.S. involvement can be traced to May 12, 1992, when Boutros-Ghali visited the White House and alerted President Bush to the growing crisis in Somalia.[22] Boutros-Ghali informed the president that the weak Western response to the famine in Somalia was lowering U.S. prestige in the Middle East, which had been greatly boosted during the Gulf War. In the region, the perception was growing that the West was turning a blind eye to Somalis because they were Muslims. Although the Bush administration had committed some $240 million in food aid to Somalia, starting in April 1991, the food was clearly not reaching the most desperate people.[23] In response to the secretary-general's plea, President Bush, at the end of July 1992, ordered an airlift from Kenya, which would continue until the roads to Somalia could be opened. In spite of the airlift, insufficient food was reaching the most stricken parts of Somalia, and more and more Somalis were suffering from severe hunger and malnutrition and were dying of starvation and disease.

By the first week of November 1992, the crisis had brought massive famine and television pictures from CNN of starving and sick children. President Bush was receiving reports that relief efforts were not succeeding and that thousands were dying each week. Deliberations began in the White House, the State Department, and the Defense Department about how to deal with the increasingly desperate situation. Officials from relief organizations were lobbying Bush administration officials, including Acting Secretary of State, Lawrence Eagleburger, and Undersecretary of State for International Security Affairs, Frank Wisner, with demands that action be taken. In particular, the relief specialist, Fred Cuny, lobbied Paul Wolfowitz, the Undersecretary of Defense for Policy Planning, for a humanitarian operation. Cuny told Wolfowitz that the mission to save Somalis should be similar to Operation Provide Comfort that had helped to relieve the Iraqi Kurds in April 1991.[24]

Only in the middle of November 1992, did U.S. officials begin to consider the option of sending ground forces to Somalia. On November 15, 1992, the Deputies Committee (including deputies to the Secretary of State and Secretary of Defense) met at the Pentagon and devised a plan for an expanded UN presence. Undersecretary of State Wisner proposed that the United States organize a coalition under UN command and provide logistics, but no ground forces. Accordingly, the Deputies Committee proposed to President Bush a compromise option, with an expanded UN presence with ground forces from Canada, Belgium, and other NATO allies, but not from the United States. However, opponents of "option one-and-a-half" argued that Canada and Belgium would not commit troops unless the United States did. Four days later, on Thursday, November 19, 1992, Admiral David Jeremiah, Vice Chairman of the Joint Chiefs of Staff argued strongly that the greatest chance of success lay in having the United States carry out the relief effort itself with a division or so of troops. For the first time, massive deployment appeared on the table as an option. However, on that day, Admiral Jeremiah did not persuade the rest of the Deputies Committee. Joint Chiefs of Staff Chairman Colin Powell remained against the involvement of U.S. ground forces. However, Powell made it clear that he wanted complete command and control by the United States if ground forces were to be committed.[25]

Boutros-Ghali dispatched a letter to Security Council members urgently asking for ideas or initiatives to stem the mounting humanitarian disaster. Upon receiving the letter on Tuesday, November 24, President Bush asked the Pentagon to come up with a much bolder plan. Dropping his opposition to intervention, Colin Powell requested the formulation of a plan of action based upon the principle of decisive intervention in which U.S. forces would intervene massively and leave quickly. A meeting of top members of the National Security Council convened at the White House on Wednesday, November 25. At the meeting, option one-

and-a-half was the main topic of discussion. However, the meeting rejected this option, because it had been confirmed that Canada and Belgium would not commit troops unless the United States did. Colin Powell then laid out plans for Operation Restore Hope, which involved putting a substantial number of U.S. troops on the ground to take charge of the country and to make sure that the food reached the starving Somalis. President Bush approved the plan. He did so even though there was no prospect for the mission to be finished by the time he left office on January 20, 1993.[26]

After the meeting, President Bush dispatched Acting Secretary of State Eagleburger to the UN to meet with Boutros-Ghali and make the offer of U.S. troops. The United States would launch Operation Restore Hope on condition that the force was under U.S. command, included sizeable contingents from other national armies, and be authorized under Chapter VII of the UN Charter to use force when necessary. Upon receiving the offer, Secretary-General Boutros-Ghali recommended the U.S. proposal to the Security Council on November 29. On December 3, the council agreed to the terms and approved and authorized Operation Restore Hope, in the guise of the United Task Force (UNITAF), and invoked Chapter VII of the UN Charter.[27]

President Bush's support for the New World Order and Boutros-Ghali's proposal for peace enforcement and humanitarian intervention, outlined in *An Agenda for Peace,* had brought the two together in support of Operation Restore Hope. In addition, the two continued to be embarrassed by the lack of response to ethnic cleansing by the Bosnian Serbs. Boutros-Ghali had failed in Somalia with his undermining of Sahnoun's mediation efforts, the weakness of UNOSOM I, and the intransigence and unreliability of the warlords and faction leaders. Bush was embarrassed by the fact that the mass starvation of Somali children now characterized the "new world order."

Without Boutros-Ghali's letter and Colin Powell's "decisive intervention" option, it is unlikely that Bush would have opted for massive deployment. President Bush, with his proposal for Operation Restore Hope answered the secretary-general's plea for action in the boldest possible way. If President Bush's advisors harbored reservations about a "Somalia quagmire," he preempted them by selecting the strongest possible option. Thus, he surprised many administration officials, especially top State Department staff, who had proposed a far more modest plan. The president was not being realistic when he assumed that U.S. forces could arrive in December and be withdrawn by January 19, 1993.

The United States committed 24,000 troops to ensure the provision of humanitarian relief. While the United Task Force (UNITAF) or Operation Restore Hope proceeded with Chapter VII powers to use force if necessary to complete the mission, the United States had less free rein than during the Gulf War. Unlike Operation Desert Storm, where the UN provided a blank check to free Kuwait, the United States was required to work closely with UN agencies in Somalia and at UN headquarters in New York. This arrangement created friction between the United States and the secretary-general over the goals of the mission. Early on, a significant difference arose over the disarming of Somali factions, which the U.S. military declared that it was most reluctant to do. Boutros-Ghali would continue to focus on the point, which would lead to disaster ten months later in UNOSOM II.

U.S. Marines landed in Mogadishu on December 9, 1992, and soon the entire contingent of 24,000 U.S. troops came ashore. Eventually, more than 20,000 additional troops from twenty other countries joined U.S. forces, and Japan contributed $100 million to help pay for the operation.[28] President Bush visited the troops in January 1993. Before he left office on January 20, 1993, the U.S.-led multilateral operation had succeeded in supplying humanitarian relief and helping to curb the famine and starvation. However, UNITAF ignored Boutros-Ghali's requests and made little effort at disarming or demobilizing Somalia's warring factions. Furthermore, the relief operation had concentrated on delivering food, when medical supplies for the malnourished were in the greatest need.

In launching the Somalia mission, President Bush made a series of statements, which seemed to constitute a doctrine for U.S.-led humanitarian intervention in cooperation with the UN. On Friday, December 4, 1992, President Bush addressed the American people, announcing the commitment of U.S. troops to rescue the people of Somalia. "I want to emphasize that I understand the United States alone cannot right the world's wrongs, but we also know that some crises in the world cannot be resolved without American involvement, that American action is often necessary as a catalyst for broader involvement of the community of nations."[29]

On January 5, 1993, President Bush spoke at West Point and supported interventionism in cases where the national interest was not at stake in order to support a democratic peace and less than vital interests:

However, in the wake of the Cold War, in a world where we are the only superpower, it is the role of the United States to marshal its moral and material resources to promote a democratic peace. Similarly, we cannot always decide in advance which interests will require our using military force to protect them. The relative importance of an interest is not a guide: military force may not be the best way of safeguarding something vital, while using force may be the best way to protect an interest that qualifies as important but less than vital. Using military force makes sense as a policy where the stakes warrant, where and when force can be effective, where no other policies are likely to prove effective, where its application can be limited in scope and time, and where the potential benefits justify the potential costs and sacrifice. Once we are satisfied that force makes sense, we must act with the maximum possible support. The United States can and should lead, but we will want to act in concert, where possible involving the UN or other international grouping. The United States can and should contribute to the common undertaking in a manner commensurate with our wealth, with our strength. Nevertheless, others should also contribute militarily, be it by providing combat or support forces, access to facilities or bases, or over-flight rights. Similarly, others should contribute economically.[30]

After the caution displayed by the Bush administration in the Bosnia and Haiti crises of 1992 and with weeks to go in the administration, the decision to intervene and to declare a doctrine of intervention was indeed surprising. Clinton and his advisors had little foreign policy experience and virtually no knowledge of the Somalia situation. In addition, the Clinton transition team was in the process of adopting a policy of "assertive multilateralism" that was just as idealistic or even more so than Bush's "new world order." Therefore, President Bush was, indeed, dropping a potentially dangerous foreign policy initiative into President Clinton's lap. While the Bush administration consulted Clinton, the president-elect had little or no basis for vetoing or even disagreeing with President Bush's decision.

UNOSOM II: Peace Enforcement and Nation-Building

In spite of limited aims, Operation Restore Hope, with the humanitarian intervention of the United States and forces from around the world, helped to end a famine, saved thousands of lives, and was the high water mark of the "new world order." However, President Bush's decision to intervene meant that the United States maintained a major presence in Somalia when the new, inexperienced and idealist Clinton administration came to office on January 20, 1993. President Clinton's "assertive multilateralism" went beyond President Bush's U.S.-led "new world order" and committed the United States to even closer collaboration with the UN. One outcome of this policy was the acceptance of dual leadership in Somalia by the U.S. government and by the secretary-general. In the first months of 1993, both the Clinton administration and Boutros-Ghali began to push the mission away from a humanitarian operation and toward peace enforcement, disarmament, and nation-building. "Mission Creep" had begun.

With the impending withdrawal of UNITAF, the Security Council, on the advice of the secretary-general, created UNOSOM II with Resolution 814 on March 26, 1993. UNOSOM II was granted a Chapter VII mandate, which enabled it to enforce cease-fires and seize weapons from warring factions, as well as to protect ongoing humanitarian relief efforts. In addition to the assertive peace enforcement tasks, UNOSOM II was expected to make peace through the delicate process of mediating among the warlords, bringing about a cease-fire, establishing an interim government, and restoring civil order throughout Somalia.[31]

The mandate given to UNOSOM II was a "tall order," especially since able and active diplomats, such as Mohamed Sahnoun and UNITAF's Ambassador Robert Oakley, had achieved only partial success in their peacemaking efforts. The new SRSG and Chief of UNOSOM II, the retired U.S. Admiral Jonathan Howe, lacked the diplomatic skills of his predecessors, and his assistants proved to be unhelpful. In addition, military command of UNOSOM II was placed largely in the hands of two U.S. generals who were accustomed to using force aggressively and not judiciously.

From its inception, UNOSOM II made diplomatic missteps. At the end of March 1993, two peace agreements emerged from the Addis Ababa conference, one which circumvented the warlords and the other which recognized their power and fiefdoms. UNOSOM II accepted and promoted the rebuilding of government from the local level upward, with minimal participation from the warlords. UNOSOM II's approach directly contradicted that of the warlords and, especially, General Mohamed Farah Aideed who expected to eventually become president of Somalia under the second agreement. Thus, a struggle for power began between Aideed and UNOSOM II. Boutros-Ghali and the Americans saw Aideed as the principal obstacle to peace and an adversary, while Aideed viewed the secretary-general and the UN as usurpers of his right to unify and rule Somalia. Thus began the "war of the air waves," with Aideed's Radio Mogadishu attacking UNOSOM II and with the much weaker UN radio station attempting to defend the mission and blame Aideed for its shortcomings. The struggle escalated as UNOSOM II began a campaign to inspect weapons and disarm the warlords.

On June 5, 1993, Pakistani peacekeepers conducted a surprise weapons inspection of Aideed's forces in Mogadishu. Believing they were under attack Aideed's forces opened fire and killed twenty-four blue helmets. Thus, began the four-month-long "Battle of Mogadishu." In response to the killings, the Security Council passed Resolution 837, which blamed Aideed for the clashes and called for his arrest and closing Radio Mogadishu.[32]

UNOSOM II forces attacked Radio Mogadishu and Aideed's military installations, intensified the campaign to disarm his faction, and dispatched forces to capture him. Admiral Howe requested and received the assistance of U.S. Army Rangers in the attempt to capture Aideed. In the meantime, the peace process was halted, as political reconciliation talks were stopped.

As the fighting between UNOSOM II and Aideed's forces continued, the Clinton administration and the UN failed to act to restore the peace process or to provide extra protection for the blue helmets. On October 3, 1993, U.S. Rangers were carrying out an operation against Aideed's forces when eighteen were trapped and killed. Subsequently, mutilated and naked American bodies were dragged through the streets of Mogadishu and filmed by CNN. The immediate outcry in the U.S. Congress led President Clinton to announce, on October 6, the withdrawal of U.S. forces from Somalia by March 31, 1994. In the meantime, U.S. forces retreated to fortified positions and were reinforced for their protection. Subsequently, contingents from other countries stood down as well. Ambassador Oakley returned to Mogadishu to negotiate with Aideed for the withdrawal of U.S. forces and the return of a captured American soldier. On November 16, 1993, the Security Council canceled the arrest warrant against Aideed. Aideed had won his war with the UN.[33]

Surprisingly, Boutros-Ghali continued to plea for peace enforcement efforts, including the disarmament of warring factions, to be sustained. UNOSOM II officials continued to act as if the mission could be resumed, especially as U.S. troops had been reinforced. Such behavior on the secretary-general's part revealed how zealously he was involved in the Somalia mission and that he did not understand the dramatic reversal of U.S. policy on Somalia and on the role of the UN in conflict management in general.

After the defeat of UNOSOM II's efforts at peace enforcement and nation-building, the mission was reduced to protecting humanitarian operations. The UN hoped that ongoing peacemaking efforts would bring a cease-fire among the warring factions and that peace-building efforts at the district level would lay the foundation for a new Somali state. However, General Aideed and other warlords still believed that they could seize control of Somalia through force, so they continued fighting each other and the UN. Finally, on November 4, 1994, the Security Council voted to terminate UNOSOM II by March 31, 1995.[34]

Pakistani, Bangladeshi, and Egyptian forces were the last to withdraw from Somalia. As U.S. ships arrived to pick them up, the warring clans scrambled to seize their military equipment. With the end of UNOSOM II, Somalia continued to be racked by violence and civil war. On a positive note, the specter of famine had receded and only occasionally has threatened Somalis since the early 1990s.

In 1993, "assertive multilateralism" and ambitious U.S. plans for the UN collided in Somalia with the reality of shrinking U.S. interests in the wake of the Cold War in a unipolar world with no superpower rivalry. In addition to the Somalia debacle, the exponential growth of the UN peacekeeping budget awakened the U.S. Congress and the Clinton administration toward a sober reassessment of the U.S.-UN relationship. Consequently, in October 1993, the Clinton administration balked at paying for a higher level of peacekeeping forces in Rwanda (UNAMIR), although additional blue helmets might have prevented the genocide of April-May 1994 from occurring. As a result of the Somalia experience and in the midst of the Rwandan genocide, the Clinton administration issued Presidential Defense Directive 25, a directive against U.S. involvement in peace enforcement operations. In sum, the killing of eighteen Americans destroyed Clinton's "assertive multilateralism" policy and led to the restoration of realism in U.S. foreign policy. The U.S. Congress and Clinton administration distanced itself from Secretary-General Boutros-Ghali and his *An Agenda for Peace*.

Both President Bush and President Clinton were unfortunate in having Boutros-Ghali as a partner in the Somalia operation. Starting in 1992, many Somalis perceived him and the UN as adversaries. By mid-1993, many saw UNOSOM II as an occupying force. With hindsight, Boutros-Ghali carried too much baggage in the Somalia crisis and was much too assertive. He should have kept a lower profile in Somalia and allowed his

Special Representative, Mohamed Sahnoun, to mediate among the warlords. Instead, Boutros-Ghali undermined and removed Sahnoun and antagonized Mohamed Farah Aideed and other warlords. The secretary-general pushed for disarmament and pacification of the warlords, when it was clear that this was an impossible task. Instead of attempting to work with the warlords, he urged UNOSOM II to confront them. While U.S. forces aggressively fought Aideed and precipitated the killing of the eighteen U.S. Army Rangers, Boutros-Ghali had pushed for the mandate that made such a scenario possible. With hindsight, President Clinton might have been wiser to maintain Operation Restore Hope and UNITAF longer in Somalia and forestalled the creation of UNOSOM II and the active involvement of Boutros-Ghali. President Clinton should not have agreed to UNOSOM II and its peace enforcement and nation-building terms of reference.

Conclusion: Failure in Angola and Somalia

In 1992, the UN undertook six missions (including Bosnia) where, for one of the first times, warring factions were either still fighting or were not fully committed to peace. In the three that succeeded, the chiefs of mission were skillful enough to adjust the timetables and the operations in order to hold elections and compel the parties (except the Khmer Rouge) to cooperate. In both Angola and Somalia, the chiefs of mission were not as skillful. However, given the lust for power of Savimbi and UNITA and Aideed and other warlords, it is unlikely that any amount of skill would have led to cooperation and peace. In Angola, the UN did what it could to bring about peace, but Savimbi deceived the peacemakers and broke two different agreements. In Somalia, the UN antagonized the warlords, but it is doubtful that peace would have been achieved, even if the UN had worked with the warlords.

The failure of the Angolan missions was unfortunate, but not damaging to the UN as the collapse of UNOSOM II was. In 1992, the collapse of UNAVEM II was blamed on the Security Council and the peacemakers rather than on the mission itself. In fact, the failure of the mission had a positive impact in preparations for ONUMOZ in Mozambique. Furthermore, the blame for failure in Angola ultimately fell on Savimbi and UNITA, with his betrayal of UNAVEM III. In contrast, the failure of UNOSOM II was disastrous, as Boutros-Ghali and the UN were blamed for the death of the eighteen U.S. Rangers, and it alienated the U.S. Congress and, to a lesser extent, the Clinton administration. The collapse of UNOSOM II led to UN inaction in the Rwandan genocide. UN failure in Somalia, combined with that in Bosnia, touched off the process that led to the end of Boutros-Ghali as secretary-general and to the chronic UN budget crisis of the 1990s.

Notes

1. Dennis C. Jett, *Why Peacekeeping Fails* (New York: St. Martin's Press, 1999), 64

2. Jett, *Why Peacekeeping Fails,* 70

3. UN Security Council Resolution 696, May 30, 1991.

4. Yvonne C. Lodico, "A Peace that Fell Apart: The United Nations and the War in Angola," in *UN Peacekeeping American Policy, and the Uncivil Wars of the 1990s,* William J. Durch, ed. (New York: St. Martin's Press, 1996), 111.

5. Margaret Joan Anstee, *Orphan of the Cold War: The Inside Story of the Collapse of the Angolan Peace Process, 1992-3* (New York: St. Martin's Press, 1996), 19.

6. UN Security Council Resolution 747, March 24, 1992.

7. Anstee, *Orphan of the Cold War*, 30.

8. Lodico, "A Peace that Fell Apart," 114.

9. Lodico, "A Peace that Fell Apart," 118-19.

10. Lodico, "A Peace that Fell Apart," 119.

11. Anstee, *Orphan of the Cold War*, 199.

12. "The September 1992 Elections," in *History of Angola: Virtual Tour,* <http://www.angola.org/> Angolan Government Web site.

13. UN Security Council Resolution 976, February 8, 1995.

14. Lodico, "A Peace that Fell Apart," 126.

15. UN Security Council Resolution 1075, October 11, 1996.

16. UN Security Council Resolution 1118, June 30, 1997.

17. UN Security Council Resolution 733, January 23, 1992.

18. UN Security Council Resolution 767, July 24, 1992.

19. Samuel Makinda, *Seeking Peace from Chaos* (Boulder, Colo.: Lynne Rienner, 1993), 63.

20. Mohamed Sahnoun, *Somalia: The Missed Opportunities* (Washington, D.C.: U.S. Institute for Peace, 1994), 39. Also, Jonathan Stevenson, "Hope Restored in Somalia," *Foreign Policy* no. 91 (Summer 1993), 148.

21. Peter B. Levy, *Encyclopedia of the Reagan-Bush Years* (Westport, Conn.: Greenwood Press, 1996), 255.

22. Fred Barnes, "Last Call," *New Republic,* December 28, 1992, 11.

23. Herman J. Cohen, "Update on Operation Restore Hope," U.S. Department of State Dispatch, December 21, 1992.

24. Barnes, "Last Call," 12.

25. Michael R. Gordon, "Somali Aid Plan is Called Most Ambitious Option," *New York Times,* November 28, 1992, A6.

26. Colin Powell, *My American Journey* (New York: Random House, 1995), 564-65.

27. UN Security Council Resolution 767, July 24, 1992.

28. Makinda, *Seeking Peace from Chaos*, 73. The biggest contributors were Pakistan (4,000 troops), Italy (3,800), India (3,000), and France (2,500). The African contributors were Morocco (1,250), Nigeria (550), Zimbabwe (400), Egypt (250), and Tunisia (130).

29. Barnes, "Last Call," 13.

30. Richard Haas, *Intervention: The Use of American Military Force in the Post-Cold War World* (Washington, D.C.: the Carnegie Endowment for International Peace, 1994), 201-3.

31. UN Security Council Resolution 814, March 26, 1993.

32. UN Security Council Resolution 837, June 6, 1993.

33. UN Security Council Resolution 885, November 16, 1993.

34. UN Security Council Resolution 885, November 4, 1994.

5

Genocide: Bosnia and Rwanda

The failures of the UN in Angola and Somalia proved costly, both to the peoples and states concerned and to the UN. In Angola, the civil war continued, with civilians taking the brunt of the conflict and with land mines claiming thousands of limbs and lives. In Somalia, the warlords kept fighting, no government was formed, and the threat of famine continued. The country remained divided into warlord zones, and parts of Somalia were periodically subject to warfare. The misadventure in Somalia damaged the credibility of the UN and the secretary-general. Bosnia and Rwanda, in contrast to Angola and Somalia, represented another scale in UN failure. In both cases, clear intent existed on the part of militarized groups to liquidate entire peoples from their homelands. In both cases, the UN failed to act to deter or stop genocidal conduct. States did not abide by the Convention on the Prevention and Punishment of the Crime of Genocide, which was created in the wake of the Nazi-engineered Holocaust during the Second World War.

The Genocide Convention

The 1948 Genocide Convention clearly stipulates the obligations of states, when genocide rears its head. By 1992, when "ethnic cleansing" began in Bosnia, most states, including the United States, had ratified the convention and were, therefore, required to intervene to *prevent and stop* the crime of genocide. Thus, most states were obliged to intervene in Bosnia when ethnic cleansing started in April 1992; in

Rwanda in January 1994, when firm evidence of the planned genocide emerged; and in the less-publicized case of Burundi in October 1993, when genocidal killings commenced. From 1992-94, when genocidal acts were at their greatest, the UN possessed a convention to deter or stop genocide. The tragedies and UN inaction that occurred in Bosnia, Rwanda, and Burundi reflected the reluctance of states, including the United States and other powers, to intervene in the "internal affairs" of another state. Only after genocide had consumed tens of thousands of victims was action taken. By then, UN action was too little and too late to be effective. The only alternative was to try to punish the perpetrators in war crimes tribunals ex post facto and deter future genocidal conduct.

Yugoslavia and Bosnia

Before ethnic cleansing and genocidal behavior in Bosnia began, there had been nearly a year of conflict in Yugoslavia as the federal republic disintegrated. The crisis in the Balkans that erupted in 1991 was the product of the end of the Cold War and the transformation of states throughout the former communist bloc, including the 1989 "Velvet Revolution" in Czechoslovakia and the 1990 merger between East and West Germany. In 1991, the Soviet Union and Yugoslavia broke apart. Yugoslavia had been the federation of the autonomous entities of Serbia, Montenegro, Macedonia, Croatia, Slovenia, and Bosnia-Herzegovina and an artificial creation with a tumultuous history among federation components. In 1980, the death of Yugoslavia's communist patriarch, Marshal Josip Broz Tito, led to a federal power struggle, which featured rising tensions between Serbia and Croatia, the two most prominent entities in Yugoslavia. Tensions escalated in the mid-1980s with the rise to power of a Serb Communist, Slobodan Milosevic, who turned ultra-nationalist. He declared his intention of making Serbia the dominant state in Yugoslavia, thereby provoking alarm among the other constituent republics.

In 1990 and early 1991, eighteen months of dialogue proceeded on Yugoslavia's future. While Milosevic predicted and even desired the divorce of Serbia from Slovenia and Croatia, Slovenian and Croatian leaders initially made clear that they were not rejecting all forms of Yugoslav union. In December 1990, a plebiscite was held in Slovenia, in which its citizens voted in favor of independence. Croatia held its referendum on May 19, 1991 on the question of independence from

Yugoslavia, and 94 percent of the Croats opted for independence, while most Serbs living in Croatia had boycotted the vote.[1] In response to the plebiscites, the Yugoslav central government sought to keep the federation together, even offering a more confederal arrangement. However, Croatia and Slovenia had already traveled too far down the road of independence to turn back. On June 25, 1991, Slovenia and Croatia declared independence from Yugoslavia.

In other parts of Eastern Europe, the Soviet Union had offered little resistance to change in 1989 and 1990. However, the Yugoslav government offered more opposition to emerging changes within its boundaries. In response to Slovenia's plans for independence, the Yugoslav federal government prepared to send the Yugoslav National Army (JNA) to prevent Slovenia from seceding by blocking the mobilization of territorial defense forces. The JNA's reaction to the secession was the "critical event" that started the war in Slovenia. Before the JNA action, talk of secession was mostly a tool in a political dispute. During this time, Slovenia had anticipated Yugoslav resistance, and made preparations to create a defense force in preparation for any resistance. The Slovene defense forces surrounded Yugoslav army barracks to prevent them from suppressing the independence movement. The JNA made preliminary preparations for operations on June 26, 1991. The Yugoslav federal government proclaimed the Slovenian declaration of independence illegal and ordered the JNA to capture and hold strategic targets like border checkpoints and airports. Air strikes commenced against Slovenian targets. The JNA High Command was hoping that a show of force should be sufficient to persuade the Slovene government to retract its declaration and act as a warning to Croatian leaders.[2]

In June 1991, the international community, headed by the European powers and European organizations, became involved in conflict management in Yugoslavia. At the urging of the German government, the foreign ministers of the Western European Union, on June 27, requested the Conference for Security and Cooperation in Europe (CSCE) to dispatch an investigating team to Yugoslavia. The CSCE agreed to let the European Community act on its behalf. The EC "Troika," foreign ministers Gianni de Michelis from Italy, Jacques Poos from Luxembourg, and Hans van den Broek from the Netherlands, were sent to negotiate an end to the hostilities.[3] On the island of Brioni, Yugoslavia on July 7, 1991 they issued a joint declaration which committed the European Community both to monitoring and offering assistance in the negotiating process among the Yugoslav republics, which was scheduled to start by August 1.

The Yugoslav government out-maneuvered the negotiators, when, on July 18, it offered to remove Yugoslav forces from Slovenia in three months. This signaled Yugoslavia's approval of an independent Slovenia. The EC Troika's success did not signal any recognition of the EC's peacemaking capabilities, but the willingness of the Yugoslav Federal Army High Command and Serbian representatives in the Yugoslav state presidency to abandon Slovenia.

The EC Troika's demands for CSCE monitors and the possibility of extended negotiations would have tied up the JNA's resources and prevented it from acting in its most important theaters of operations, in Croatia and Bosnia. The Brioni Accords also indicated to the Yugoslav government that it was foolish to get trapped in negotiations, when more could be gained on the battlefield. The Brioni Accords served notice that the political infighting between the presidents of the Yugoslav Republics now had become a fight between the leaders of newly emerging states. The Brioni Accords and the JNA's agreement to withdraw quickly, was a victory for the Serb nationalists over the remaining "Yugoslavists" in the military. By abandoning Slovenia, the JNA was also discarding all visions of Yugoslavia. Instead, it sought a "Greater Serbia," which some ultra-nationalists leaders projected to be Serbia, Vojvodina, Montenegro, Kosovo, and Bosnia-Herzegovina, as well as parts of Romania, Bulgaria, Hungary, Croatia, and Albania.[4] Since the EC favored the independence of Slovenia, the JNA became concerned about possible international interference in the Croatian and Bosnian theaters. After studying international intervention strategy, the JNA concluded that the major international players were unlikely to achieve the political consensus necessary to intervene in Yugoslav territory.[5]

The threat of force against Slovenia had inflamed the situation in other parts of Yugoslavia. With Slovenia "lost" to independence, the JNA turned its attention to attacking other former republics in order to fortify Serb interests. The Serb-led Yugoslav government turned next to Croatia, with a different view than it had of Slovenia. Croatia had a 12 percent Serb minority that was concentrated in the provinces of Krajina, near the Adriatic Sea, and Eastern Slavonia, which bordered on western Serbia. The Serbs in these regions and those in Serbia feared the repercussions of Croatian nationalism that came with the decision to become independent. Following a referendum in Serb-inhabited regions of Croatia from August 9 to September 2, 1990, of the 756,781 Serbs who voted, 756,549 voted for autonomy from Croatia.[6] A "Serbian Autonomous Region of Krajina" was declared, while the Croatian government tried to prevent the Krajina Serbs from arming themselves. However, General Ratko Mladic of the JNA was able to circumvent the Croatians and arm the Krajina Serbs. Subsequently, they declared their separation from Croatia on March 16, 1991, and, within a month, clashes between armed Serbs and Croatian police developed into a serious conflict. Croatia's fledgling military was formed in the spring of 1991, as the JNA split into a largely Serbian and Montenegrin "JNA" and a Croatian armed force, the Croatian National Guard (ZNG). Many of the Croatians had been more technically proficient members of the JNA, which benefited the ZNG. However, the JNA still had significantly more weapons, which left the Croatians on the defensive for several years.

By August 1991, only four months after the successful conclusion of Operation Desert Storm, Serbian aggression against Croatia was challenging George Bush's "new world order." On September 25, 1991, the United Nations became involved in the conflict. The Security Council in Resolution 713 ordered an embargo on weapons to any part of Yugoslavia as a way to control the spread, intensity and severity of the conflict. The resolution also called for humanitarian assistance and for pressure to be placed on the aggressors.[7]

When the JNA entered Croatia in the summer of 1991, it was under the guise of protection for the Serb minority that faced persecution by the Croatians. However, the JNA intervened in order to begin a campaign of "ethnic cleansing." Units took calculated actions, designed to maximize the conflict between Serbs and Croats and then induced non-Serbs to vacate their homes and flee. This genocidal conduct, plus the twin dangers of escalation and the conflict spilling over, caused the Security Council to become involved. However, the United States, the UN and the European Community found it difficult to take decisive action against Serbian aggression in Croatia. Months after the thwarting of Iraqi aggression against Kuwait and the declaration of a "new world order," the United States and the council began to lose credibility.

Milosevic and his associates formulated the strategy of "ethnic cleansing" with the intention of evicting non-Serbs from the territory of "Greater Serbia." In 1991, the Serbian population in the proposed Greater Serbia comprised only 52.5 percent of the population. In order to become the undisputed majority, a large portion of the non-Serbian population had to be expelled. Therefore, in the Croatian regions of Krajina and Eastern Slavonia, where Serbs were the majority, Croats were terrorized and driven from their homes. Images of ethnic cleansing first appeared on television in 1991, as Croatian fighters allowed foreign journalists to roam freely around their lines. At their own risk, reporters could effectively go wherever they wanted and thus became witnesses as to the barbarity of Serb irregular forces and the JNA.[8] The most visible Serb onslaught was from August through November 1991 on the Eastern Slavonian city of Vukovar, and the JNA made it a ghost town. In Croatia, the first signs of genocidal behavior had appeared, which would escalate to greater proportions in Bosnia, from 1992 to 1995.[9]

As the war in Croatia intensified, the EC responded by attempting to broker peace between the Yugoslav government and Croatia. After many failed attempts at negotiating a permanent cease-fire throughout the summer of 1991, the EC called for a "Peace Conference on Yugoslavia" to begin in September. Before and during the conference, both sides repeatedly violated cease-fires. Peace conference delegates included officials of the Yugoslav state presidency and the Yugoslav federal government, the presidents of the Yugoslav republics, EC officials, and the conference chairman, former British foreign secretary, Lord Carrington. On October 18, 1981, he proposed a plan, which expressed the international community's desire to keep the remaining Yugoslav republics together. Carrington's original plan would have created a free association of sovereign and independent republics within their previous internal borders. In addition, this proposal envisaged a special autonomous status for a national or ethnic group forming a majority in an area of each of these republics. The plan also called for a separate legislative body, judiciary, educational system and the displaying of separate national emblems, as well as international monitoring. The Carrington Plan was "too little and too late," because the Croatian and Slovenian republics had already proposed autonomy earlier in 1991 and then had moved beyond it toward their own declarations of independence. After the initial, largely negative reactions, Carrington continued to modify his plan. However, it became apparent that the reluctance of the Yugoslav parties to accept the deal was based more on their own agenda than a willingness to agree to arbitration. With the expiry of the three-month "moratorium" on their independence on October 8, Slovenia and Croatia reiterated their declarations of independence. Subsequently, Milosevic rejected Lord Carrington's proposal saying that it would abolish Yugoslavia as a state, which had existed for seventy years.[10]

Meanwhile, Macedonia's referendum on independence paved the way for its departure from the Yugoslav Federation and for a UN preventive deployment force. Subsequently, the issue of independence was becoming more prevalent in Bosnia. As the situation in the Balkans continued to deteriorate, Carrington persevered in his role as chief diplomat. He consulted the EC's Arbitration Commission of the Conference on Yugoslavia to determine the legality behind the claims of the various parties. Carrington hoped that, if the issues were legally clarified, the correct course of action could be taken by the EC. The commission in effect legalized the change of external or international borders of the Yugoslav state "in the process of dissolution." The commission applied a principle, which had been used in border cases involving former European colonies. In effect, the commission unreservedly sided with Croatia and Slovenia by effectively legitimizing their secession. The commission ruled against Serbia and Montenegro, declaring that the Yugoslav state, which the Serbian and Montenegrin governments claimed to represent, had no legal basis.

As 1991 wore on, the EC's involvement in the Balkans shifted from negotiator to facilitator, as it recognized Slovenia and Croatia. Germany, a member of the EC and a traditional supporter of Croatia and Slovenia, pushed the EC to recognize the fledgling states. Although the other powers of the EC, particularly the United Kingdom and France, were not enthusiastic about Croatian and Slovenian independence, the politics of the EC affected their decision. Because of Germany's "post-unification euphoria" and its ties to Croatia and Slovenia, disagreement within the EC on the issue threatened to alienate Germany and hinder other areas of cooperation, such as the Maastricht Treaty. Thus, for the EC, placating Germany and maintaining unity became a top priority.[11] The EC set up the Badinter Commission at the end of 1991 to consider applications for recognition by the EC from any Yugoslav republic seeking independence. This paved the way for Slovenia and Croatia to be formally recognized. On the other hand, the commission rejected independence for Kosovo, while Bosnia was allowed to conduct a referendum in order for the EC to gauge Bosnian feelings toward independence.[12]

On January 2, 1992, just as Boutros Boutros-Ghali assumed the office of secretary-general, the UN negotiator, Cyrus Vance, succeeded in negotiating the withdrawal of the JNA from Croatia and introducing UN peacekeepers to monitor the situation. The UN had appointed Vance on October 8, 1991. The peacekeeping force, called the United Nations Protection Force (UNPROFOR), would be deployed to separate belligerents in Croatia and to protect Croats in "safe havens" in majority Serb areas, such as Krajina, and in Eastern Slavonia, where the JNA was the occupying force. While the UN had succeeded in achieving a cease-fire in Croatia, the UN proved to be shortsighted about the overall instability in the region. In fact, the truce set the stage for the expansion of the war into Bosnia, where the battlefield in the ethnic war would feature Croatian and Serbian nationalists who intensified hostilities and their quest for territorial gain.

Bosnia

In Bosnia-Herzegovina, the Bosnian Muslims and Croats were pursuing their own plans for independence, which led to a referendum from February 29 to March 1, 1992. Anticipating such a move, the Bosnian Serbs declared a republic on January 9, which the Izetbegovic government did not recognize. As the February 29 referendum approached, the Bosnian Serb leader, Radovan Karadzic, appealed to his fellow Serbs to boycott. Subsequently, a majority of Serbs complied. The result of the referendum was a comfortable majority of 62.7 percent of mainly Muslims and Croats in support of independence.[13] Alija Izetbegovic, who had served as the president of Bosnia under the Yugoslav federation, used the results of the referendum to proclaim independence for Bosnia-Herzegovina on March 3, 1992. However, the Bosnian Serbs continued to strongly oppose independence and began to mount armed resistance. On March 27, Karadzic announced that the Bosnian Serb Republic was attaching itself to what was left of Yugoslavia.

In spite of the warning signs, the Bosnian Muslims and Croats went ahead with the referendum and with plans for independence. In the face of violent Serb opposition, the Muslims and Croats knew that an independence plebiscite was one of the conditions stipulated by the EC Badinter Commission in order for Bosnia to receive diplomatic recognition. It was not designed to bring Bosnian Muslims and Croats together with Bosnian Serbs. Supporters of independence hoped that they could emulate the mostly successful independence processes in Slovenia and Croatia and that the EC, Germany, and other powers would then recognize and support Bosnia. Since Croatian recognition appeared to have limited the scale of the war in Croatia, EC leaders and diplomats hoped that recognition of Bosnia-Herzegovina might prevent the conflict from escalating into a full-scale war. However, their calculations proved to be wrong, and the EC remained paralyzed as the war escalated in intensity and horror.

In 1991, Karadzic had begun to make preparations to ensure that his designs on power would not be threatened. He began to implement and coordinate a plan with Slobodan Milosevic to create a "shadow army" for the Bosnian Serbs. In January 1992, JNA officers were transferred to Bosnia. Milosevic and Karadzic calculated that, when Bosnia declared independence and the JNA would be asked to withdraw, Bosnian Serb officers would be permitted to stay as citizens. Subsequently, they would be able to legally work with Karadzic in fighting the war.[14]

Independence would not come as "easy" for Bosnia as it did for Macedonia and Slovenia or even Croatia. Already, President Izetbegovic had recognized the instability in the area when he asked the UN to send peacekeepers on November 12, 1991. On December 22, he appealed again to the UN to prevent civil war from consuming Bosnia. However, the UN did not respond. The rejection of the February 29-March 1, 1992 referendum results by the Bosnian Serbs signaled the beginning of the war that would be waged by Serb military forces against Bosnia and the assault on Sarajevo, the capital of Bosnia and the most ethnically diverse city in Yugoslavia. As Bosnian Serb militias began to surround Sarajevo, Karadzic asked the JNA to intervene and support them. At this point the JNA refused, and along with the Bosnian police, helped to forestall the blockade of Sarajevo. On April 6, 1992, Bosnia-Herzegovina formally declared independence, was recognized by the EC and the United States, and gained a seat at the UN. On that date, the JNA and police permitted Bosnian Serb paramilitaries to begin the shelling of Sarajevo. Ethnic cleansing, especially against "Bosniak" Muslims in Eastern Bosnia, commenced.

With the start of the Bosnian conflict, the Balkans situation continued to deteriorate. As in the case of Croatia, the UN recognized a need to intervene, based on the duty to keep peace, preserve borders, protect minorities, and provide humanitarian assistance to civilians suffering from the vagaries of war. However, these objectives overlapped, creating confusion. Some states, mainly European, argued that conflict should be contained. Other states and international agencies stressed the need to deliver food and medicine to those trapped by war. Some, such as the Islamic states, even argued for intervention on the side of the Bosnian regime and for punishing the Bosnian Serbs. Secretary-General Boutros-Ghali argued against intervention and for mediation. In addition, the international community was experiencing interstate rivalries, especially between Russia, which supported Serbia, and the West. The result of the mixture of intentions and motivations was gridlock, in which the bare minimum was agreed upon and implemented. After considerable debate and delay, the UN, by mid-September 1992, decided to contain the crisis, ensure delivery of humanitarian supplies, and set up "safe havens" but allowed the Bosnian Serbs to continue to shell Sarajevo and ethnically cleanse.

In 1992, as ethnic cleansing mounted and as the "new world order" came into question, the Bush administration did not want to become the power primarily involved in the Balkans. At the time, U.S. attention was centered on rescuing Russia after the demise of the Soviet Union and on post-war Iraq. The EC's initiative in dealing with the Croatian conflict and determination, contained in the Maastricht Treaty, to forge a "Common Foreign and Security Policy," led the Bush administration to believe that the EC could resolve the Bosnian conflict itself. In addition, Bush officials, such as Acting Secretary of State Lawrence Eagleburger, had opposed the breakup of Yugoslavia and were not sympathetic to the breakaway republics, including Bosnia. In the final analysis, the Bush administration decided that the former Yugoslavia was not as important to the U.S. national interest as Kuwait and Saudi Arabia and that the costs of reversing Serbian aggression were unacceptably high. Administration officials believed that intervention in the former Yugoslavia could sink the United States and the UN into a Vietnam-style quagmire. Thus, Bush chose to intervene in Somalia in December 1992, where the perceived costs were low, instead of in Bosnia in August, where the costs were estimated to be much higher.

The Security Council, Secretariat, and other organs of the UN adopted the view that the Europeans should be given the opportunity to handle both the negotiations to end the conflict and to supply the peacekeeping elements that would be required. Four of the Permanent Five (P-5) members of the council, the United States, Russia, France, and the United Kingdom, had an interest in the conflict and its outcome. The P-5's failure to agree on a position, which proved to be a serious abdication of responsibility, was reinforced in the early stages by the view of the secretary-general. Boutros-Ghali believed that Bosnia was a situation when Chapter VIII of the Charter, on cooperation between regional and global organizations, could be tested. In a number of his reports, the secretary-general had proposed an extended role for regional organizations in the maintenance of international peace and security, and the obvious regional organizations in Europe were the EU and the CSCE.[15]

Televised images of the shelling of Sarajevo, the home of the 1984 Winter Olympic Games, prompted the UN to act in June 1992. Negotiations with the Bosnian government and with the Bosnian Serb authorities led to an agreement to reopen Sarajevo Airport. The London Conference on the Former Yugoslavia adopted a declaration on the concentration of heavy weapons around Sarajevo, many of which had been shelling the city. The Security Council was prepared to act on the declaration when the secretary-general intervened. Subsequently, he reported that more than 10,000 military observers would be required, and the council hesitated at following through with the proposal. Boutros-Ghali demonstrated a lack of decorum by chiding the council for their preoccupation with a "rich man's war" and "ethnic cleansing" in the former Yugoslavia, while neglecting war and famine in Somalia.[16]

As the summer of 1992 wore on, ethnic cleansing intensified throughout areas designated as part of the new Bosnian Serb Republic. Serb forces swept through village after village, rounding up Muslim men and boys, raping women, and burning houses. Tens of thousands of Bosniak Muslims were taken away to concentration camps where many of them died and where women were repeatedly raped. Photographers and even some television crews were able to gain access to some of the concentration camps and broadcast footage of emaciated Muslim prisoners. In response to the mounting humanitarian disaster and, with winter not far off, the Security Council decided to act. On August 13, 1992, the council passed Resolution 770, which called for the delivery of humanitarian assistance by "all measures necessary," under Chapter VII of the UN Charter. Resolution 770 authorized UNPROFOR to use force, if necessary, but only if one of the parties was blocking the UN aid deliveries. UNPROFOR was not authorized to subdue the forces that were causing the humanitarian crisis.[17]

Lord David Owen became the EC negotiator in August 1992, and, at the London Conference of August 26-28, 1992, he assumed responsibility for negotiating peace in Bosnia. The London Conference recognized the territorial integrity of Bosnia-Herzegovina and identified Serbia and Montenegro as aggressors, calling for the introduction of UN peacekeeping forces into Bosnia in order to maintain a cease-fire in the area. Although the London Conference was correct in condemning the Serbs and although concessions were gained from the Bosnian Serbs, Lord Owen recommended the use of sanctions and not force to bring peace to Bosnia. Owen's recommendation was one of a series of mixed signals that the international community was sending that did not deter, but actually encouraged, those committing the atrocities.

Once the peacemakers had passed their resolutions, they consulted the military leaders who would be responsible for implementation. NATO and the U.S. Joint Chiefs of Staff estimated that at least 60,000 heavily armed troops would be necessary to deliver aid and that 400,000 troops would be needed to pacify Bosnia. With the prospect of a major ground war and heavy casualties, Western leaders retreated from the type of action that would be required to alleviate humanitarian suffering. They did not seriously entertain the possibility of committing hundreds of thousands of soldiers to put an end to the most vicious warfare that Europe had witnessed since Hitler's legions had ravaged the continent fifty years earlier.

As a consequence, the Security Council changed course and, on September 14, 1992, adopted Resolution 776, which authorized the United Kingdom and France to lead European NATO members in a humanitarian mission to Bosnia, under the aegis of UNPROFOR. The Security Council withdrew the Chapter VII powers that it had authorized under Resolution 770 and only provided UNPROFOR with limited rules of engagement. In October 1992, the Security Council authorized a "no fly zone" over Bosnia, which had little impact on the largely ground-based Serb forces.[18]

Thus, began the UN's three-year foray into Bosnia. By November 1992, UNPROFOR was deploying more than 8,000 troops to Bosnia and escorting convoys of food and medicine. Serb and Croat forces immediately began the practice of blocking food and medicine from reaching civilians in order to apply pressure to the Bosnian government and its supporters. Consequently, an airlift to Sarajevo operated for three years, until April 1995, through which more food was delivered than via road.

The Bosnian Serbs continued to pound Sarajevo and threaten other enclaves, so that many civilians who received aid were subsequently killed in mortar or artillery attacks or through incursions. For three years, the United States, EC, and UN stood by as atrocity-after-atrocity was committed and as the Serbs consolidated the gains made through ethnic cleansing. The Security Council passed resolution after resolution but soon lost credibility as no actions were taken against the Bosnian Serbs.

The Geneva Conference followed the London Conference, where UN representative, Cyrus Vance, joined Lord Owen, as a lead negotiator. The purpose was to discuss ways of implementing the agreements and recommendations of the London Conference. However, the Geneva Conference marked a major shift in the international community's assessment of the situation in the Balkans as Vance and Owen dropped references to the Serbs as aggressors and introduced the notion of "three warring factions." In September, the Bosnian Croats had broken with the government and were attempting to carve out part of Bosnia and attach it to Croatia. As the government counterattacked, it gave some observers the impression that all three sides were taking aggressive action. The conference's identification of three aggressors and placing of the government of Izetbegovic in Sarajevo on the same level with the Serb and Croat insurgents laid the basis for negotiating the partition of Bosnia and essentially rewarded aggression.

The Geneva Conference culminated in the Vance-Owen plan of October 1992, which was on the table through January 1993. The Vance-Owen plan expressed the view that Bosnia was an independent entity with three aggressors, who must be equally blamed for the war they were waging. Previously, Vance and Owen had recognized Izetbegovic's government and its sovereignty over all of Bosnia. Now they were willing to recognize ethnic enclaves, secured by force, and downplay Bosnian sovereignty. Initially, all three parties had agreed to the Vance-Owen plan. However, in January 1993, the Bosnian Serbs rejected the plan, because it provided them with only 49 percent of Bosnia and required them to give up a considerable amount of captured territory that had been acquired through ethnic cleansing. The Serbs had the upper hand in the conflict and could not be persuaded to compromise. Furthermore, they blamed the EC for the disintegration of Yugoslavia and the scheme for Bosnian independence and were in the mood for revenge rather than cooperation.[19]

With the collapse of the Vance-Owen plan, Owen and a new UN envoy, Thorvald Stoltenberg, began to explore the establishment of three republics, which amounted to partition. In opposition, the Clinton administration offered a new proposal, "lift-and-strike," which strongly supported the Bosnian government. In the spring of 1993, the new Secretary of State Warren Christopher came to Europe to propose fortifying the Bosnian government against the Bosnian Serbs by lifting the arms embargo, supplying arms to the Bosnian government, and launching air strikes against Bosnian Serb positions. EC leaders rejected the proposal because they were afraid that conflict escalation might harm their peacekeepers on the ground in Bosnia. Christopher did not press the NATO allies. Instead, the Clinton administration sought to implement more modest measures that might aid the Bosnian government. The United States led in pushing through a proposal in the Security Council for a war crimes tribunal for the former Yugoslavia, which would especially target Bosnian Serb leaders who had been responsible for ethnic cleansing.[20]

The United States joined with Germany in pressing for an end to fighting between Croats and Muslims and succeeded in establishing a

Muslim-Croat federation in 1994. The United States also led the way in circumventing the arms embargo, helping to strengthen the Croatian Army and the Bosnian government. Two years of aid helped to tilt the balance of power toward Croatia and the Bosnian government in the summer of 1995.

Between the spring of 1992 and the summer of 1995, the world watched as Bosnia suffered through more than three agonizing years of horror. In the spring of 1993, the Bosnian Serbs launched new attacks in the eastern part of the country against Bosniak Muslim enclaves. In April 1993, the Security Council passed a resolution declaring Srebenica a "safe haven."[21]

Soon, five additional enclaves, including Sarajevo, were declared safe havens. UNPROFOR troops were stationed in the safe havens and could call for air strikes to defend their positions, but they were not authorized to defend the safe havens. UNPROFOR was counting largely on Serb "respect" for the safe havens and for the UN to keep them safe. In the meantime, the Security Council tightened economic sanctions against Serbia and Montenegro, the two biggest supporters of the Bosnian Serbs.

In January 1994, Yasushi Akashi, fresh from his UNTAC success in Cambodia, arrived in Zagreb, Croatia to become UNPROFOR Special Representative. Immediately, he was faced with a new crisis. On February 5, 1994, a Bosnian Serb mortar attack killed 68 and wounded 197 in a Sarajevo marketplace. In response, the UN created a "weapons exclusion zone," which required the Bosnian Serbs to move their mortars and artillery out of range of Sarajevo. NATO air strikes were authorized to attack heavy weapons, which could be used to attack civilians, left inside the exclusion zone. UNPROFOR brought more forces into Bosnia, especially from Islamic countries, until the number of troops exceeded 22,500.[22]

British Lieutenant General Sir Michael Rose became the new Force Commander. Rose and Akashi started to pursue a course of using more force, but only enough to deter the Bosnian Serbs without provoking them into escalation. The use of limited force in peacekeeping became known as employing "wider peacekeeping."[23] However, UNPROFOR's balancing act proved unsuccessful and alienated both the Bosnian Serbs and the Bosnian government and its supporters. Even limited NATO air attacks on Serb positions were met with retaliation, as UNPROFOR hostages were taken and safe havens threatened in retaliation. Thus, Akashi and Rose reined in NATO air strikes. The Bosnian government and its supporters, such as the United States and the Islamic states, complained that Akashi and Rose were appeasing the Bosnian Serbs. In the meantime, Bosnian government forces began to use Sarajevo and other UNPROFOR safe havens, as bases from which to launch attacks against Bosnian Serb positions. As 1994 ended, UNPROFOR found itself in an increasingly untenable position in Bosnia.

In the spring and summer of 1995, the growing confrontation between the resurgent Bosnian government and the Bosnian Serbs, with UNPROFOR caught in between, came to a climax. The Bosnian Serbs increased violations of the exclusion zone and threatened some of the safe havens. On May 24, the Serbs received an ultimatum to withdraw from the exclusion zone. When they refused, NATO launched air strikes. In retaliation, the Serbs seized hundreds of UNPROFOR hostages, killed 71 civilians in a mortar attack on Tuzla, and withdrew weapons from Sarajevo collection points. On July 12, the Serbs attacked the Srebenica "safe haven," brushed past Dutch UNPROFOR troops, and seized thousands of Muslim men and executed them. On July 25, the Serbs overran the Zepa "safe haven."

The Serb offensive against Srebenica finally caused the United States and its NATO allies to act. A concerted air campaign was mounted against Bosnian Serb forces. The Netherlands, Britain and France formed a Rapid Reaction Force of more than 10,000 heavily armed troops to ensure the overland delivery of food and the protection of the four remaining safe havens. In late July, the Croatian army began an offensive against the Krajina, which brought the expulsion of 200,000 Serbs, undid much of UNPROFOR's work in Croatia, and spilled over into Bosnia. The Bosnian Serbs were thrown on the defensive and began to seek a negotiated settlement.

In August, the United States undertook a diplomatic initiative, with Assistant Secretary of State Richard Holbrooke opening negotiations with Milosevic over the future configuration of Bosnia and with the United States leading NATO in preparing to use force. The UN role was reduced, and blue helmets withdrew from areas where they could be taken hostage. Advancing Croatian and Bosnian forces were pushed the Serbs back in western Bosnia. On August 28, mortars attacked the Sarajevo marketplace, killing thirty-seven and wounding eighty. Once the UN established that the Serbs were responsible, NATO unleashed a two-week air campaign that attacked hundreds of military targets. UNPROFOR switched from a peacekeeping to a peace-enforcement role, as UN Rapid Reaction Force tanks and artillery shelled Serb positions around Sarajevo. The combination of territorial and materiel losses compelled the Bosnian Serbs to capitulate on September 15, 1995.

With the forceful ending of Bosnian Serb aggression, the diplomatic process advanced. In Geneva, Holbrooke secured agreement on a political framework, which guaranteed Bosnian sovereignty, with 51 percent of the land going to the Muslim-Croat Federation and 49 percent to an autonomous *Republika Srpska*. He also succeeded in lifting the siege of Sarajevo. During the first three weeks of November 1995, Holbrooke managed the Dayton "proximity" peace talks at Wright-Patterson Air Force Base in Ohio, which brought together the presidents of Bosnia, Serbia, and Croatia and the leaders of the Bosnian Serbs. The talks were aimed at consolidating the Geneva political framework, drawing the boundaries of Bosnia, and agreeing on the repatriation of refugees/displaced persons. The talks came close to breaking down, but Holbrooke compelled the parties to stay until an agreement was reached. On November 21, 1995, the Dayton Agreement was initialed, and then signed in Paris. Responsibility for implementing the agreement was given to NATO, which had sufficient forces (more than 50,000) and rules of engagement to compel the parties to comply. On December 20, 1995, UNPROFOR ceased operating in Bosnia, as NATO's Implementation Force (IFOR) was deployed.

Genocide in Bosnia

Ethnic cleansing by Serbs was obviously genocide, albeit on a smaller and less comprehensive scale than the killing of six million Jews by Nazi Germany. While the Serbs did not plan to exterminate all Bosniak Muslims, a plan was implemented that wiped them out of large sections of territory and that sought to partition Bosnia out of existence. Serbs in Croatia conducted ethnic cleansing in Krajina on a smaller scale. Confronted with genocidal behavior, the United States and the EC did not react, as they were obliged to do under the Genocide Convention. The result was three agonizing years in which the Bosnian Serbs tortured and bludgeoned Muslims, as the UN delivered humanitarian aid. Finally, as Serb behavior became increasingly monstrous, the NATO allies finally reacted. By 1995, the Europeans and the United States both had learned their lesson. Subsequently, when Serbia engaged in similarly genocidal behavior in Kosovo in 1997-99, the

NATO allies forced Serbia to relinquish control over Kosovo. Also, slowly, but surely the perpetrators of ethnic cleansing were brought before the War Crimes Tribunal for the Former Yugoslavia in The Hague. Genocidal behavior in Europe was no longer tolerable.

Rwanda

From April to June 1994, more than 800,000 Rwandans were killed, mainly hacked to death, by Hutu extremists, who were attempting to exterminate Tutsi and moderate Hutu.[24] Six months earlier, in Burundi, the Tutsi-led army assassinated the Hutu president and killed Hutu in large numbers. A "creeping genocide" continued, in which more than 70,000 died. In both Rwanda and Burundi, NGOs and UN workers provided UN Headquarters with ample warning that genocide was imminent and supplied evidence once the killings began. In spite of warnings, the international community failed to intervene to prevent or stop genocide. In particular, the Rwandan failure delivered another blow to the UN under Boutros-Ghali, after the setbacks in Bosnia and Somalia.

In both Rwanda and Burundi, Belgian colonizers had elevated and consolidated the position of the Tutsi as the "ruling elite" over the majority Hutu. In 1959, an uprising by militant Hutu led to the killing of tens of thousands of Rwandan Tutsi and forced hundreds of thousands more to flee to Uganda, Burundi and the Congo. Rwandan Hutu elites established Hutu hegemony that lasted until 1990. In the 1980's, the children and grandchildren of 1960s Tutsi refugees fought alongside Yoweri Museveni in liberating Uganda from the tyrannical regime of Milton Obote in 1986. Several Tutsi officers continued to serve in leadership positions in the Ugandan National Resistance Army (the NRA). In three years, they formed the Rwandan Patriotic Front (RPF) in order to return to their homeland through guerrilla warfare. In October 1990, the RPF began cross-border incursions from Uganda into northern Rwanda and challenged Hutu hegemony and the regime of President Juvenal Habyarimana. The regime, backed primarily by France, built up its military and counterattacked in 1991.

From 1990-93, RPF military activity continued and intensified. RPF incursions resulted in two contradictory outcomes. They helped to spur the rise of Hutu extremist groups and anti-Tutsi violence. However, they did succeed at forcing President Habyarimana to the negotiating table. Peace talks in Arusha, Tanzania, between the RPF and the government resulted first in a UN mission to monitor the Ugandan-Rwandan border (UNOMUR) in June 1993 and, in August, the Arusha Accords. In August 1993, the RPF activity apparently had brought victory for exiled Tutsi, as well as moderates inside Rwanda, who wanted reconciliation between Hutu and Tutsi. Their euphoria was short-lived.

From 1990 onwards, RPF activity and the threat posed to Hutu hegemony succeeded at providing an ideological basis for radical Hutu groups.[25] In particular, Hutu in the north of Rwanda, close to the border with Uganda, were afraid of the advancing RPF. Extremist elements in the Habyarimana government and in society played upon traditional Hutu fears, extremists told farmers that the Tutsi had returned to seize Hutu land. In reality, the Habyarimana regime was a principal exploiter of Hutu farmers.[26] Through increasingly pervasive Hutu extremist propaganda, all Tutsi were equated with the RPF and, therefore, with the expropriation of Hutu land. Habyarimana and his cronies spread anti-Tutsi messages through the media. Moderate newspapers were closed and replaced by anti-Tutsi newspapers, which confused the public and inspired hatred. For instance, *Kangura* ("Wake It Up") replaced *Kanguka* ("Wake Up"). Football (soccer) fan clubs were used to indoctrinate youths and induce them to join anti-Tutsi militias, called the *interahamwe* ("those who attack together") The *interahamwe* would form the spearhead and backbone for massive killings and a campaign of genocide.

In 1991, less than a year after RPF military activity began, a number of Rwandan human rights NGOs reported on killings by Hutu militias and arrest and torture by the Habyarimana regime. As massive human rights abuses continued, indigenous NGOs called on their international counterparts to act. In November 1992, a delegation of international NGOs, including Human Rights Watch, arrived in Rwanda, where they were shown mass graves and further evidence of genocidal activity. In January 1993, the delegation reported that the Habyarimana regime had engaged in acts of genocide and called for the dissolution of the Hutu militias. The UN Human Rights Commission's Special *Rapporteur* on Executions confirmed that massive human rights abuses were taking place. In response to mounting evidence, the United States cut aid to Rwanda, and many European Union countries protested. By April, the Rwandan government admitted that it had been responsible for the abuses. Afterwards, genocidal activity diminished. Subsequently, the international community chose to believe President Habyarimana's promises to reform and relaxed its guard, rather than monitoring compliance by the regime and the militias.

On August 4, 1993, the Arusha Peace Accords were signed. The RPF, after fighting for almost three years and establishing a foothold in Rwanda, had compelled the Habyarimana regime to agree to a power-sharing arrangement. The accords included a broad-based "government of national unity," comprised of the RPF and the Habyarimana regime, and for Rwandan refugees to return from neighboring Tanzania, Burundi, and Uganda. Representative members of the ruling and opposition parties would be allowed to enter the new government, with elections to be called in a short time. The military would be composed of RPF units and the Rwandan Armed Forces (FAR), with the demobilization of some FAR units. The Arusha Accords led some international observers to blithely think that Rwanda was a prime example of a country where ethnic reconciliation and peaceful, democratic government were assured.

The Arusha Accords called for monitoring of the agreement by UN observers and peacekeepers. Subsequently, on October 5, 1993 (two days after the eighteen U.S. Army Rangers died in Mogadishu), the Security Council authorized the United Nations Assistance Mission for Rwanda (UNAMIR). However, the Security Council decided to establish UNAMIR provisionally for an initial period of only six months. Balking against the mushrooming peacekeeping budget, the United States and other Security Council members resisted funding a major operation in Rwanda. As a result of "peacekeeping fatigue," they added the proviso that UNAMIR would be extended only if progress were made in implementing the Arusha Accords. The initial monitoring force was to consist of only 1,400 military personnel, eventually expanding to 2,165. The force was small compared to the more than 8,000 troops that were being recommended by the UN Department of Peacekeeping Operations (DPKO) for Rwanda and the 5,500 approved for ONUMOZ in Mozambique. In addition, UNAMIR was to be less involved in demobilizing FAR and RPF forces than ONUMOZ had been in Mozambique. Thus, the probability of resumed hostilities was great.[27]

In October 1993, the cease-fire commenced between the FAR and RPF, and a demilitarized zone was established by December. However, even as UNAMIR began to deploy, signs were emerging that Rwanda was becoming increasingly more volatile. Then, on October 21, in Burundi, the Tutsi army assassinated the Hutu president, Melchior

Ndadaye, and began a massive wave of killing. Fleeing Burundi, 300,000 Hutu refugees poured into Rwanda.[28] The UN did not respond, especially in the wake of the setback in Somalia. The Burundian killing and influx of refugees led the Hutu extremists to remobilize their base. An extremist radio station, *Radio Mille Collines*, incited Hutu by telling them that they were going to be killed, like their counterparts in Burundi, and that they should kill Tutsi. Hutu militias resumed killing Tutsi civilians after an eight-month hiatus. Submitting to Hutu extremist pressure, Habyarimana failed to implement the Arusha Accords and establish a government of national unity.

While the international community saw the Arusha Accords as the start of peace in Rwanda, Hutu extremists declared that they were a Tutsi ploy to dominate Hutu. As UNAMIR troops entered Rwanda to monitor the agreement, extremists lashed out at their presence and goal. Hasan Ngeze, the publisher of *Kangura* proclaimed that UNAMIR was nothing but a tool "to help the RPF take power by force," and he explicitly warned UNAMIR to "stay out of the way."[29] Ngeze advised readers how to combat UNAMIR, reminding them that peacekeepers were generally "cowardly" and were inclined to stand by and watch whenever violence occurred. Ngeze based his views on the UN's failure to retaliate after the killing of the eighteen U.S. Army Rangers in Somalia. He proclaimed that the UN mandate would be ended and that U.S. and European leaders, who were not willing to commit more lives and resources, would abandon Somalia to its own self-destruction. Ngeze predicted that the killing of UNAMIR peacekeeping troops would force the UN to leave Rwanda.

In December 1993 and January 1994, Hutu extremist activities, including the killing of Tutsi civilians, intensified. On January 11, 1994, Canadian General Romeo Dallaire, the UNAMIR Commander, sent an urgent fax to the Under-Secretary-General for Peacekeeping Operations Kofi Annan. The fax requested permission for UNAMIR to provide protection to a FAR officer and *interahamwe* member, who had confessed to a plot that planned to exterminate Tutsi. The informant revealed that the *interahamwe* were compiling lists of Tutsi names, gathering arms in Kigali, the capital city, and receiving training from FAR officers in order to conduct an extermination campaign. The mandate of UNAMIR provided for monitoring the Arusha Accords, which included keeping Kigali as a weapons free zone. The informant was willing to show UNAMIR where the plotters had cached their weapons in exchange for protection for himself and his family.

Iqbal Riza, Annan's deputy, replied to Dallaire. Riza stated that the UN could not offer protection for the informant, but that Dallaire could order UNAMIR to seize the weapons. However, without protection from UNAMIR, the informant would not reveal the location of the weapons. Dallaire was ordered to warn President Habyarimana of the potential plot and the dangers of violating the Arusha Accords. On January 13, Iqbal Riza presented the fax to Kofi Annan and Boutros Boutros-Ghali. However, neither official reacted to plans for genocide by ordering a UN response, nor did they send the fax to the Security Council.[30]

UN Headquarters ignored General Dallaire's urgent fax, instead, ordering him to comply with the UNAMIR mandate and monitor the Arusha Accords. However, Dallaire was unable to fulfill UNAMIR's mandate, as Habyarimana, feeling pressure from Hutu extremists, failed to implement power-sharing. In an effort to allay growing fears among UNAMIR leaders, Colonel Theoneste Bagosora, a top military planner who was also in the extremist *akazu*, formed a "crisis committee." He sought to reassure General Dallaire and the SRSG to Rwanda, Jacques Roger Booh-Booh that a new government was being formed that would "uphold" the accords.[31]

From January to April 1994, efforts to revive the Accords were frustrated by the growing violence and the specter of genocide. Meanwhile, Dallaire and UNAMIR were not permitted to disarm the Hutu militias in order to prevent genocide. Instead, the Security Council continued to threaten to withdraw UNAMIR, if the transitional process did not progress. However, growing aggression by Hutu extremists and rising anti-Tutsi violence in Kigali made it impossible to install a transitional government, which would have included RPF leaders. Neither the Security Council nor the secretary-general responded to these developments. Nor did the UN respond to warnings by indigenous human rights NGOs of impending genocide. Extremist radio and newspaper propaganda continued to distort facts, incite a cadre of anti-Tutsi fanatics ready to join the militias, and raise animosities to a genocidal level.

Genocide, April-July 1994

On April 6, 1994, Hutu extremists shot down the plane carrying President Habyarimana and Burundi's President Cyprien Ntaryamira at Kigali airport, as the two leaders returned from peace talks in Arusha.[32]

What appeared at the time to be a plane crash sparked killings of Tutsi and moderate Hutu by Hutu extremists that, in a matter of weeks, became a massive genocide. The "crash" served a dual purpose for the anti-Tutsi forces. It eliminated Habyarimana, who they viewed as a traitor to "Hutu power" for agreeing to the Arusha Accords. Secondly, on April 6, some reports claimed that RPF rebels might have downed the plane carrying Habyarimana, giving extremist forces an excuse to suppress the Tutsi, who were blamed for the killing of the Hutu leader. Within minutes after the plane was downed, the *interahamwe* mobilized to establish roadblocks around Kigali and began a campaign of genocide.

On April 7, the *interahamwe* attacked Rwanda's prime minister, Agathe Uwilingiyamana, and the ten Belgian bodyguards dispatched from UNAMIR to protect her. Before she became prime minister, Uwilingiyamana had been a member of the opposition who had been in favor of the Arusha Accords. Her support for the accords led to death threats and an assassination plan ordered by the *akazu* and executed by the *interahamwe*. Her bodyguards were armed, but they were not permitted to fire unless they faced imminent harm. When the Armed Forces of Rwanda (RAF) soldiers and *interahamwe* appeared, they were so numerous that they surrounded and disarmed the peacekeepers without a shot being fired. The prime minister was able to escape over the wall of her housing compound, with her family, to a neighbor's yard. The UNAMIR soldiers were taken to Camp Kigali, where they were tortured and killed. At the same time, the military was able to search for the prime minister. It is reported that, when found, she was killed in front of her children.[33]

The slaying of the Rwandan prime minister and ten Belgian blue helmets did not provoke the UN to take action. Instead, as Ngeze predicted, the killings had the same impact as those in Mogadishu, causing the UN to cower and withdraw. On April 14, 1994, one week after the murder of the ten Belgian blue helmets, Belgium withdrew 420 soldiers from UNAMIR, precisely as the Hutu extremists had hoped. Belgian soldiers, aggrieved by the cowardice of their leaders and the defeat of their mission, shredded their blue UN peacekeeping berets on the tarmac at Kigali airport.[34] Soon afterwards, several hundred Bangladeshi troops left, while the rest of UNAMIR was confined to barracks.

As the UN shrank from its obligations under the Genocide Convention, the wholesale extermination of Tutsi and moderate Hutu civilians accelerated and spread to the countryside. During the first three weeks, hundreds of thousands were killed, mainly out of the view of the UN, the media, and NGOs. By and large, the few hundred blue helmets of the UN based in Kigali were impotent in the face of the slaughter. Foreign governments rushed to close their embassies and sent forces to evacuate their nationals. While some peacekeepers disobeyed orders and tried to evacuate Rwandans fleeing the genocide, most were ordered to assist with the evacuation of Westerners and little else. Even with the withdrawals and the initial international paralysis, General Dallaire continued to press for action to stop the genocide. After the genocide was over, he would testify that if he had received armored vehicles and other equipment, he could have halted the genocide with a contingent of 1,500 men.[35] As the UN and Western forces failed to act, the RPF broke the cease-fire and attempted to come to the rescue of the Rwandan Tutsi and moderate Hutu.

In response to the events in Rwanda, Secretary-General Boutros-Ghali presented three options to the Security Council in response to the massacres. The first was peace enforcement, with an immediate and massive reinforcement of UNAMIR with thousands of troops and the invocation of Chapter VII of the Charter in order to coerce opposing forces into a cease-fire and to stop the killings. The second was partial retreat, with a small UNAMIR contingent, which would remain to try to bring about a cease-fire. The third was a complete retreat.[36] As the Security Council debate commenced, Boutros-Ghali continued to refer to the "civil war" between the RPF and the regime and to "mutual killings." He did nothing to convince the Security Council that genocide was taking place, which obliged the United Nations to act. The secretary-general favored the second option. On April 21, the Security Council decided to authorize partial withdrawal, and the secretary-general acted to reduce UNAMIR to 250 soldiers and confine them to barracks.[37]

The second wave of withdrawals dashed hopes that the Security Council would upgrade UNAMIR to a peace enforcement mission in order to stop the genocide. Thus, the killings continued unabated. In the weeks following the death of President Habyarimana, unprecedented rates of murder were attained. In the first two weeks, an estimated 300,000 Rwandans were killed, a rate of 20,000 per day, and over 90 days an estimated 800,000 were killed, almost 9,000 people per day. However, mass graves discovered in subsequent years pushed the number killed even higher. The extermination of 20,000 people per day was one of the most intense homicidal events in human history, much faster than the Nazi's pace in killing six million Jews in the period from 1942-45.[38]

While the killings continued, human rights NGOs and the New Zealand Mission to the UN continued to push the Security Council and the Secretariat to admit that genocide was occurring and to take action. Images appeared on CNN and other television networks showing glimpses of the genocide. A particularly memorable image was that of bloated bodies flowing down a river from Rwanda into Tanzania, which resulted from exhortations by Hutu extremist leaders to "send the Tutsi back to Ethiopia via the nearest river."[39] "Hutu power" propaganda had revived myths from the colonial era that the Tutsi descended from Ethiopian conquerors. Thus, extremist followers dumped corpses in the river that flowed eastward into Tanzania. Media coverage of the carnage prompted public outcry that began to motivate Western governments, especially that of New Zealand, to act. The U.S. government was aware of the genocide and its tremendous humanitarian cost from early April 1994. However, it took the media's exposure of the genocide to trigger belated U.S. government response.

For most of April and May 1994, the United States continued to resist involvement in Rwanda. On May 5, 1994, the Clinton administration issued Presidential Decision Directive 25, which placed strict limits on the types of peacekeeping operations that the United States would support. With PDD-25, it became clear that the United States was reluctant to support any peace enforcement operation, such as UNOSOM II, that involved intervention without a permanent cease-fire. As the leading force on the Security Council and with the capability of reaching Rwanda quickly, the United States could have acted to stop the genocide by providing military resources. In fact, some members of the Clinton administration began calling for such action. However, Congress, the military, and the State Department remembered the Somalia debacle and were not willing to allow the United States or the UN to become involved in committed to another volatile conflict. Pentagon and State Department officials felt that if any peace enforcement operation went badly, the United States would be the only power capable of rescuing UN forces. The voices of caution prevailed and successfully pressed for the withdrawal of most of UNAMIR and a decision not to commit any U.S. troops or U.S. assets.

After much pressure by NGOs and the media, New Zealand's call for peace enforcement and a change of position by Boutros-Ghali, the

Security Council finally accepted a compromise proposal on May 17, 1994. The proposal called for a phased insertion of 5,500 African UNAMIR troops and the establishment of safe areas. Ethiopia announced that it was ready to send troops, while Congo-Brazzaville, Ghana, Malawi, and Mali, as well as Nigeria, Senegal, Zambia, and Zimbabwe were prepared to commit troops if the UN paid.[40] However, the United States and France refused to grant UNAMIR Chapter VII powers and failed to fund or equip an African force. Thus, the African UNAMIR II force could not be deployed. Amazingly, the United States and the Security Council failed to accept New Zealand's demand for acknowledgement that genocide was occurring.[41]

As May dragged on into June, the genocide continued. However, RPF troops advanced on Kigali, which caused tens of thousands of Hutu to flee. With no prospect for deployment of the African UNAMIR force, France offered to stabilize Rwanda. France had been the principal supporter of the Habyarimana regime and the FAR's main source of supplies and training. On June 22 the Security Council authorized French intervention with Chapter VII powers.[42] On June 23, France launched "Operation Turquoise." Quickly, more than 2,000 troops established safe havens in southwest Rwanda, where the RPF was not present. These safe havens had the effect of protecting mainly Hutu, who were fleeing from advancing RPF forces. Among the displaced who came under French protection were former Rwandan government officials and thousands of Hutu "genocidaires." In terms of saving the main targets of the genocide, Tutsi civilians, the French saved less than 10,000. In contrast, the RPF offensive saved approximately 25,000 Tutsi with the capture of Kigali and thousands more.[43]

On July 4, 1994, the RPF captured Kigali and, by July 15, had moved to take the rest of the country, except for the French zone in the southwest. Approximately a million Hutu fled westward to Zaire in mid-July. The UN High Commission for Refugees (UNHCR) began to coordinate a massive humanitarian relief operation from Western countries to the millions of refugees, and a UN Rwanda Emergency Office did the same for the millions of internally displaced people inside the country. A majority of the Rwandan population was either internally displaced or refugees. More than 3,500 UNAMIR II troops were deployed in the French zone in order to prevent more Hutu from fleeing the country and to allow French forces to withdraw.[44]

On August 21, French forces withdrew, and UNAMIR II assumed control and began to work with the RPF's "government of national unity." With the establishment of a War Crimes Tribunal for Rwanda, UNAMIR II also assisted in investigating and arresting suspected *genocidaires*. With the RPF in control, 600,000 Tutsi refugees from Uganda began to return to Rwanda, which fulfilled the RPF's original goal. Many Tutsi took over land that had been vacated by fleeing Hutu. The RPF victory was pyrrhic, in that 800,000 people, mainly Tutsi, had died in the process.[45]

By August 1994, an estimated 1.7 million refugees had fled to Tanzania, Zaire, and Burundi. After helping to establish refugee camps and dealing with a deadly cholera outbreak, UNHCR and other aid organizations helped to sustain the refugees. While aid organizations tried to be apolitical, they soon found that the politics of the camp impinged on their work. Interspersed among the Hutu refugees were forces of both the FAR (the former Rwandan army) and the *interahamwe* that had been responsible for the genocide. The FAR and Interahamwe were still armed and controlling the Hutu population inside the camps, just as they had done in Rwanda. The Hutu *genocidaires* began to organize in the refugee camps in Zaire for a guerrilla campaign against the RPF regime and for an eventual return to power in Rwanda. The UNHCR appealed to the Mobutu regime in Zaire and to the Security Council to disarm the extremist forces and provide security. However, they did not comply. Consequently, the UN increasingly earned the distrust of the RPF regime in Rwanda. Attacks from Zaire and from the southwestern safe areas intensified. In April 1995, RPF forces attacked into the southwestern zone. In June 1995, the Rwanda government requested the withdrawal of UNAMIR II.

In January 1998, Secretary of State Madeleine Albright, the U.S. UN Ambassador in 1994, apologized to Rwandans for U.S. failure to act to stop the genocide. In March, President Clinton traveled to Kigali for a three-hour visit and also apologized. In November 1999, Secretary-General Kofi Annan apologized both for his own failure to act and for the UN. The most interesting facet of the apologies was the resolve expressed not to let genocide happen again. Whether or not action will be taken against genocide in the future remains to be seen.

"Creeping Genocide" in Burundi

In contrast to the three-month bloodbath in Rwanda, the genocide in Burundi proceeded intermittently. In Burundi, the Tutsi army maintained dominance over the Hutu. In 1972, the army led in the genocidal killing of over 200,000 Hutu civilians. With the wave of "democratization" that swept Africa in 1990, Burundi underwent what appeared to be a successful transition to multi-party democracy, which culminated in the election of President Ndadaye on June 1, 1993. However, the army's coup and assassination of the president on October 21, 1993 derailed what seemed to be a most encouraging process, and a "creeping genocide" commenced. In the three weeks after the coup and assassination, the army killed massive numbers of Hutu and drove nearly a million from their homes. More than 50,000 people were slaughtered in three weeks. In response, Hutu rebels struck and killed Tutsi civilians, which led to civil war and a series of retaliatory slayings. Within two years, the "creeping genocide" resulted in more than 20,000 additional deaths. NGOs provided ample evidence of genocide.[46]

When UNAMIR was established for Rwanda in October 1993, the Security Council was unwilling to become involved in Burundi. While NGOs called for UN intervention in Burundi, the council was suffering through the Somalia debacle and a major case of "peacekeeping fatigue." Furthermore, the Tutsi-dominated army opposed any intervention in the "sovereign affairs" of Burundi. Without peacekeepers, the UN and other third parties had to suffice with peacemaking and mediation. Boutros-Ghali dispatched Ahmedou Ould Abdallah to be his special representative in mediating the Tutsi-Hutu conflict. The United States sent Howard Wolpe, the former chair of the House of Representatives Sub-Committee on Africa, and other envoys. The mediators helped to prevent the waves of killings from exploding into full-blown war and Rwandan-style genocide. By January 1994, mediators had convinced the Tutsi-led army to relinquish control to civilian politicians, who were primarily Hutu. A new president, Cyprien Ntayamira, a Hutu, was elected by Parliament. He died in the plane that was shot down by Hutu extremists in Kigali and that also killed Rwandan President Habyarimana on April 6, 1994. Sylvestre Ntibantuganya, a Hutu, became interim president.

The Rwandan genocide of April-July 1994 reverberated through Burundi but did not precipitate another wave of genocide. Instead, on September 10, 1994, the Hutu party, the Democratic Front of Burundi (FRODEBU), agreed to share power in a government of national unity. At the same time, attacks by Burundian Hutu militias on the Tutsi-led army escalated into revenge killings, which culminated in the murder of a UNHCR field officer. In October, Sylvestre Ntibantuganya was elected president and Anatole Kanyenkiko, a Tutsi, became prime minister and formed the government of national unity. Subsequently, a pro-Tutsi party, the Union for National Progress (UPRONA), began to incite opposition against the government and, in January 1995, called for its overthrow. The Security Council condemned the UPRONA provocation. In retaliation, the newspaper owned by a Tutsi extremist and former president, Jean-Baptiste Bagaza threatened the lives of SRSG Abdallah and the U.S. Ambassador, Robert Krueger.[47]

In July 1996, the Tutsi-led army, headed by former dictator Pierre Buyoya, again intervened in a coup. The Organization of African Unity (OAU), led by Burundi's neighboring coastal state, Tanzania, moved to impose sanctions. This action was most significant, because it represented one of the first times that the OAU had imposed sanctions against a military dictatorship, which was abusing human rights. All of the states that surrounded Burundi, including the Tutsi-led RPF regime in Rwanda, agreed to cooperate by imposing sanctions. At the same time, mediators from the UN, OAU, United States, and neighboring states sought to persuade Buyoya to relinquish power to a government of national unity. Former Tanzanian President Julius Nyerere became the OAU mediator and assumed a leading role in the peace process. However, progress was slow because pressure on the Buyoya regime lessened in 1996-97. One source of pressure, the armed Hutu opposition, which had sprung from FRODEBU, had been weakened by the outbreak of fighting in Zaire in September 1996. FRODEBU fighters were forced from their bases in Zaire by the Banyanmulenge Tutsi during the fighting from September through November and were compelled to cross through Burundi on their way to new bases in Tanzania. Thus, the peace process became protracted. Finally, in October 1999, President Nyerere died and was replaced by the former South African president, Nelson Mandela, with the peace process still in progress.

Genocide Prevention and the Civil War in Zaire/Congo

After the Rwandan cataclysm of 1994, many of the Hutu *genocidaires* of the *interahamwe* and the FAR escaped to eastern Zaire and began plans for a counteroffensive to regain control of Rwanda and annihilate the remaining Tutsi. They found fertile ground for their plans and for the recruitment of fighters in the refugee camps, where more than a million Hutu were congregated. UNHCR and other aid agencies coordinated the feeding and maintenance of Hutu refugees, which unintentionally aided the *genocidaires*. The Hutu extremists began training guerrillas, launching incursions into Rwanda, and killing "disloyal" refugees. In spite of these activities and complaints from UNHCR and the RPF regime, President Mobutu of Zaire did little or nothing to stop these activities. Mobutu's inaction and the sovereignty of Zaire were masking preparations for genocidal activities, and the behavior of the *genocidaires* posed a grave threat to the sovereignty and survival of Rwanda. Consequently, the RPF regime was prepared to fight for its very existence and, if necessary, to violate the sovereignty of Zaire. At the same time, the RPF cemented its long-standing alliance with Uganda in preparation for war.

In 1996, anti-Tutsi sentiments and activities intensified in eastern Zaire. Mobutu's troops renewed their periodic harassment of the Banyamulenge, ethnic Tutsi living in South Kivu Province of Zaire. Mobutu threatened to remove their citizenship and expel them from Zaire. In October 1996, responding to rising persecution, the Banyamulenge began a counteroffensive against Zairian government forces. Soon they were joined by troops from the RPF's Rwandan Patriotic Army (RPA) that crossed into Zaire. Uganda provided logistical support and military advisors. The counteroffensive met little resistance, as Mobutu's troops fled. Subsequently, the RPA, Ugandans, and Banyamulenge did not stop their advance and moved north to attack Hutu extremist forces in and around the refugee camps. By November 1996, the offensive succeeded in breaking up the camps and routing the extremists. With the grip of the extremists broken, 600,000 refugees came streaming home into Rwanda.[48] The *genocidaires* and tens of thousands of refugees fled further westward into Zaire. The RPA and other forces pursued them in order to exact revenge and to eliminate the threat of renewed anti-Tutsi genocide. The flight of the refugees and massacre of thousands of Hutu comprised a new man-made humanitarian problem.

As the crisis in eastern Zaire intensified, Canada stepped forward and offered the Security Council its services in leading a humanitarian and peacekeeping operation in the African Great Lakes region. France offered to assist the Canadians, with the ulterior motive of preserving the Mobutu regime. On November 9, 1996, the Security Council authorized the Canadians to investigate the modalities for establishing an operation, and several countries, including the United States, assisted.[49]

A major incentive for the Canadian-led operation disappeared soon afterward, with the disbanding of the refugee camps and the return of 600,000 Hutu to Rwanda. Canada determined that support for its proposed mission had diminished. Only France remained supportive, especially because it was increasingly concerned about the precarious position of the Mobutu regime. As Boutros-Ghali left office and Kofi Annan became secretary-general, the UN could no longer manage the conflict in Zaire.

As the counteroffensive began, other forces opposed to Mobutu began to join the RPA, Ugandans, and Banyamulenge Tutsi. The Rwandans brought Laurent Kabila from obscurity in Tanzania to head the anti-Mobutu rebellion. Kabila had been a supporter of Prime Minister Patrice Lumumba until the latter's assassination in 1961 and had become a guerrilla leader for more than two decades. At the start of 1997, the multinational, multi-ethnic force began to march across Zaire in a campaign to seize power from Mobutu in Kinshasa. Mobutu's forces put up little resistance and demonstrated that the government's exercise of sovereignty was ephemeral. As the rebels approached Kinshasa, troops from Angola joined them. The Angolans intended to put an end to Mobutu's support for UNITA's rebellion. Finally, in May 1997, President Nelson Mandela and South Africa stepped in to negotiate Mobutu's removal from power and the installation of Kabila as President of the Democratic Republic of the Congo.

Rwanda's violation of Zaire's sovereignty in October 1996 led to a multilateral intervention, involving several African states and peoples that, temporarily, reduced threats to Rwanda, Uganda, and Angola and to the Banyamulenge Tutsi. Rwanda had strongly indicated that sovereignty would not stop intervention to prevent genocide or other manmade humanitarian disasters. However, the Rwandan-organized intervention did not lead to peace but to a new cycle of violence. Kabila turned against the Banyamulenge Tutsi, Rwanda and Uganda in 1998, and the latter responded by attempting to overthrow Kabila. In the end, Rwanda was more secure from Hutu extremists than before 1997. However, extremists continued to launch attacks from the Congo into Rwanda. Furthermore, the Congo had been turned into a battleground, in which armies from at least six different countries and at least three different rebel movements created their own spheres of influence.

The Yugoslav and Rwandan Criminal Tribunals

Genocidal activities in the former Yugoslavia and Rwanda led to the establishment of the first international criminal tribunals since the Nuremberg trials that convicted Nazi leaders after the World War II. Although the international community had failed to stop genocide, the Security Council decided that the perpetrators should be punished. It was hoped that the capture, trial, sentencing, and incarceration of the criminals would deter further ethnic cleansing and other genocidal activity. In both cases, the tribunals got off to shaky starts and made slow and halting progress.

In August 1992, the UN Human Rights Commission created a "Special *Rapporteur*" and, in October 1992, the Security Council established a "Commission of Experts" to investigate crimes in the former Yugoslavia that violated the 1949 Geneva Conventions. The *Rapporteur* and commission both issued reports on the extent of the devastation and dislocation caused mainly by Serb forces and apportioned blame for crimes that were committed. After the Special *Rapporteur* and commission revealed the extent of the crimes and after considerable pressure by the United States, Islamic states, and the secretary-general, the Security Council moved to establish the International Tribunal for Crimes in the former Yugoslavia on May 25, 1993. The peace enforcement provisions of Chapter VII of the UN Charter were invoked.[50]

In August, the council nominated judge candidates, in September, the General Assembly elected eleven judges for a four-year term, and in November, the tribunal convened for the first time and spent the first six months adopting rules. Finally, in July 1994, the Security Council appointed Judge Richard J. Goldstone as the Tribunal's Prosecutor. Judge Goldstone had played a key role in initiating South Africa's Truth and Reconciliation Commission (TRC) and was called on to bring the former Yugoslavia's war criminals to prosecution.

A principal problem for the Tribunal was that most of the suspects lived under Bosnian Serb or Serbian protection. When the Dayton Accords and NATO peacekeeping came into effect at the end of 1995, it was hoped that the culprits could be apprehended. However, the capture of suspected war criminals was not NATO's main priority. After a slow start, the tribunal began to make progress in 1996, during Secretary-General Boutros-Ghali's final year in office, with Canadian jurist Louise Arbour as prosecutor. The first case involved a Bosnian

Serb, Dusan Tadic, who was tried, convicted, and sentenced to twenty years in prison in May 1997. In November 1996, the tribunal announced that seventy-five persons had been indicted, including the leaders of the Bosnian Serbs, Radovan Karadzic, and Ratko Mladic, who remained at large. Slowly, NATO forces in Bosnia, especially the British, began to apprehend the suspects and bring them to trial.[51]

The Security Council set up the International Criminal Tribunal for Rwanda in November 1994 and selected Arusha, Tanzania, as the site. The tribunal came after a Commission of Experts found more than ample evidence of genocide against Rwandan Tutsi from April to July 1994.[52]

The RPF regime in Kigali, Rwanda supported the tribunal, except for the absence of the death penalty, and started its own national criminal proceedings against thousands of Hutu extremists who had been captured in Rwanda. The absence of a regime, like Serbia's, that would protect leading *genocidaires* made it easier for the tribunal and Rwanda to extradite suspects to be tried. One exception was President Moi of Kenya, who gave refuge to more than 10,000 Rwandan Hutu. The tribunal suffered from other problems, including an inefficient administration and difficulties in attracting judges and a prosecutor to Arusha. As a result, it took more than three years to get trials started.

In February 1996, the first indictments were handed down, including one for Georges Rutaganda, who was said to have played a major role in planning the genocide. In January 1997, Colonel Bagosora, another principal planner of the genocide, and Professor Ferdinand Nahimana, the creator of *Radio Mille Collines,* were among four prominent suspects who were extradited from Cameroon. In July 1997, President Moi approved the extradition from Kenya of seven *genocidaires,* including Hasan Ngeze, the publisher of *Kangura*, and Jean Kambanda, the Prime Minister of the Interim Government, who succeeded the murdered Prime Minister Agathe Uwilingiyamana in April 1994. In sum, the Rwandan Tribunal proved to be more successful in punishing the leaders of genocide than the tribunal for the former Yugoslavia.[53]

Conclusion: The UN and Genocide

In the former Yugoslavia and the Great Lakes of Africa and, particularly, in Bosnia and Rwanda, the UN failed to prevent or stop genocide. In both cases, the UN and its member states failed to heed the warnings of human rights NGOs and other evidence that genocidal activities were being planned, once they were under way, denied that they were genocidal in nature and required intervention. The UN and the United States did not heed the information from NGOs and the media, partly because they did not want to be compelled to intervene, as required by the Genocide Convention. As a result, Bosnia slowly suffered for three long years, while Rwanda quickly became a horrifying river of blood.

In the former Yugoslavia, ethnic cleansing by Serbs in Croatia foreshadowed what would happen in Bosnia. UNPROFOR troops on the ground in Croatia witnessed ethnic cleansing and concentration camps and could have moved to prevent similar occurrences in Bosnia. Learning from Croatia and Bosnia, the UN deployed a successful prevention force in Macedonia. In the case of Rwanda, the UN knew that the pogrom in Burundi and the Arusha Accords were provoking Hutu extremists. The personnel of UNAMIR recognized the beginning of the genocide campaign of the *interahamwe* and other "Hutu power" groups. However, the Security Council was so content with the success of the Arusha Accords that it became complacent in responding to the tensions that lurked beneath the surface of the peace agreement, and the council left UNAMIR powerless. The negligence of the council, including the United States, allowed UN personnel and nearly one million civilians to be killed in ninety days, with little or no response.

As a consequence of the events in the former Yugoslavia and African Great lakes region, the UN intensified its exploration of ways to prevent or stop internal conflicts and genocide. The UN Office for the Coordination of Humanitarian Affairs (OCHA) and UNHCR developed early warning systems to increase the UN's ability to respond to internal conflicts. The UN Development Programme identified nations at risk of internal strife, caused by ethnic competition for resources or by widening class differences. The UN, World Bank, and other agencies focused on the correlation between deepening economic crisis and ethnic conflict. However, it has been difficult to translate early warning into preventive action. The Security Council has authorized only one preventive deployment operation. The UNPREDEP mission to the Former Yugoslav Republic of Macedonia sought to preserve territorial integrity and internal cohesion in the face of Serbian threats. In responding to the problems of preventive deployment and stopping genocide, the secretary-general, The Netherlands, and a few other "good UN citizens" proposed a "UN rapid reaction force." However, the United States and other states rejected the proposal, as they distanced themselves from Boutros-Ghali and assertive multilateralism.

The British, after their experience in Bosnia, devised measures that would protect safe havens by force and rescues potential victims of ethnic cleansing and genocide. These measures came to be known as "wider peacekeeping," because they entailed more enforcement than "Chapter VI-and-a-half" peacekeeping and not the enforcement powers authorized under Chapter VII. In 1999, NATO intervened, without Security Council approval, in Kosovo to stop anther episode of genocidal ethnic cleansing by Serbia against Kosovar Albanians. It appeared that the lessons of Bosnia and Rwanda had been learned.

In spite of the major successes scored by the UN in Cambodia, Mozambique, Central America, and Haiti from 1992-94, the UN and Boutros-Ghali had been seriously damaged by failures in Somalia, Bosnia and Rwanda. The sagging reputation of the UN led the United States to distance itself from Boutros-Ghali and his agenda. In stopping genocidal conduct, the United States and other states turned to regional organizations and powers and looked less to the UN. As the United States and other states shifted direction, Boutros-Ghali was left in their wake.

Notes

1. Robert Donia, *Bosnia and Hercegovina: A Tradition Betrayed* (New York: Columbia University Press, 1994), 225.

2. Aleksandar Pavkovic, *The Fragmentation of Yugoslavia: Nationalism in a Multinational State* (New York: St. Martin's Press, 1997), 134.

3. James Gow, *Triumph of the Lack of Will: International Diplomacy and the Yugoslav War* (New York: Columbia University Press, 1997), 50.

4. Christopher Bennett, *Yugoslavia's Bloody Collapse: Causes, Course and Consequences* (New York: New York University Press, 1995), 160.

5. Donia, *Bosnia and Hercegovina,* 221.

6. Donia, *Bosnia and Hercegovina,* 223.

7. UN Security Council Resolution 713, September 25, 1991.

8. Bennett, *Yugoslavia's Bloody Collapse,* 163.

9. Norman L. Cigar, *Genocide in Bosnia: The Policy of 'Ethnic Cleansing'* (College Station: Texas A&M University Press, 1995), 40-41.

10. Pavkovic, *The Fragmentation of Yugoslavia,* 148.

11. Stanley Hoffmann, *The Ethics and Politics of Humanitarian Intervention* (Notre Dame, Ind.: University of Notre Dame Press, 1996), 40.

12. Bennett, *Yugoslavia's Bloody Collapse,* 179-80.

13. Sabrina P. Ramet, *Balkan Babel: The Disintegration of Yugoslavia from the Death of Tito to Ethnic War* (Boulder, Colo.: Westview Press, 1996),

246.

14. Laura Silber and Allan Little, *Yugoslavia: Death of a Nation* (New York: Penguin Books, 1997), 217-18.

15. Spyros Economides and Paul Taylor, "Former Yugoslavia," in *The New Interventionism 1991-1994: United Nations Experience in Cambodia, Former Yugoslavia, and Somalia,* James Mayall, ed. (Cambridge: Cambridge University Press, 1996), 65-66.

16. Boutros Boutros-Ghali, *Unvanquished: A U.S.-UN Saga* (New York: Random House, 1999), 55.

17. UN Security Council Resolution 770. August 13, 1992.

18. UN Security Council Resolutions 776 and 781, September 14 and October 9, 1992.

19. Ramet, *Balkan Babel,* 248-50.

20. UN Security Council Resolutions 808 and 827, February 22 and May 25, 1993.

21. UN Security Council Resolution 819, April 16, 1993.

22. William J. Durch and James A. Schear, "Faultlines: UN Operations in the Former Yugoslavia," in *UN Peacekeeping, American Policy, and the Uncivil Wars of the 1990s,* William J. Durch, ed. (New York: St. Martin's Press, 1996), 239.

23. Durch, "Faultlines," 241.

24. Howard Adelman and Astri Suhrke, eds., *The Path of a Genocide: The Rwanda Crisis from Uganda to Zaire* (New Brunswick, N.J.: Transaction Publishers, 1999), xviii.

25. Neil Jeffery Kressel, *Mass Hate: The Global Rise of Genocide and Terror* (New York: Plenum Press, 1996), 107.

26. Fergal Keane, *Seasons of Blood: A Rwandan Journey* (London: Viking, 1995), 23.

27. UN Security Council Resolution 872, October 5, 1993.

28. Allison Des Forges, "Burundi: Failed Coup or Creeping Coup?" *Current History* May 1994, 206-7.

29. Philip Gourevitch, *We Wish to Inform You That Tomorrow We Will be Killed with Our Families: Stories From Rwanda* (New York: Farrar, Straus and Giroux, 1998), 100.

30. Gourevitch, *We Wish to Inform You,* 103-6.

31. Gourevitch, *We Wish to Inform You,* 113.

32. Kressel, *Mass Hate* 90.

33. Gourevitch, *We Wish to Inform You,* 114.

34. Gourevitch, *We Wish to Inform You,* 150.

35. Holly Burkhalter, "A Preventable Horror?" *Africa Report* November-December 1994, 18.

36. Report of the Secretary-General on the United Nations Assistance Mission for Rwanda, S/1994/470, April 20, 1994.

37. UN Security Council Resolution 912, April 21, 1994.

38. Adelman, *The Path of a Genocide*, xviii.

39. Keane, *Seasons of Blood*, 15.

40. J. Matthew Vaccaro, "The Politics of Genocide: Peacekeeping in Rwanda," in *UN Peacekeeping, American Policy, and the Uncivil Wars of the 1990s,* William J. Durch, ed. (New York: St. Martin's Press, 1996), 384.

41. UN Security Council Resolution 918, May 17, 1994.

42. UN Security Council Resolution 929, June 22, 1994.

43. Vaccaro, "The Politics of Genocide," 387. However, the RPF was unable to save more than 800,000 innocent victims who were slaughtered between April and July.

44. Vaccaro, "The Politics of Genocide," 393.

45. Adelman, *The Path of a Genocide*, xviii.

46. Richard A. Sollom and Darren Kew, "Humanitarian Assistance and Conflict Prevention in Burundi," in *Vigilance and Vengeance: NGOs Preventing Ethnic Conflict in Divided Societies,* Robert I. Rotberg, ed. (Washington, D.C.: Brookings Institution Press, 1996), 245.

47. Sollom, "Humanitarian Assistance," 240.

48. Abbas H. Gnamo, "The Rwandan Genocide and the Collapse of Mobutu's Kleptocracy," in *The Path of a Genocide,* Howard Adelman and Astri Suhrke, eds. (New Brunswick, N.J.: Transaction Publishers, 1999), 346.

49. UN Security Council Resolution 1078, November 9, 1996.

50. UN Security Council Resolutions 780 and 827, October 6, 1992 and May 25, 1993.

51. Yves Beigbeder, *Judging War Criminals: The Politics of International Justice* (London: MacMillan, 1999), 156.

52. UN Security Council Resolution 955, November 8, 1994.

53. Beigbeder, *Judging War Criminals*, 180.

6

Sovereignty Eroded? Iraq, Arms Control, and Human Rights

The defeat of Saddam Hussein's Iraq in the 1991 Gulf War, following Iraq's audacious 1990 invasion of Kuwait, provided the UN with the opportunity to intervene strongly in the internal affairs of a sovereign member state. Not since the end of the Second World War and the occupation of Germany, Japan, and Austria had the sovereignty of a state been so systematically suspended. In particular, the cease-fire agreement gave the UN the power to intrude into Iraqi missile, nuclear, chemical, and biological weapons programs. Iraqi attacks on their Kurdish and Shiite populations provoked the United States and its allies to set up "no-fly zones" and guarantee the autonomy of the Kurdish area in the north. The struggle with Saddam Hussein and his regime represents as important a story about the UN under the secretary-generalship of Boutros Boutros-Ghali as the successes and failures in peacekeeping and peace enforcement. In 1990, Saddam Hussein demonstrated to the world that "aggressors" in the mold of Hitler still existed. Subsequently, Saddam would continue to act as a useful foil for the UN. For much of the decade, member states concurred that Iraq had to be contained and that Saddam's war machine and weapons of mass destruction had to be counteracted. Vicariously, Saddam's weapons programs and obstruction of inspectors provided major powers with an incentive to push for greater arms control efforts.

UN involvement with Iraq began after Saddam Hussein's 1980 decision to invade Iran. In response, the Security Council passed a resolution, urging Iraq and Iran to cease-fire, withdraw to pre-war boundaries, and negotiate.[1] When Iran stopped the invasion in 1981 and launched wave after wave of counterattacks, Saddam Hussein ordered the use of chemical weapons against Iranian soldiers and installations. Chemical weapons were used, even though Iraq had acceded to the 1925 Geneva Protocol that banned the use of such weapons between signatory nations. Iraq also launched missile attacks on Iranian cities. In 1986, UN Secretary-General Pérez de Cuéllar became the principal mediator in negotiations, which brought an end to the war by 1988. In that year, Saddam Hussein ordered a military campaign, featuring chemical weapons, against the Kurdish population, which was accused of consorting with the Iranians. Especially with the Kurds, Saddam Hussein demonstrated the propensity for launching indiscriminate attacks on civilian targets, through the use of Scud missiles. Consequently, UN member states were aware of Iraq's development of weapons of mass destruction when Iraq invaded Kuwait on August 2, 1990.

After Iraq invaded Kuwait, the Security Council, led by the United States, passed a raft of resolutions. The first resolutions, 660, 661, and 662, condemned the invasion, called for immediate Iraqi withdrawal, and imposed sanctions. The council also demanded that Iraq permit the departure of third-state nationals (who could have been held as hostages) from Kuwait and Iraq. On August 18, the council passed resolution 665, expanding the sanctions against Iraq and authorizing maritime forces to take measures to ensure strict compliance. As the sanctions tightened, the council launched investigations into concerns that neighboring states, such as Jordan, as well as Iraqi civilians would suffer.[2]

From August through November 1990, the Bush administration constructed an international coalition against Iraq. By November, the administration had concluded that sanctions would not work against Iraq and pushed for the use of force. On November 29, the Security Council passed Resolution 678, authorizing UN member states, cooperating with Kuwait, to use "all necessary means to uphold and implement" the council's resolutions on the situation.[3]

Iraq was given a deadline of January 15, 1991 to fully comply with all Security Council resolutions. In less than four months, the Bush administration had guided the council from supporting sanctions to authorizing the U.S.-led coalition to use force.[4]

At the end of November 1990, the council expressed concern that Iraq was attempting to alter the ethnic balance in Kuwait to its favor by expelling Kuwaitis and importing Iraqis. In December, the General

Assembly passed a resolution concerning the lack of human rights in occupied Kuwait. In six weeks, the international community's patience with Iraq expired, and the Gulf War began on January 16, 1991. The day after, the Permanent Representative of Kuwait presented a letter to the President of the Security Council stating that the deadline of Resolution 678 had expired and that Kuwait was exercising its right to self-defense with the cooperation of friendly states.[5]

Before the Gulf War commenced, the United States and its allies were understandably concerned over Iraq's weapons of mass destruction. Reports appeared concerning Iraq's nuclear weapons program, which was estimated to be within two years of being operational. Suspicions also rose over a biological weapons program. Concern was especially great over Saddam Hussein's demonstrated willingness to order the use of chemical weapons.[6]

As a result, U.S. and coalition military planners targeted weapons of mass destruction for air strikes. Along with associated facilities, they were attacked repeatedly throughout the war in an attempt to prevent Iraq from using such weapons. While Iraq did not use its weapons during the war, it did use its medium-range missile capability against Israel and coalition forces in Saudi Arabia. The war ended on March 2, 1991, with Iraq's weapons programs damaged but still largely intact.

When Saddam Hussein submitted to the coalition and accepted a cease-fire, he agreed to open weapons sites to international inspectors. In formulating the cease-fire resolution 687, approved on April 3, 1991, the Security Council established the institutions and procedures for eliminating Iraq's weapons programs and maintaining sanctions in order to compel disarmament. The rest of the resolution dealt with Iraq's relations with Kuwait. Iraq was expected to recognize Kuwait and pay reparations for Kuwaitis who had been harmed and for property damage. Subsequently, the UN Iraq-Kuwait Observer Mission (UNIKOM) was set up to monitor Iraq's behavior along the frontier with Kuwait. In addition, the resolution provided the basis for humanitarian relief from the impact of sanctions in Iraq, which was to culminate almost five years later in the "oil-for-food" program.[7]

After Saddam Hussein dispatched forces to crush rebellions by Kurds and Shiites and created a humanitarian crisis, the Security Council took further action against Iraq. In response, the council passed resolution 688 on April 5, which condemned Iraq's gross mistreatment of the Kurdish and Shiite populations in northern and southern Iraq. The resolution paved the way for Operation Provide Comfort, an international humanitarian action to alleviate the suffering of tens of thousands of Kurdish civilians who had fled from Iraqi forces.

Resolution 688 provided the basis for no-fly zones in northern and southern Iraq. In April 1991, a no-fly zone was established above the thirty-sixth parallel in northern Iraq to protect the Kurds. In August 1992, the southern no-fly zone was created, below the thirty-second parallel in southern Iraq to protect the Shiites.[8]

The UN Special Commission (UNSCOM)

Resolution 687 called for the disarmament of Iraq, with part C specifically covering unconventional weapons. Iraq was required to destroy and undertake never to use, develop, construct, or acquire unconventional weapons or ballistic missiles with a range greater than 150 kilometers. UNSCOM was established to verify Iraq's compliance with the resolution, with the Swedish diplomat, Rolf Ekeus, at the helm. UNSCOM was given two basic functions. The first was to inspect and oversee the destruction or elimination of Iraq's chemical and biological weapons and ballistic missile capabilities and the associated production and storage facilities. Second, UNSCOM was to monitor Iraq over the longer term to ensure continued compliance with the resolution. Finally, UNSCOM was charged to work with the International Atomic Energy Agency (IAEA) in dismantling Iraq's nuclear weapons program.[9]

Iraq was required to declare the locations, amounts, and types of proscribed weapons and allow on-site inspections of those sites. UNSCOM undertook this task through inspections of notified sites and by no-notice inspections of suspected facilities. Many of these suspected facilities were identified through military intelligence, provided mainly by the United States. The institution and enforcement of the no-fly zones to protect the Kurds and Shiites proved to be a valuable source of intelligence, as well as a way to threaten the use of force. UNSCOM's task proved to be complex and difficult and lasted far longer than the original estimate, made by Ekeus, of six months. At the zenith of its operations, because of the scope of its tasks, UNSCOM employed over 200 people, had a headquarters in New York, a permanent monitoring station in Baghdad equipped with five helicopters for no-notice visits to inspection sites, and a field office in Bahrain.[10]

Due to its record during the Iran-Iraq war, Iraq could not deny that it had a ballistic missile or chemical weapons capability. However, despite the suspicions of western intelligence, Iraq denied completely that it possessed biological weapons or a nuclear weapons program. During its first four years of its existence, UNSCOM was able to discover that, not only was the chemical weapons program much larger than Iraq had admitted, but that Iraq also had large biological and nuclear weapons programs. During this period, because of these discoveries and with the information that had been furnished by Iraqi authorities, UNSCOM was able to gain access to Iraq's weapons of mass destruction programs and supervise the dismantling of some of the weapons and associated production and testing facilities. However, due to a deliberate Iraqi policy of obstruction and deception, many weapons and facilities went undetected and unscathed. As part of this policy, Iraq would announce that it had unilaterally destroyed all of a certain type of weapon, while concealing a substantial quantity of the same weapon.

In June 1991, an inspection by IAEA inspectors discovered evidence that Iraq, indeed, was within two years of acquiring full nuclear capability, even though Iraq had ratified the 1968 Non-Proliferation Treaty (NPT). The United States and its coalition partners were disturbed by the discovery and called for a tough response. When joining the IAEA in inspection activities, UNSCOM was prepared for Iraqi deception and first focused on keeping track of Iraq's missiles and chemical weapons. While the inspectors were able to gain access to Iraqi sites and achieved a number of successes, they soon discovered that Iraq had set a course of systematically violating resolution 687 and obstructing the work of UNSCOM. Just as Iraq had failed to abide by its responsibilities as signatory to the Geneva Protocol and the NPT in the 1980s, it chose to evade compliance with Security Council resolutions during the 1990s.

By the end of 1991, UNSCOM had already conducted six ballistic missile inspections, as well as seven nuclear (with IAEA), six chemical, and two biological weapons inspections of Iraqi facilities.[11] On the sixth ballistic missile inspection, the team visited fixed Scud launchers, supervised the destruction of "supergun" long-range artillery components, and discovered that Iraq had sought to repair items destroyed during a previous inspection. UNSCOM destroyed other missile-related equipment and transporters. At the same time, the Iraqi Resident Representative in Vienna transmitted to the Director General of the IAEA information on Iraq's nuclear program. This was the first instance of Iraqi compliance with UNSCOM under Security Council resolution 715 of October 11, 1991.[12]

On December 20, the Security Council, following consultations about Iraq's compliance record, announced that the sanctions regime would stay in place without modification.[13] Every sixty days for more than a decade, the council continued to find that there was no reason to alter the sanctions regime in any significant way.

Iraq and the UN under Boutros-Ghali

Boutros Boutros-Ghali, as a top Egyptian foreign policymaker acting in the wake of Egypt's peace agreement with Israel, had worked to improve relations with Saddam Hussein's Iraq during the 1980s. When Boutros-Ghali became secretary-general in January 1992, he expressed empathy with Iraq and its people, issuing a statement expressing concern about the plight of civilian Iraqis who were being harmed by sanctions and emphasizing the importance of putting the humanitarian relief operation into place. At the same time, UNSCOM inspections and the struggle with Iraq were already well under way.

On January 31, Boutros-Ghali was joined by the Security Council's heads of state or government, led by President Bush, who emphasized the importance of the full implementation of all Iraq-related resolutions pertaining and Iraqi compliance with those resolutions, UNSCOM, and the IAEA. They also expressed concern for the humanitarian situation of Iraqi civilians. In response, the UN launched the Inter-Agency Humanitarian Program for Iraq, with shipments of food and medicine to beleaguered Iraqis and with initial requirements of $143.2 million.[14]

In the course of subsequent talks, the UN proposed an "oil-for-food" program. In response, Iraq continued to object for the next four years to the oil-for-food formula and demanded greater freedom in using its oil revenues. In the meantime, not enough food and medicine was making it to the Iraqi people, who suffered horribly.

At the end of January, UNSCOM dispatched a special mission to confirm Iraq's agreement to Security Council resolutions and to urge disclosure of information on chemical and biological weapons and ballistic missile programs. In particular, UNSCOM was attempting to tighten the disarmament regime, after it had received information in December 1991 that Iraq was concealing a substantial ballistic missile force. In spite of the revelations, UNSCOM continued to experience difficulties with gaining access to the program. On February 14, Ekeus, in a letter to Iraq's Minister for Foreign Affairs, Tariq Aziz, identified ballistic missile production, repair facilities, and related equipment within Iraq and demanded their destruction under UNSCOM supervision. In a report to the Security Council, Ekeus and UNSCOM concluded that Iraq was not prepared to give unconditional agreement to the destruction of ballistic missile-related facilities and equipment and other obligations. The Security Council weighed in by stating that Iraq's continued failure to acknowledge all of its obligations, its rejection of the two plans for ongoing monitoring and verification, and its failure to provide full disclosure of its weapons capabilities constituted a "material breach of the relevant provisions" of resolution 687.[15]

Consequently, a special mission, headed by Ekeus, held high-level talks with the Iraqi government in an attempt to secure its unconditional agreement to implement all obligations under resolutions 687, 707, and 715. At the end of February, UNSCOM conducted another (its eighth) ballistic missile inspection of Iraqi facilities, and teams cataloged prohibited items and attempted to verify the destruction of ballistic missile production and repair facilities and equipment, as directed by Ekeus. However, Iraq refused to destroy the missiles and components specified by UNSCOM. As a result, the inspection team was withdrawn from Iraq, and Ekeus brought the issue to the attention of the Security Council, reporting that he had not secured Iraq's unconditional agreement to implement all of its obligations.[16]

Iraq reiterated that it had provided all the information required by Security Council resolutions. While Iraq did not reject an ongoing monitoring and verification regime, it objected to the indefinite duration of the privileges, immunities, and facilities granted to UNSCOM and the IAEA and the infringement of Iraqi sovereignty. Once again, Iraq questioned the authority of UNSCOM and the items to be destroyed under resolution 687. In response, the Security Council reaffirmed that it alone was to determine which items were to be destroyed and warned Iraq of the consequences of continued noncooperation. The Security Council debated Iraq's compliance, and the council president reaffirmed that Iraq had not yet complied fully and unconditionally with council resolutions and stated that Iraqi authorities had to do so immediately. A March 19 statement by Iraq, in response to the council, declared the existence of eight, yet undeclared ballistic missiles, as well as chemical weapons and associated materials. Iraq claimed that most of the undeclared items were "unilaterally destroyed" in 1991 and that it was willing to carry out the additional necessary destruction of the remaining weapons. The March 19 declaration was part and parcel of the Iraqi plan of deception.[17]

In the chemical weapons area, UNSCOM made some progress in dismantling Iraq's massive program. During its seventh chemical inspection of Iraqi facilities, UNSCOM verified the delivery of chemical bomb-making equipment to a central destruction facility under construction at Al Muthanna and concluded that additional tests of the procedure for the destruction of nerve agents would be necessary. In February and March 1992, the first chemical weapons destruction team destroyed 463 nerve agent-filled rockets (approximately 2.5 tons of agent). Even so, UNSCOM inspectors believed that Iraq had concealed its best equipment and chemicals.[18]

Iraq's human rights record was found to be consistently poor by UN inspectors. In March, the UN Commission on Human Rights expressed its concern at the violations of human rights and fundamental freedoms committed during the occupation of Kuwait and condemned massive violations of rights carried out inside Iraq. In addition, the Security Council voiced its concern at human rights abuses being perpetrated by Iraq against its population. At this time, representatives of Iraq, Kuwait, France, Saudi Arabia, the United Kingdom, and the United States, with the International Committee of the Red Cross (ICRC) as a neutral intermediary, began meeting to identify missing Kuwaitis and effecting the release of those being held. On March 17, 1992, the Governing Council of the UN Compensation Commission adopted criteria for the processing of additional categories of claims against Iraq, covering individuals with losses exceeding $100,000 and the claims of corporations, international organizations, and governments.[19]

On March 19, the Security Council informed Iraq of its willingness to authorize the regime to sell petroleum and petroleum products in order to purchase food and medicine. The council would do so as soon as Iraqi authorities were prepared to proceed in accordance with resolutions 687, 707, and 715. A second round of discussions was held in Vienna between the UN Secretariat and Iraqi representatives on arrangements for the proposed sale of petroleum to finance the purchase of goods for humanitarian purposes. In spite of these initial efforts, Saddam Hussein continued to resist the oil-for-food program for four more years, as the plight of Iraqis deteriorated.

On April 9, following the incursion of an Iranian aircraft into Iraqi airspace, Iraq called for a halt to all aerial surveillance flights, stating that the safety of the pilots and aircraft could be in danger. In response, Ekeus expressed his concern at the implied threats to the safety of the commission's pilots and aircraft. The Security Council reaffirmed the right of UNSCOM to conduct aerial surveillance over Iraq, called upon Iraq to ensure that its military forces did not interfere with or threaten the safety of the commission's aircraft and personnel, and warned the

Iraqis of serious consequences should they fail to comply. Backing down, Iraq asserted that it did not intend to carry out any military operation aimed at UNSCOM surveillance activity.[20]

In the meantime, UNSCOM conducted its ninth ballistic missile inspection of Iraqi facilities. Teams were charged with verifying the destruction of facilities and equipment cited by Ekeus in his February letter, as well as Iraq's March 19 claims of having unilaterally destroyed eighty-nine ballistic missiles and associated equipment in 1991. After UNSCOM conducted undeclared inspections of sites throughout Iraq, Ekeus, in a letter of April 4 to Iraq, detailed additional items to be destroyed or to verify as having been destroyed. In spite of these efforts, UNSCOM was still experiencing difficulty discovering how many missiles Iraq possessed. Also, UNSCOM teams continued to supervise the destruction of ballistic missile production equipment, monitoring the destruction of forty-five items and ten buildings.[21]

In April, UNSCOM teams monitoring preparations for the destruction of chemical weapons at the Al Muthanna site provided technical guidance for the construction of a mustard agent incinerator and a large-scale nerve agent hydrolysis plant. Also they supervised the transfer of all chemicals usable for the manufacture of ballistic-missile propellant to the site for destruction. During a chemical inspection (its eighth) of Iraqi facilities, UNSCOM teams visited fourteen sites to verify the destruction of chemical weapons items that Iraq declared it had destroyed unilaterally. On June 18, UNSCOM's Chemical Destruction Group started its operations in Iraq. In June and July, the second joint chemical and biological inspection team visited undeclared sites and supervised the destruction of chemical bomb-making equipment. In September, UNSCOM commissioned the Al Muthanna hydrolysis plant, designed to destroy nerve agent.[22]

At the end of March, the IAEA presented to Iraq a list of buildings and equipment to be destroyed at the Al Atheer-Al Hateen site. In April, the IAEA conducted its eleventh nuclear inspection of Iraqi facilities and supervised the destruction of equipment and facilities at Al Atheer, Iraq's nuclear weaponization research and development center. The IAEA plan for the dismantling of uranium enrichment production capabilities at the Tarmiya and Ash Sharqat sites was prepared and communicated to Iraq. In May and June, the twelfth IAEA inspection at Al Atheer removed what was believed to be the last highly enriched uranium from Iraq. In September, an IAEA team sampled Iraqi streams, canals, and swamps to find nuclear weapons materials.[23]

In May, UNSCOM conducted its eleventh ballistic missile inspection of Iraqi facilities. Teams continued attempts to verify the destruction of additional chemical warheads and ballistic missiles, as claimed in Iraq's declaration of March 19, 1992. They also continued to take inventory of material designed for the construction of the BADR-2000 (medium-range ballistic missile), to verify the destruction of additional missile-related items in the Iraqi arsenal, and to identify five sets of Iraqi-manufactured missile-guidance components, which were to be removed. UNSCOM inspectors attempted to find documents related to the construction of facilities associated with the missile program. Iraq engaged in further deception, when it informed Ekeus that it had already disclosed or was imminently ready to disclose its full nuclear, chemical, biological, and ballistic missile programs, as required by resolution 687 and that it was ready to reach a practical solution to the monitoring program required by resolutions 707 and 715.[24]

UNSCOM experienced its next crisis, starting on July 5, 1992, when an inspection team in pursuit of documents about the ballistic missile program was refused access to the Ministry of Agriculture. In response, the Security Council demanded that Iraq grant the team immediate access to the ministry as required by resolution 687. Through seventeen days of a very hot July, UNSCOM's ballistic missile inspection team maintained a close watch outside the building, awaiting access to the site. On July 22, the team was withdrawn, following an attack on one of its members. Access was finally permitted on July 28, when a thorough inspection was conducted. Evidence gathered from the ministry demonstrated that, during the period the team was denied entry, the Iraqis had removed important items from the building.[25]

In 1992, Iraq continued to cause difficulties in the Kurdish and Shiite zones and along the border with Kuwait. In response, the Security Council pressed Iraq to finally repudiate all claims to Kuwait and fulfill its obligation under resolution 687 to accept the inviolability of borders drawn by the Boundary Demarcation Commission. On July 16, a member of the UN Guards Contingent was murdered in the northern Iraqi governorate of Dohuk. In response, Boutros-Ghali called for an investigation, and the council condemned the murder, expressed concern at the deterioration of security conditions affecting UN personnel in Iraq, and demanded the cessation of attacks against them.[26]

In August 1992, the southern no-fly zone below the thirty-second parallel was added to the one that already existed in the north. The southern zone was imposed as Shiite Muslims continued to come under attack from the Iraqi military. However, the lack of ground forces in support of "Operation Southern Watch" severely restrained the ability to protect the Shiites. In 1996, the no-fly zone was moved upward to the thirty-third parallel after additional attacks against the Shiites. In contrast to the south, Kurdish militias and UN Guards effectively established autonomy for the Kurds in the north.[27]

UNHCR scaled down its refugee and relief operations, having fully implemented the Emergency Relief Program and the first phase of rehabilitation in the three northern governorates of Iraq where the Kurds lived. UNHCR's activities and some assets were handed over to the UN Children's Emergency Fund (UNICEF), the UN Development Programme (UNDP), and other agencies in order to sustain rehabilitation efforts. At the end of September, Iraq announced that it had no objection to the UN mounting a relief operation for the Kurds in northern Iraq during the winter.[28]

In November 1992, Iraq sent a high-level delegation to the Security Council's review of Iraq's compliance with resolutions 687, 707, and 715. At the beginning of the meeting, the council stated that Iraq had not fully complied with all of its obligations. Iraq reiterated its position that economic sanctions should be removed, because of the suffering that sanctions were imposing on Iraqis and due to the high proportion of obligations that had been fulfilled. Iraq submitted to the council a detailed account of its activities in conjunction with UNSCOM and IAEA inspections and measures it had taken to implement resolution 687, part C. After debating Iraqi compliance, the council reiterated its support for the statement made at the opening of the meeting, called on Iraq to take appropriate actions immediately to comply fully and unconditionally with its obligations. and announced that there was no agreement that the conditions existed for modifying the sanctions regime. Once again, Iraq's efforts to lift sanctions had been rebuffed.[29]

The Clinton Administration, the UN, and Iraq

At the end of 1992 and beginning of 1993, as the United States and UN were focused on Somalia and as the presidency passed from George Bush to Bill Clinton, Iraq stepped up its military activities and defied resolutions 687 and 688. Iraq fighters breached the no-fly zones on several occasions, and in December 1992, an Iraqi fighter was shot down when it entered one of the exclusion zones. In January 1993, Iraq fomented two crises. On January 2, some 200 Iraqi soldiers entered the former naval base at Umm Qasr in the demilitarized zone (DMZ), without UNIKOM authorization, ostensibly to retrieve Iraqi property. Five days later, Iraqi authorities informed UNSCOM that the UN would no longer be permitted to use its own aircraft to transport personnel and equipment between Iraq and its base in Bahrain. In response, the Security Council demanded that Iraq permit UNIKOM and UNSCOM to use their own aircraft to transport personnel and equipment and that Iraq abide by all relevant UN resolutions. The President of the Security Council wrote to Boutros-Ghali concerning Iraqi incursions into the DMZ and expressed council members' insistence on the removal, by January 15, of six Iraqi police posts on Kuwaiti territory.[30]

On January 10, the Iraqis who had entered the DMZ forced their way into six ammunition bunkers at Umm Qasr and removed most of their contents, including weapons and armaments slated for destruction. In response, the council condemned Iraq for removing the equipment and other materials from the Kuwaiti side of the DMZ and declared that Iraq's actions toward UNIKOM and UNSCOM constituted "material breaches" of resolution 687.[31]

On January 13, the United States, the United Kingdom, and France punished Iraq by staging air raids on anti-missile sites and radar bases in the south. Four days later, U.S. planes fired missiles at an industrial complex in suburban Baghdad, and, the next day, the United Kingdom and the United States launched air strikes against radar sites in southern and northern Iraq. Later, in June 1993, the United States followed with more air attacks, after former President Bush was threatened by Iraq before an April 1993 visit to Kuwait.

As the air strikes took their toll, the Iraqi operation to retrieve property from Kuwait ended, and the six Iraqi police posts on Kuwaiti territory were withdrawn. On January 18, Boutros-Ghali recommended strengthening UNIKOM to give it the capacity to deal with small-scale violations of the border and with problems that might arise from the demarcation of the boundary. The next day, he reported that Iraq had agreed to a resumption of UNSCOM flights. On February 5, the council adopted resolution 806, strengthening UNIKOM and widening its mandate to permit it to take direct physical action to prevent or stop violations of the DMZ.[32]

On May 20, the Iraq-Kuwait Boundary Demarcation Commission submitted its final report on the boundary between Iraq and Kuwait. At the commission's final session, Boutros-Ghali confirmed that a precise, well-defined and verifiable demarcation of the entire boundary had been accomplished. On May 27, the Security Council adopted resolution 833, reaffirming the decisions of the commission and underlining the council's guarantee of the boundary's inviolability.[33]

On June 6, in a letter to the secretary-general, Iraq outlined objections to the work of the Boundary Commission. However, ten days later, Iraq reversed itself and joined Kuwait in accepting the decisions of the commission. On June 28, the council, in response to Iraq's letter reaffirmed the legality and finality of the provisions of the commission and reminded Iraq of the boundary's inviolability.[34]

In November 1993, Kuwait reported on Iraqi actions against Kuwaiti territory and nationals and against UNIKOM officers on patrol. The Security Council held Iraq responsible for violations of the boundary and demanded that Iraq prevent any future violation. In February 1994, Boutros-Ghali reported to the President of the Security Council on his efforts to resolve the issue of Iraqi citizens and their assets found to be in Kuwaiti territory following the demarcation of the boundary. In response, the council adopted resolution 899, deciding that compensation could be made to Iraqi citizens for the loss of assets resulting from the demarcation of the boundary.[35]

In 1993 and 1994, the disarmament of Iraq proceeded unevenly, with the IAEA making substantial progress on the nuclear front and with UNSCOM confronting difficulties in uncovering Iraq's biological weapons program. In June 1993, UNSCOM reported on Iraq's noncompliance with monitoring efforts, including its refusal to permit helicopter surveillance during on-site inspections and the installation of monitoring cameras at two rocket test sites. In addition, Iraqi authorities refused to transport chemical-weapons-related equipment to a designated site for destruction under UNSCOM supervision. In response, the Security Council demanded that Iraq accept the installation by UNSCOM of monitoring devices at the rocket engine test sites and transport chemical-weapons-related equipment to the UNSCOM-designated destruction site. It warned of the danger of refusing to comply with part C of resolution 687. In response, Iraq provided UNSCOM with further information on how it would continue to comply with missile, chemical, and biological monitoring.[36]

In July, after high-level meetings between UNSCOM and Iraq, Ekeus reported to the Security Council that Iraq had agreed to allow installation of the monitoring cameras but not their operation by UNSCOM. In addition, Ekeus reported that Iraq had removed and was

destroying, under UNSCOM supervision, all chemical-weapons production equipment and precursor chemicals from its site at Al Fallujah.
In early September, at talks in New York between Iraq, UNSCOM, and
the IAEA, Iraq agreed to the operation of the monitoring cameras
installed at rocket engine rest stands, and the cameras were subsequently installed. By November 1993, it appeared that Iraq was finally
admitting that it could no longer resist the UNSCOM/IAEA inspection
regime. On November 26, Iraq accepted Security Council resolutions
707 and 715 of 1991, in which the council had approved plans for the
ongoing monitoring and verification of Iraqi compliance with the
disarmament provisions of resolution 687.[37]

In January 1994, Iraq made its first declarations to UNSCOM under
resolution 715 about dual-purpose capabilities that could produce
chemical and biological weapons or missiles and notified the commission that previous compliance declarations should be considered as
having been submitted under resolution 715. From March to May,
UNSCOM conducted baseline inspections of dual-purpose facilities in
Iraq. On April 19, Iraq submitted to UNSCOM detailed information on
its imports of precursor chemicals and equipment for the production of
chemical weapons. In May and June, UNSCOM conducted verification
inspections of Iraq's biological weapons program in order to develop
an inventory of biological dual-purpose equipment and to mark and
photograph relevant equipment in order to provide a baseline of data
against which to determine equipment use, modification and transfer.
In July, Iraq updated its declarations to UNSCOM of dual-purpose
capabilities in the chemical, biological, and missile areas.[38]

In March 1994, the IAEA announced that all irradiated nuclear fuel
had been removed from Iraq. In April, high-level talks between
UNSCOM, IAEA, and Iraqi officials took place in Baghdad. Progress
in preparation for ongoing monitoring and verification was assessed,
and a joint statement was issued. Four months later, the IAEA established a continuous presence in Iraq in order to monitor and verify
compliance. On May 10, following high-level technical talks in Vienna, the IAEA and Iraq issued joint statements acknowledging Iraq's
cooperation in facilitating the mission of IAEA.[39]

In September 1994, UNSCOM and Iraq resumed high-level technical talks in Baghdad to review Iraq's biological weapons capability and
activities since 1986. At the beginning of October, UNSCOM announced that the system for ongoing monitoring and verification of

Iraqi compliance with the disarmament provisions of resolution 687 was provisionally operational, subject to a period of testing.

In March 1994, the UN Commission on Human Rights expressed strong condemnation of the massive violations of human rights in Iraq and called upon Iraq to release all persons arbitrarily arrested and detained, including Kuwaitis and nationals of other states. The commission requested the secretary-general, in consultation with the special rapporteur, to facilitate the sending of human rights monitors to locations that would enhance information flows and the independent verification of reports on Iraq's human rights situation. Kuwait reported that it had handed over to the ICRC the files of 627 prisoners, detainees, and missing persons about whom it was seeking information from Iraq.

In March, the Governing Council of the UN Compensation Commission decided the priority of payment, payment mechanisms, distribution of payments, and transparency, and in June, the commission paid $2.7 million to 670 claimants from 16 countries who had suffered serious injury or whose relatives had been killed. Monitors from the UN Centre for Human Rights visited Kuwait to gather further information on missing persons. In July, Iraq resumed its participation in the meetings of the Tripartite Commission, which formed a Technical Subcommittee on Military and Civilian Missing Prisoners. In October, Kuwait submitted to Boutros-Ghali a list of property, which was still to be returned, including property belonging to the Kuwaiti armed forces, the central bank, the central library, and government ministries and departments. The claims of victims of the Iraqi invasion of Kuwait continued to be met. In October 1995, the UN paid $82 million to 2,577 serious personal injury or death claimants from 41 countries and Palestine and, in December, $2.4 million to 720 claimants from nineteen countries and Palestine.[40]

In 1994, Iraq became more assertive in its relations with the UN, and several countries began to assist Iraq in evading sanctions. On July 1, Boutros-Ghali, in an effort to fortify the monitoring of sanctions, wrote to the foreign ministers of twenty countries that had been the principal importers of Iraqi crude petroleum before Iraq's invasion of Kuwait. In the letter, he sought information from companies on any importation of Iraqi petroleum and products on or after June 1, 1990. In spite of his action, evasion of sanctions continued.

On October 6, Iraq threatened to cease cooperation with UNSCOM and IAEA and moved 10,000 troops to within thirty miles of the border with Kuwait. At this time, the Security Council declared Iraq's threatened withdrawal of cooperation from UNSCOM and IAEA as unacceptable and renewed UNIKOM's mandate for a further six-month period. Nevertheless, reports mounted that substantial numbers of Iraqi troops were being deployed even closer to the Kuwait border. In response, the council requested UNIKOM to increase its vigilance and reiterated that Iraq must comply fully with all relevant resolutions. In addition, the council adopted resolution 949, condemning Iraq's large-scale military deployment toward the Kuwait border and demanding a complete withdrawal.[41]

After resolution 949 and threats from the United States, the United Kingdom, and France, Iraq announced that, as of October 12, it had withdrawn its troops to their previous positions and affirmed its readiness to resolve the issue of its recognition of Kuwaiti sovereignty. The council resolved that Iraq should not re-deploy these troops to the south of the country and that Iraq should resume full cooperation with UNSCOM. On November 10, 1994, reversing its nonrecognition of Kuwait, an Iraqi Revolution Command Council decree and a National Assembly declaration confirmed Iraq's "irrevocable and unqualified recognition of the sovereignty, territorial integrity and political independence of the state of Kuwait."[42]

In addition, Iraq recognized the international boundary between Iraq and Kuwait, as demarcated by the Iraq-Kuwait Boundary Demarcation Commission, and Iraq's respect for the inviolability of that boundary. The Security Council welcomed Iraq's recognition of Kuwait and its commitment to respect Kuwait's sovereignty, territorial integrity, and borders. In a matter of days, Saddam Hussein had moved from a threatened invasion of Kuwait to full recognition.

In April 1995, a seminar of international biological weapons experts, convened by UNSCOM, concluded that Iraq had an undeclared and full-scale biological weapons program. UNSCOM reported that the system for ongoing monitoring and verification of Iraqi compliance with the disarmament provisions of resolution 687 was operational. At the beginning of May, UNSCOM convened a seminar of international chemical weapons experts, and it concluded that Iraq had not adequately disclosed its pre-1990 chemical weapons program. On July 1, Iraq admitted to once having had a full-scale offensive biological weapons program, and, in early August, Iraq gave UNSCOM a written account of its pre-1990 biological-weapons program that still denied efforts to weaponize biological warfare agents. However, on July 17,

Saddam Hussein threatened to end all cooperation with UNSCOM and the IAEA, if there was no progress toward the lifting of sanctions and the oil embargo. Iraq set the end of August 1995 as the deadline.[43]

From April 1991 to mid-1995, the UN and, in particular, UNSCOM, seemed to have made considerable progress in Iraq, albeit after considerable struggle. However, on the weapons of mass destruction front, Iraq was still concealing more than it had disclosed. By mid-1995, UNSCOM was fully aware that the Iraqis were not providing the required assistance and were resisting as much as possible. Due to Iraq's refusal to allow UNSCOM access to a number of sites, there were deep suspicions that the Iraqis were trying to conceal large amounts of materiel from inspectors. Three particular incidents had underscored these suspicions. The first followed the inspection of a suspected nuclear facility and the removal of documents, when an IAEA team was besieged in a car park for a number of days in September 1991. The second was the July 1992 confrontation in front of the Ministry of Agriculture building and the subsequent withdrawal of UNSCOM investigators from Iraq. The third was when UNSCOM was prevented from installing monitoring cameras at two missile test sites in July 1993 and when the Iraqi government eventually backed down under threat of international military action. Evidence also emerged that Saddam Hussein had started a new weapons of mass destruction program apart from the old one and was using his network of presidential palaces for concealment.[44]

UNSCOM suspicions were to be confirmed fully in August 1995, following the dramatic defection of Saddam Hussein's son-in-law, General Hussein Kamel Hassan Al-Majid.

The Kamel Defection and Crisis in UN-Iraq Relations

General Kamel, the head of the Military Industrial Organization in Iraq and the director of Iraq's "special weapons" of mass destruction programs and ballistic missile program, and his brother Saddam were married to daughters of Saddam Hussein. On August 7, 1995, all four defected from Iraq to Jordan. Immediately after he defected, Kamel revealed how Iraq was deliberately and systematically misleading the UN weapons inspection team. The most startling aspect of his revelations was how successful the Iraqis had been at concealing their weapons. He provided detailed information on the concealment and deception operation and, most alarmingly, on the true extent of the nuclear weapons program. It was now obvious that, not only was the Iraqi regime concealing information from UNSCOM, but that it had also lied about the "destruction" of its entire operational ballistic missile capability in the summer of 1991. Kamel's revelations shocked many of the UN weapons inspectors who thought that most of the material had been surrendered and who were prepared to brief the Security Council accordingly. Rather than wrapping up UNSCOM and giving Iraq its seal of approval, the new information proved that Iraq still possessed a large arsenal weapons of mass destruction and presented UNSCOM with a new challenge. Suddenly, UNSCOM acquired the knowledge to more aggressively combat Iraqi deception and to demand proof that weapons had been destroyed.

Ten days after the defection, on August 17, Iraq reversed itself and made sweeping admissions about its weapons programs. Iraq admitted that it did, indeed, produce biological weapons, that it had a crash program to acquire nuclear weapons, that it had made greater progress than previously thought in producing the nerve agent VX, and that it had produced more ballistic missiles inside the country than previously declared. Rather than accepting responsibility, the Iraqi government blamed the concealment on General Kamel. At the same time, Iraq removed its threat to end cooperation with UNSCOM and the IAEA at the end of August. On August 20, Iraq handed over to UNSCOM and the IAEA some "680,000 pages of printed materials, computer disks, videotapes, microfilm and microfiche, and various items and materials relating to its past banned weapons programs."[45]

The Iraqi regime could do little more than plead ignorance of the concealment activities and make the gesture of surrendering "newly discovered" information. However, at the same time, a damage-control exercise was initiated, which, in effect, became a continuation of the deception and concealment program. As UNSCOM renewed its inspections, Iraq began a new campaign of obstruction.[46]

In September, an IAEA inspection team met with Iraqi scientists, engineers, and support staff involved in the nuclear program and obtained further information. In October, during the next IAEA inspection, the state of knowledge of Iraqi scientists and engineers in centrifuge enrichment and weaponization technologies was discussed in order to ensure that ongoing monitoring and verification efforts were properly focused. On December 7, the Sanctions Committee forwarded to the Security Council a proposal for a mechanism to monitor Iraq's exports and imports of dual-purpose capabilities, once sanctions were lifted.[47]

From Boutros-Ghali to Annan and UN-Iraq Relations

As Boutros-Ghali began his final year as secretary-general, it seemed that the UN had made major breakthroughs in disarming and controlling Iraq. However, the high hopes for the UN mission soon evaporated, as did Boutros-Ghali's expectations of a second term.

From December 26 to 29, 1995, Secretary-General Boutros-Ghali made an official visit to Kuwait to inspect UN operations. There he met with the Emir, the crown prince, and prime minister, other government officials, and representatives of Kuwaiti development funds and other international organizations. Also, he visited UNIKOM forces on the Kuwaiti side of the Iraq-Kuwait border and addressed a joint meeting of the National Assembly Committees for Foreign Affairs and for the Protection of Human Rights. During the visit, Boutros-Ghali urged the Kuwaiti leadership to take a more "flexible stance" toward Iraq.[48]

In regard to Iraqis who were suffering from the effects of sanctions, the Under-Secretary-General for Humanitarian Affairs wrote to UN member states and other potential donors in December 1995, asking them to contribute urgently and substantially to fund UN humanitarian activities in Iraq. In addition, Iraq edged closer to finally accepting the UN "oil-for-food" proposal. On January 29, 1996, Iraq accepted Boutros-Ghali's invitation to enter into discussions with the UN Secretariat on implementation of the "oil-for-food" formula contained in Security Council Resolution 986 of 1995.[49]

Boutros-Ghali announced that talks on oil-for-food would begin on February 6. On that date, discussions on the implementation of the resolution began at UN Headquarters in New York. The talks led to the inauguration of the "oil for food" program, finally, after five years of sanctions had ravaged the Iraqi population.

In July 1996, Iraq threatened the Kurdish safe haven in northern Iraq and Shiite areas in the south. In response, in July and August, U.S. planes struck Iraqi anti-aircraft missile sites in a series of attacks in the no-fly zones in both southern and northern Iraq. In August and September, Iraqi armed forces ignored the air strikes and deployed in the Kurdish safe haven in northern Iraq. Subsequently, the United States launched missile attacks in southern Iraq and extended the no-fly zone to the thirty-third parallel, close to Baghdad. France broke ranks with the United States and the United Kingdom and refused to participate in patrolling the extended zone. In addition, the Iraqi government complained about and questioned the legitimacy of the no-fly zones, claiming that there were no Security Council resolutions authorizing enforcement. Iraq asserted that the no-fly zones were an infringement of sovereignty and that the rationale for the no-fly-zones was ambiguous. The United States argued that, because resolution 688 stipulated that Iraq could not harm its own people, it provided the legal basis for these zones. However, nations, such as Russia, joined with Iraq and stated that the zones were not been backed by specific UN resolutions.

When Boutros-Ghali left office as secretary-general in January 1997, the UN mission in Iraq had accomplished many of its goals. Iraq had recognized Kuwait, and the UN was making progress toward seeing that victims of the 1990 invasion were compensated. The United States and its allies were maintaining no-fly zones to protect the Kurds and Shiites against Iraqi air power, and the Kurds were operating an autonomous region in the north. UNSCOM and IAEA had destroyed a large proportion of Iraq's nuclear and chemical weapons and missile programs. The Kamel defection had revealed the extent of Iraq's biological program and remaining nuclear, chemical, and missile assets. In spite of Iraq's continuing outlaw behavior, the regime could not be shamed into complying with UNSCOM and IAEA, and the regime continued resisting inspections and the destruction of weapons. Also, Iraq resumed rebuilding its weapons of mass destruction programs.

Although there had been consensus within the Security Council during the early part of UNSCOM's existence, this support gradually declined as the inspections and the associated punitive sanctions were increasingly prolonged. In particular, by the time Boutros-Ghali was replaced by Kofi Annan, three of the permanent members, France, Russia, and China, were pressing for the lifting of sanctions. Extensive economic interests in Iraq motivated France and Russia, and China had been supplying weapons technology in the 1980s and wished to resume. In December 1996, France stopped patrolling the no-fly zones, claiming that changes made in the mission meant that it no longer served humanitarian purposes. Russia was already moving to reestablish its special relationship with Iraq. There is evidence that a Russian member of UNSCOM, with encouragement from Moscow, supplied information forewarning Iraq of UNSCOM's inspection plans.[50]

In opposition to Russia, China and France, the other two permanent members, the United States and the United Kingdom, remained staunchly in favor of sanctions, inspections, and no-fly zones. In doing so, the United States and the United Kingdom differed in their motives. The Clinton administration was seeking to remove Saddam Hussein from power, while both the Major and Blair governments merely wanted Iraq to live up to its obligations under resolutions 687 and 688.

In July 1997, Richard Butler replaced Rolf Ekeus as head of UNSCOM and served until 1999. Butler took a harder line toward the Iraqi regime and its noncompliance, and the first UNSCOM report of under his supervision, issued in October 1997, was more critical of Iraq than any previous report. In the same month, the first crisis involving Butler started over Iraqi demands that American arms inspectors with UNSCOM should be dismissed and over objections to UNSCOM insistence that presidential palaces should be inspected for records and weapons materials. By February 1998, the crisis had escalated to the point where the United States and the United Kingdom were on the verge of using force. As an air campaign was about to be launched, Secretary-General Annan visited Baghdad and, after difficult negotiations, was able to defuse the crisis. However, Iraqi intransigence soon returned. As there was still no improvement in the situation, Butler became increasingly pessimistic in his briefings to the Security Council.

In June 1998, U.S. F-16s fired a missile at a radar site in southern Iraq. In August, Saddam Hussein reiterated that Iraq would cease cooperating with UNSCOM. The United States and the United Kingdom were now faced with attempting to coerce Iraq to submit. By its own rhetoric, the United States had been maneuvered into a position where it would have to use force if Iraq did not submit. On the other hand, the United Kingdom was concerned by the growing support for Iraq within the Security Council and was seeking a means for UNSCOM to regain the initiative in order to uncover and destroy Iraq's concealed WMD capability. There was, however, little room for compromise and, with the differing positions of the main players, the scene had been set for an armed confrontation. For three months, the United States refrained from taking action. As matters came to a head in early November 1998, Kofi Annan was able to achieve yet another compromise. However, Iraq's compliance was short lived, and the United States and the United Kingdom initiated a four-day air campaign, Operation Desert Fox, on December 16, 1998. This sealed the fate of UNSCOM, as Iraq refused to allow the weapons inspectors to return.

Conclusion

For a decade, the UN intervened in the internal affairs of Iraq, an aggressor nation in the mold of Germany and Japan in the 1930s and 1940s. The UN applied sanctions, authorized the use of force, investigated and destroyed weapons of mass destruction, and provided humanitarian relief and protection to victims of a brutal regime. On the weapons of mass destruction front, the IAEF dismantled Iraq's nuclear weapons program. UNSCOM oversaw the destruction of nearly 40,000 chemical weapons, 690 tons of chemical weapons agents, more than 3,000 tons of precursor materials, and numerous pieces of production equipment, as well as 48 long-range missiles and a similar number of chemical and conventional warheads.[51]

In spite of the UN's many accomplishments, Iraq was not occupied, like Germany and Japan had been. Without foreign forces on Iraqi soil, the dictator, Saddam Hussein, had the opportunity to resist the UN and eventually split the consensus on the need to contain Iraq and interfere in its internal affairs.

Iraq's roguish behavior had two opposing effects on arms control efforts. On the one hand, the United States and other major powers mobilized to push for verifiable arms control. Initiatives included the 1993 Chemical Weapon Convention (CWC), the indefinite renewal of the NPT, the promulgation of the Comprehensive Nuclear Test Ban Treaty (CTBT), and moves toward a tougher biological weapons convention. On the other hand, Iraq's deceptive behavior in relation to the UN raises a greater and more fundamental problem, which concerns the UN's ability to respond to the proliferation of weapons of mass destruction. The UN cannot expect states to relinquish WMD programs, if the protection that is normally offered in international arms control treaties is negated by rogue nations, such as Iraq, which deliberately flout treaties and UN agencies and proceed to develop and maintain such weapons.

The declining determination within the Security Council to disarm Iraq will make it increasingly more difficult in the future to stop an aggressor nation from developing WMD programs. What makes such a scenario even more worrying is the increasing occurrence of massive human rights abuses, including genocide, perpetrated by authoritarian states and sub-state actors. Possession of chemical and biological materials by such regimes presents a nightmare scenario. Without a solution that will re-establish UN pre-eminence, there appears to be declining hope that the UN and the United States will be able to deal effectively with a threat from weapons of mass destruction.

Notes

1. UN Security Council Resolution 479, September 28, 1980.

2. UN Security Council Resolutions 660, 661, 662, and 665, August 2, 6, 9, and 25, 1990.

3. *The United Nations and the Iraq-Kuwait Conflict: The United Nations Blue Books Series Volume IX* (New York: United Nations Department of Public Information, 1996), 178.

4. UN Security Council Resolution 678, November 29, 1990.

5. *The United Nations and the Iraq-Kuwait*, 180.

6. Avigdor Haselkorn, *The Continuing Storm: Iraq, Poisonous Weapons, and Deterrence* (New Haven, Conn.: Yale University Press, 1999), 11-13.

7. UN Security Council Resolution 687, April 3, 1991.

8. UN Security Council Resolution 688, April 5, 1991.

9. *The United Nations and the Iraq-Kuwait*, 195-96.

10. *The United Nations and the Iraq-Kuwait*, 75-76. Scott Ritter, *Endgame: Solving the Iraq Problem* (New York: Simon & Schuster, 1999), 178.

11. Kathleen C. Bailey, *The UN Inspections in Iraq: Lessons for On-site Verification* (Boulder, Colo.: Westview Press, 1995), 120-21.

12. UN Security Council Resolution 715, October 11, 1991.

13. Statement by the President of the Security Council concerning the sanctions regime imposed against Iraq and humanitarian conditions of the civilian population in Iraq, S/23305, December 20, 1991.

14. *The United Nations and the Iraq-Kuwait*, 59.

15. Statement by the President of the Security Council concerning UNSCOM's special mission to Baghdad, February 21-24, 1992, and Iraq's compliance with relevant Security Council Resolutions, S/23663, February 28, 1992.

16. *The United Nations and the Iraq-Kuwait*, 82-83.

17. *The United Nations and the Iraq-Kuwait*, 129.

18. Bailey, *The UN Inspections in Iraq*, 35.

19. Decision 7 taken by the Governing Council of the United Nations Compensation Commission: Criteria for additional categories of claims, S/AC.26/1991/7/Rev.1, March 17, 1992.

20. *The United Nations and the Iraq-Kuwait*, 129.

21. *The United Nations and the Iraq-Kuwait*, 128.

22. *Third Report of the Executive Chairman of UNSCOM*, S/24108, June

16, 1992.

23. *The United Nations and the Iraq-Kuwait*, 129.

24. *The United Nations and the Iraq-Kuwait*, 129-30.

25. *The United Nations and the Iraq-Kuwait*, 85-86.

26. Statement by the President of the Security Council concerning the murder of a member of the United Nations Guards Contingent in Iraq on July 16, S/24309, July 17, 1992.

27. Sarah Graham-Brown, *Sanctioning Saddam: The Politics of Intervention in Iraq* (London: I.B. Tauris, 1999), 108-9.

28. *The United Nations and the Iraq-Kuwait*, 130.

29. Statement by the President of the Security Council concerning Iraq's compliance with the relevant council resolutions, S/24839, November 24, 1992.

30. *The United Nations and the Iraq-Kuwait,* 132.

31. *The United Nations and the Iraq-Kuwait,* 133.

32. UN Security Council Resolution 806, February 5, 1993.

33. UN Security Council Resolution 833, May 27, 1993.

34. Statement by the President of the Security Council concerning the Iraq-Kuwait Boundary Demarcation Commission, S/26006, June 28, 1993.

35. UN Security Council Resolution 899, March 4, 1994. See also Report of the Secretary-General on the Return of Kuwaiti Property Seized by Iraq S/1994/243, March 2, 1994.

36. *The United Nations and the Iraq-Kuwait,* 134.

37. Anthony H. Cordesman, *Iraq and the War of Sanctions: Conventional Threats and Weapons of Mass Destruction* (Westport, Conn.: Praeger, 1999), 211.

38. *The United Nations and the Iraq-Kuwait,* 135-36.

39. *The United Nations and the Iraq-Kuwait,* 136.

40. *The United Nations and the Iraq-Kuwait,* 136, 138.

41. UN Security Council Resolution 949, October 15, 1994.

42. *The United Nations and the Iraq-Kuwait*, 136.

43. *The United Nations and the Iraq-Kuwait,* 137.

44. Cordesman, *Iraq and the War of Sanctions*, 180.

45. *The United Nations and the Iraq-Kuwait*, 138.

46. Ritter, *Endgame*, 91.

47. *The United Nations and the Iraq-Kuwait*, 138.

48. Boutros Boutros-Ghali, *Unvanquished: A US-U.N. Saga* (New York: Random House, 1999), 258-59.

49. UN Security Council Resolution 986, April 14, 1995.

50. Ritter, *Endgame*, 136-42.

51. Cordesman, *Iraq and the War of Sanctions*, 552.

7

The Mega-Conferences: Rio, Vienna, Cairo, Copenhagen, and Beijing

The United Nations under Boutros Boutros-Ghali featured five "mega-conferences," on the environment, human rights, population, social development, and women. The mega-conferences were attended by thousands of delegates from all parts of the globe and by significant numbers of heads of government and state. Before the main conferences, NGO forums usually convened, which brought together more actors than at the main conference proceedings, including concerned people and organizations from civil society from many nations of the world. Once the main conferences commenced, the UN Secretariat usually permitted NGOs to send representatives and make an impact on the proceedings. The quality and quantity of participation in the conferences indicated that the issues involved had steadily gained in importance over the two decades since the first wave of conferences in the early 1970s. At most of the conferences, heated debates took place over a range of issues. The best-known debates were initiated by the Vatican and by Islamic states at the 1994 Cairo Population Conference over abortion rights and contraception. In addition, debates between North and South occurred at each conference over a range of development and human rights issues. In retrospect, the mega-conferences made a major impact, furthering international regimes pertaining to the environment, human rights, women, and population and demonstrating that the UN was not only concerned with peace and security, but also about a wide array of issues.

The UN Secretariat was charged with the formidable task of organizing and coordinating the mega-conferences and the NGO forums, involving thousands of delegates, organizations, and many complex issues. In addition, the Secretariat was in the process of organizing eight multi-dimensional peace operations to Cambodia, Bosnia, and other hot spots. As a result, from early 1992 until late 1995, the UN was busier than at any time in its history. In January 1992, Boutros-Ghali took office and stepped into a maelstrom of activity, immediately becoming the most tasked secretary-general in the UN's five decades. Besides overseeing conference preparations and peace operations, the new secretary-general played a "hands-on" role in producing *An Agenda for Peace*. In addition, as the June 1992 Rio Conference on the Environment (the "Earth Summit") approached, Boutros-Ghali was called upon to assist with conference preparations, help preside at the conference, and work to persuade President Bush and other leaders to attend.

This chapter provides a description of the mega-conferences, particularly during the secretary-generalship of Boutros Boutros-Ghali. It also analyzes the main conference issues, as well as the proceedings and politics involved, and underlines the point that the UN is multi-dimensional, dealing with more than just peace and security issues. In examining each conference, an historical analysis is provided, then issues, proceedings and politics are considered, and finally the aftermath is discussed. The chapter closes with an assessment of the overall impact of the conferences, especially on the growth of international "regimes" in such areas as human rights and the environment.

The first chapter introduced the movements for the environment, human rights and women's rights and their impact on international public opinion. The movements gave rise to a dramatic expansion of international civil society, post-materialism, and "globalism" (as opposed to globalization). In addition, the chapter covered the demands of the South for socio-economic development and assistance from the North. This demand was made manifest at the UN in the 1990s with *An Agenda for Development*, issued by Boutros-Ghali and the UN Secretariat. Environmental, human rights, and women's movements gave rise to the first wave of global conferences in the 1970s and, in concert with the development lobby, the larger second wave in the 1990s. The 1990 Children's Summit in New York was the first mega-conference in the second wave, pre-dating the arrival of Boutros Boutros-Ghali at the UN, and gave rise to the Convention on Children's Rights.

Rio, 1992

Of all the UN conferences, the "Earth Summit" in Rio de Janeiro proved to be the one with the largest size and broadest scope. The summit represented a quantum leap beyond the first global environment conference in Stockholm twenty years earlier. With the Rio conference, the UN sought to help governments rethink economic development, find ways to halt the destruction of natural resources, and stop the pollution of their countries and the planet. Starting in 1990, hundreds of thousands of people from all walks of life and from all parts of the globe were drawn into the "Rio process" at the local, national, and international levels. The growing activism of people and organizations influenced many government leaders. Subsequently, most leaders decided to go to Rio and participate in the Earth Summit. At Rio, leaders were confronted with a number of difficult decisions and with clashes of interests. They were asked to be visionaries in dealing with forecasts, for instance, about global warming and in authorizing investments of public funds to manage problems that would only manifest themselves when they (the leaders) had departed their positions. At Rio, leaders made commitments toward ensuring an environmentally sound planet for the long-term

The first "Earth Day" was held in April 1970 and marked a watershed in the environmental or "green" movement. Before Earth Day, the emphasis of countries was placed on economic growth and industrialization and not on environmental protection, and the relationship between development and environmental degradation was not on the international agenda. As the environmental movement gathered momentum in the United States and Europe in the 1960s toward the first Earth Day and as scientific evidence of environmental degradation grew, leaders in most industrialized countries became aware of the damage that was being caused by unregulated industrialization. They also became cognizant of the rising tide of public opinion in favor of environmental protection. As a result, leaders began to act in their own countries and on the international level. The combination of the environmental movement and visionary leaders in the North (or West) provided the impetus for the first UN conference on the environment in 1972.

At the 1972 UN Conference on the Human Environment in Stockholm, participants placed on the agenda the need to regulate the industrialization process in order to preserve the environment. After the Stockholm conference, member states set up the United Nations Environment

Program (UNEP) to coordinate environmental protection efforts by various UN agencies. Since that time, UNEP has attempted to act as a global catalyst, stimulating action by governments and NGOs to protect the environment.[1]

In the wake of the Stockholm conference, the green movement continued to grow in influence in the North, and strides were made to combat air, water, and waste pollution. However, UNEP and other international agencies accomplished little in the 1970s, especially in the South and the communist East, in the way of convincing governments to integrate the environment into policy making and socio-economic planning. Despite efforts in Europe and North America, the overall global environment continued to deteriorate. Problems, such as desertification, deforestation, and water pollution grew more serious, while the destruction of natural resources accelerated at an alarming rate. The Brazilian rain forests became the most notable victim of uncontrolled economic expansion.

In 1983, the UN set up the World Commission on Environment and Development and appointed Gro Harlem Brundtland, who had just finished her term as the first woman prime minister of Norway, as its head. The commission put forward the concept of "sustainable development" as an alternative approach to the standard economic growth models.[2] Sustainable development was intended to meet the growth-oriented needs of the short run, especially for the South, without compromising the ability of future generations to meet their own needs.

In the 1980s, environmental degradation grew as an issue, thanks to the green movement and the emergence of ozone depletion and global warming as earth-threatening problems. However, pollution was still seen by many, including some in the industrial North, as a side effect of industrial growth, with only a limited impact. The green movement attempted to convince governments that environmental management was not merely a side effect but was essential for global survival. Progress was made when revelations emerged in the mid-1980s that the ozone hole in the Southern Hemisphere was threatening the health and well being of millions, that chlorofluorocarbons (CFCs) were the major source of ozone depletion. Further progress was made when it was revealed that the source of depletion could be replaced with relatively little cost. At the same time, many leaders in the South came to understand that environmental protection was a matter of national interest and global survival.

In 1987, the Brundtland report was issued by the General Assembly (GA), which considered its ramifications. After the report was released, the GA called for a major conference, which would include a discussion of the report and would attempt to adopt its recommendations. Thus, the way was cleared for the UN Conference on Environment and Development (UNCED), the "Earth Summit." In the years before the Summit, a primary challenge for UN member states was arriving at a compromise between environmental concerns, which came primarily from the North, and the development demands of the South. One task was to persuade the South to accept a definition of development, which incorporated environmental concerns. The other was to persuade the North to assist the South in achieving environmentally sound development. Thus, a primary goal of the summit was to come to a common understanding of the term "development." Summit organizers hoped that such an understanding would lead toward prevention of continued environmental deterioration, support for social and economic investment and growth, and establishment of a foundation for a global partnership between the developing and industrialized countries.

In December 1989, the process of preparing for the Earth Summit began. Maurice Strong, the first UNEP Executive Director and a business leader from Canada, was named the Earth Summit Secretary-General, led in preparations, and eventually presided over the proceedings. Two and a half years of planning, education, and negotiations among states and civil society began and led to the formulation of "Agenda 21," a wide-ranging blueprint for action to achieve sustainable development worldwide. Subsequently, Agenda 21 served as the basis for negotiation and eventual compromise at the Earth Summit.[3]

In June 1992, the Earth Summit convened. First came the NGO forum, which included more than 17,000 participants and a broad range of organizations, from Greenpeace to Brazilian Indian tribes. After the NGO forum, the summit itself began, with 108 heads of state or government attending. After considerable effort, in the weeks before the conference, U.S. President Bush was persuaded to attend. More than ten thousand journalists attended and reported on the conference. The Earth Summit featured a number of major debates. On one side, the North asserted that the South should industrialize in an environmentally sound manner, while the South demanded that the North pay for sustainable development in the South. Some European countries and "green" NGOs asserted that global warming was imminent and required drastic action, while the United States and the United Kingdom remained skeptical. NGOs wanted member states to move quickly on environmental protection, while many states balked, and some even criticized the "alarmism" of the NGOs.

The Bush administration was especially uncooperative. Until just before the Earth Summit, President Bush refused to attend. The administration claimed that the summit organizers were being unnecessarily alarmist in predicting global warming and other environmental crises. Paradoxically, Bush had campaigned for the U.S. presidency in 1988 on a platform that included combating global warming.[4] The Bush administration rejected the two landmark treaties on global warming and bio-diversity. Finally, after considerable pressure from the UN, from within the United States, and from U.S. allies, Bush relented and attended the summit. In contrast, Al Gore, who was selected as a vice presidential candidate right after the summit in June 1992, campaigned strongly in favor of the Earth Summit and the two treaties. Gore was present at the Earth Summit and issued his book on the environment in the same year. Once in office, Vice President Gore urged President Clinton to sign the conventions on global warming and bio-diversity, which he did in 1993.

At the summit, governments adopted three agreements for sustainable development. The first was a revision of Agenda 21. It provided a comprehensive program of action for global efforts in various areas of sustainable development, ranging from subsistence agriculture to "high tech" manufacturing. The second agreement was the Rio Declaration on Environment and Development, which was a series of statements defining the rights and responsibilities of states. The third agreement was the Statement of Forest Principles, which was intended to bring about a commitment toward the sustainable management of forests in Brazil, Indonesia, and other countries.[5] Two conventions were opened for signature at the summit, which provided a boost to ratification efforts by member states. They were the UN Framework Convention on Climate Change, which aimed to slow global warming, and the Convention on Biological Diversity, which was intended to stop the eradication of multitudes of species.[6]

The Agenda 21 that emerged from the Rio Summit contained numerous proposals for action. The various social and economic areas for action areas included combating poverty, changing patterns of production and consumption, and addressing demographic dynamics. Agenda 21 also included proposals for conserving and managing natural resources, preventing deforestation, and promoting sustainable agriculture, as well as protecting the atmosphere, oceans, and bio-diversity. In adopting Agenda 21, governments agreed that the integration of environment and development would lead to the increased fulfillment of basic needs, improved living standards, and better protected and managed ecosystems.

The program of action recommended ways to strengthen the part played by social groups in achieving sustainable development. These groups included women, trade unions, farmers, and children and young people, as well as indigenous peoples, the scientific community, local authorities, business, industry, and NGOs.[7]

By defining the rights and responsibilities of states, the Rio Declaration on Environment and Development complemented Agenda 21. The first of the Rio principles was that people should be the main participants in sustainable development, as well as the principal beneficiaries, and that they were entitled to healthy and productive lives in harmony with nature. The full participation of women was considered essential for achieving sustainable development. A second principle was that scientific uncertainty should not delay measures to prevent global warming and other forms of environmental degradation. A third was that states have a sovereign right to exploit their own resources but not to cause damage to the environment of other states. The 1986 Chernobyl accident and fallout, acid rain, and pollution of international waterways, such as the Rhine River, provided a sense of urgency to fulfill the third principle.[8]

Leaders from the industrialized North agreed that the South had to be assisted in moving toward sustainable development. They admitted responsibility for more than a century of pollution, which had placed great stress on the global environment. The North possessed technologies and financial resources that could assist the South. The leaders of the North accepted that sustainable development could only be achieved if poverty was eradicated and living standards raised in the South.

The Statement of Forest Principles was the first global consensus ever reached on forests. Among its provisions were that the developed countries should lead in efforts to "green the world," through reforestation and forest conservation.[9] The statement recognized that states have a right to develop forests according to their socio-economic needs, in keeping with sustainable development policies. It called for programs that would deter farmers from clearing forests and would lessen emphasis on the timber industry, as well as substitutes for wood products, such as plastic. The statement placed a spotlight on the host country, Brazil, and the incredible devastation that was occurring in the Amazon rain forests and jungles.

A number of other issues were on the agenda at Rio, including calls to help negotiate an international legal agreement on desertification. The UN made a commitment to hold talks on preventing the depletion of fish stocks, which resulted in the Agreement on High Seas Fishing.[10] The UN acted to help devise a program of action for the sustainable development of small, island developing states, which resulted in a conference on the issue. Global warming and rising seas threatened these states' survival.

At Rio, it was agreed that most financing for Agenda 21 would come from within each country. However, new and additional external funds were considered necessary if developing countries were to adopt sustainable development practices. Of the estimated $600 billion required annually by developing countries to implement Agenda 21, $475 billion was to be transferred from economic activities in those countries. A further $125 billion would be needed in new and additional funds from external sources, some $70 billion more than existing levels of official development assistance.[11]

In 1991, the Global Environment Facility (GEF) was set up to assist in the financing of Agenda 21. The World Bank, the UNDP, and UNEP were charged with implementing the GEF. The GEF provided funding for activities aimed at achieving global environmental improvement in the areas of climate change, bio-diversity, pollution of international waters, and the depletion of the ozone layer. At the Earth Summit, the GEF became the funding mechanism for activities under the Convention on Climate Change and the Convention on Biological Diversity.[12]

At the close of the summit, Maurice Strong called it an "historic moment for humanity."[13] Although compromise and negotiation had watered down Agenda 21, Strong still judged it to be the most comprehensive and potentially effective program of action ever approved by the international community. The messages of the summit concerning global climate change, rain forest preservation, sustainable development, and other issues were gaining worldwide currency, thanks to the education process that occurred beforehand and continued afterwards and to the coverage of the summit by thousands of journalists who sent their reports around the world. Many leaders submitted sustainable development plans to legislative bodies for approval. More than one hundred governments established national sustainable development councils or other coordinating bodies, and more than two thousand municipal and town governments formulated their own versions of Agenda 21.[14]

For the next three years, the Earth Summit influenced subsequent UN mega-conferences. The World Conference on Human Rights, held in Vienna in 1993, underscored the right of people to a healthy environment and the "right to development," a controversial right that had previously met with resistance from the United States and other developed states. The UN Conference on Population and Development stressed managing population growth as a means of achieving sustainable development. The

Summit on Social Development addressed the negative impact that poverty had on attaining sustainable development.

The UN Commission on Sustainable Development followed up the achievements of the Earth Summit and perpetuated the "Rio message," making ecological efficiency a guiding principle for governments and businesses throughout the world. The work of the commission was supported by meetings and activities initiated by governments, international organizations, NGOs, and transnational corporations. The UN and governments examined the production of toxic components, such as lead in gasoline, and poisonous waste. Alternative sources of energy were sought to replace the use of fossil fuels in order to reduce the threat of global warming. Public transportation systems were advocated in order to reduce vehicle emissions, congestion in cities, and pollution-related health problems, as well as to combat global warming. The commission echoed rising concern over the growing scarcity of water, especially in the Middle East.

The commission monitored the implementation of Agenda 21 and identified problems, based mainly upon reports submitted annually by governments and by review of issues, sector-by-sector and across sectors. Each year, starting in 1993, the commission examined cross-sectoral issues. First to be reviewed were elements of sustainability, such as trade and environment, patterns of production and consumption, as well as combating poverty and demographic dynamics. Second were financial resources and mechanisms. Third examined were education, science, and transfer of environmentally sound technologies, as well as technical cooperation and the building of capacity. Fourth were activities of the major groups, such as business and labor.[15]

The commission spearheaded the setting of sustainability standards. These enabled countries to gather and report the data needed to measure progress on Agenda 21. A menu of indicators was generated, from which governments could choose those appropriate to their conditions. Governments came to use the indicators in their national plans and strategies and when they came to report. The commission examined the relationship between sustainable development and projected trends in production and consumption, particularly in the developed countries, as well as the impact on trade opportunities for developing countries. It assessed the effectiveness of new policy instruments, voluntary commitments by states, and the revision of UN guidelines for consumer protection. In 1995, the commission adopted a work program on the transfer of environmentally sound technology. The program placed an emphasis on access to and dissemination of information, capacity building for managing technological change, and financial and partnership arrangements. The commission has been working with the World Trade Organization (WTO), the UN Conference on Trade and Development (UNCTAD), and UNEP to ensure that trade, environment, and sustainable development issues are addressed together.[16]

In 1995, the commission established the Intergovernmental Panel on Forests with a broad mandate covering all forest issues and dealing with conservation, sustainable development, and management. The panel submitted its final report, containing conclusions and proposals for action, to the commission's 1997 session. After pointing to an emerging freshwater crisis, the commission asked for a global assessment.

The record on financing sustainable development has been and continues to be disappointing. At Rio, donor countries from the North were requested to more than double their official assistance. However, according to the Organization for Economic Cooperation and Development (OECD), between 1992 and 1995, levels of aid fell from about $60.8 billion to $59.2 billion. However, donors continued to pledge funding for sustainable development, with some $2 billion committed to activities supported by GEF since 1992. GEF's funding activities were broadened in 1994 to include land degradation, particularly desertification and deforestation. In contrast to the stagnation in donor funding, the level of direct private investment to developing countries increased significantly, around $100 billion, far outstripping official capital flows. Accordingly, the UN's focus has shifted toward ensuring that private sector activities are environmentally sustainable.[17]

In June 1997, the General Assembly held a special session to review progress in implementing Agenda 21 in the five years since the Earth Summit. While most participants were satisfied by many of the programs and projects launched by member states, they were not pleased with the levels of funding nor by the way which glaring problems, such as deforestation or global warming were being addressed. In December 1997, a conference on global warming was held in Kyoto, Japan. Although skepticism about global warming had dissipated, the U.S. delegation, led by Vice President Gore, was not willing to reduce the production of carbon dioxide and other "greenhouse gases." Consequently, ceiling levels were agreed. As global temperatures continued to rise, as polar ice caps melted, and as seas began to rise, the international community was unable to take decisive action to deal with this most alarming threat to sustainable development.

Vienna, 1993

A year after the Rio Earth Summit, the Vienna Human Rights Conference convened. The Vienna conference was the first global review of human rights and the UN's work in a quarter of a century. Although no new conventions or treaties were signed at Vienna, the conference achieved much. Member states came to accept that women's rights are human rights and that the walls of a household could not stop measures that halted the abuse of women. The developing countries and even the few remaining communist states took steps toward acceptance of civil and political rights enjoyed in democracies. These steps were taken in spite of strong cultural relativist positions. For instance, the Malaysian Prime Minister, Mahathir Mohamed, asserted that "Asian concepts of human rights" were less concerned about individual freedoms than about community. For their part, the United States, European Union, and other states of the West came to accept social and economic rights as human rights. Finally, the position of high commissioner for human rights was created and was eventually filled, in 1997, by a forceful advocate, the former President of Ireland, Mary Robinson.

The many gross violations of human rights committed during the Second World War and, especially, the Holocaust, led the UN to pay special attention to devising measures that might prevent any repetition. Before the end of World War II, human rights advocates and democratic governments began to work to create a comprehensive body of human rights legislation and institutions. In 1948, the UN adopted the Universal Declaration of Human Rights, as well as the Convention on the Prevention and Punishment of the Crime of Genocide.

The UN created a Human Rights Commission, based in Geneva, which monitored the human rights performance of member states and served as a forum where states, intergovernmental bodies, and human rights organizations voiced their concerns about human rights. It has been the only intergovernmental body that holds public meetings on human rights violations, wherever they occur in the world, thus helping focus world attention. It has reviewed the human rights performance of countries and received complaints about violations. The commission's special rapporteurs and working groups have scrutinized the human rights situation in specific countries, or specific abuses, such as disappearances and torture. Over the years, the commission has become increasingly effective and has been aided by rising flows of information, provided by NGOs. However, the commission is still composed of fifty-three states, many which are from the South and are not fully-fledged democracies. Consequently, a major human rights abuser like China can escape votes of condemnation through the influence that it has over some member states.

In the 1960s, UN member states negotiated human rights conventions that would be legally binding on those states that ratified them. The most significant were the International Convenant on Civil and Political Rights and the International Convenant on Economic and Social Rights, which were completed and signed by a significant proportion of member states and which came into effect in 1976, almost a decade later. It was remarkable that, during the Cold War, such conventions could have been successfully negotiated. The explanation lies in the commitment of most states to the Universal Declaration of Human Rights. Also, a division of labor took place. The West focused on civil and political rights, and the South and East concentrated on social and economic rights. In 1968, the first global conference on human rights took place in Tehran and featured the divide between the "West and the rest." Unfortunately, the conference took place in Iran, a country where gross violations of human rights were occurring under the Shah.

Between 1968 and the end of the Cold War, the international movement for human rights rapidly developed. Amnesty International became the leading human rights NGO and was instrumental in bringing about the 1979 Convention against Torture. Human rights NGOs increasingly monitored the behavior of states and publicized major abuses and abusers. In 1975, the Helsinki Declaration and Final Act of the Conference on Security and Cooperation in Europe contained human rights provisions, which were agreed to by the USSR and other communist states. The door was open to NGO monitoring and human rights movements throughout the communist East. From 1977 to 1981, President Carter made human rights a guiding principle for U.S. foreign policy. The international women's movement pressed for women's rights to be recognized as human rights. The promulgation of the 1979 Convention for the Elimination of all Forms of Discrimination against Women (CEDAW) marked the first victory.

In 1989, the end of the Cold War changed the way the international community viewed human rights issues. While the UN had made great strides in defining a broad range of human rights and creating legislation, many countries and organizations argued that their implementation of conventions had been impeded by Cold War politics and that enforcement needed to be strengthened. With the end of the Cold War, many countries of the East adopted democratic principles. In addition, the "third wave" of democratization was sweeping through the South in the 1980s, and civil and political rights had gained in currency. By 1989, it had become clear that states that had promoted human rights had also demonstrated higher levels of economic growth. Governments of the West began to adopt "political conditionality," making aid contingent upon acceptable human rights performance.

It was timely, in 1989, when the General Assembly called for a world conference on human rights. In the GA, many member states had come to accept that the West had won the Cold War and that they needed to make a shift toward improving their human rights records. Many leaders in the East and South came to accept that a free press and freedom of speech were effective ways to curb corruption and promote more efficient economic development. At the same time, they continued to insist that a "right to development" was just as important as civil and political rights. Conference preparations began in 1991, two years in advance, and the process revealed how complex and divisive many human rights issues remained. As with Rio, preparatory meetings were held, and NGOs mobilized large numbers of people in support of human rights. Women's NGOs were especially active in their efforts to promote women's rights as human rights. In 1992 and 1993, as preparations concluded, Bosnian Muslims were being "ethnically-cleansed" by Serbs in a massive violation of human rights, just a stone's throw from the site of the conference in Vienna. The pictures of concentration camps reminded many delegates that the state of human rights was not satisfactory. Once the conference began, member states condemned the "genocide" in Bosnia.[18]

All told, some 7,000 participants arrived in Vienna in June 1993 to take part in the human rights conference. They included an unprecedented number of government delegates from 171 states, as well as representatives from NGOs, UN treaty bodies, academia, and national institutions. Before the main conference, more than 800 NGOs met at the NGO forum and pushed for much greater acceptance of all forms of human rights by UN member states.[19]

Tibet's Dalai Lama was excluded from the proceedings on the insistence of the Chinese government, four years after the same government had committed the Tien An Men massacre.[20]

As the representatives of member states arrived, many of them, such as the Malaysian Prime Minister, rejected NGO pressure. Consequently, the relationship between NGOs and member states was more difficult than at Rio. Much of the conference (and preparations for it) involved negotiating the Vienna Declaration and Programme of Action to guarantee that they were adopted by consensus. Unanimity was achieved by all UN member states, accepting watered down language, which endorsed "the universality, indivisibility, and interdependence of civil and political, as well as cultural, economic, and social rights."[21]

Member states from the West reached out to the South by endorsing cultural, economic, and social rights and easing pressures to accept civil and political rights. This induced member states of the South to generally accept civil and political rights as the responsibility of governments to maintain. This was something that many of them had not done previously.

At the conclusion of the conference, Secretary-General Boutros Boutros-Ghali spoke to the delegates and told them that by adopting the Vienna Declaration and Programme of Action they had renewed the international community's commitment to the promotion and protection of human rights. He saluted the meeting for having forged "a new vision for global action for human rights into the next century."[22]

UN member states agreed that, according to the United Nations Charter, the promotion and protection of all human rights were legitimate concerns of the international community. Member states made this commitment, in spite of sensitivities regarding respect for national sovereignty.

In terms of specific measures, member states welcomed the convening of emergency sessions of the Commission on Human Rights to respond to acute violations of human rights. The ethnic cleansing that was occurring in Bosnia and genocide that was to happen less than a year later in Rwanda certainly qualified for special sessions. In regard to the "right to development," the Vienna Declaration reaffirmed it as a fundamental human right and called for equitable economic relations and a favorable economic environment at the international level, as well effective development policies at the national level. The declaration also reaffirmed the rights of particularly vulnerable groups and recommended specific measures to better protect them.[23]

A major breakthrough at the conference was the acceptance of women's rights as human rights. Women's rights were emphasized in the declaration, and the conference called for the establishment of a special rapporteur on violence against women.

The Vienna Declaration called for an end to the marginalization and repression of indigenous people around the world and recommended that the General Assembly proclaim 1994-2004 as an International Decade for the World's Indigenous People. The conference pointed out that extreme poverty and social exclusion were a "violation of human dignity" and called for the combating of such poverty and participation by the poorest in community decision making. The concern for extreme poverty and social exclusion was a motive force behind the 1995 Social Summit in Copenhagen.

The Vienna Declaration made concrete recommendations for strengthening and harmonizing UN human rights bodies. In particular, the conference overcame significant opposition and adopted a call for the General Assembly to consider the establishment of a High Commissioner for Human Rights. Later in 1993, the General Assembly voted to create the position. Jose Ayala Lasso, an Ecuadorian diplomat, became the first high commissioner. During his term of office, he proved to be more of an administrator than an advocate for human rights. In 1997, Mary Robinson replaced him and became an effective and forceful proponent.

The high commissioner received a broad mandate and assumed overall responsibility for the promotion and protection of human rights and the coordination of the UN system's human rights programs. For the first few years after Vienna, much of Ayala Lasso's effort was engaged in restructuring and strengthening the part of the UN Secretariat responsible for human rights, along the lines recommended by the Vienna conference, and achieving a higher degree of professionalism and efficiency. Also, the high commissioner worked to enhance the UN's ability to respond to requests for assistance from outside the system.

The high commissioner and the UN Centre for Human Rights, as focal points for UN human rights activities, provided advisory services and technical and financial assistance and worked to improve international cooperation on human rights. They played an active role in removing obstacles to human rights and in attempting to end human rights violations. They engaged in dialogue and coordination with governments and NGOs. One practical measure taken by the high commissioner was the creation of a twenty-four-hour fax hotline that helped in monitoring and reacting quickly to crisis situations.[24]

The high commissioner and centre established a human rights database to promote rights, support the activities of human rights bodies, and develop activities to prevent rights violations. An electronically available database has made human rights monitoring more effective and less expensive.

The Vienna Declaration and Programme of Action called for increases in the funding of human rights activities. However, budget cuts in the UN Secretariat restricted the ability of the high commissioner and the Centre for Human Rights to carry out UN activities from Geneva and New York. In contrast, voluntary funding enabled increased fieldwork capacity.

A central function of the high commissioner and the Centre for Human Rights has been to service the UN Commission on Human Rights, which has continued to provide a forum for member states, NGOs, and intergovernmental organizations to voice their concern on human rights issues. The commission, with its system of special rapporteurs, as well as treaty-based bodies and working groups, has been mandated to investigate human rights abuses around the world. A new development in the area of the prevention of human rights violations has been the creation of a field presence, in the form of field operations and field offices. In 1992, there were no human rights field operations. After Vienna, UN human rights presence was established in the former Yugoslavia, Cambodia, and Central Africa (with Rwanda and Burundi as focal points).[25] New field activities have continued to be mounted and field presence has improved UN monitoring for violations and prevention of conflicts and massive violations.

In 1993, the high commissioner and the Centre for Human Rights provided assistance for the human rights components of the UN peace missions in El Salvador and Cambodia. In 1994, the UN field operation in Rwanda and the high commissioner authorized the European Union to provide specially trained and equipped personnel in the wake of the genocide. Also, the commission agreed to provide financial support to the preventive human rights action of the high commissioner in Burundi and Colombia. The high commissioner worked closely together with the Organization for Security and Cooperation in Europe (OSCE) in the implementation of the Dayton Peace Agreements in Bosnia, a program for Abkhazia (in Georgia) and one for Kosovo.[26]

As demonstrated in chapter 5, of even greater significance was the UN role in the creation of tribunals for the former Yugoslavia in 1993 and for Rwanda in 1994 to try human rights criminals. These tribunals

UNIKOM soldiers from China (third from left) and the USSR (far right) give directions to an American soldier (second from left) in the Southern Sector of the demilitarized zone. *Credit: UN Photo 158412 / J. Isaac*

Cambodians returning from refugee camps in Thailand aboard a UNHCR train as it approaches Phnom Penh. *Credit: UN Photo 159457 / P. S. Sudhakaran*

A UNPROFOR soldier watches over the confrontation line in Sarajevo. *Credit: UN/DPI Photo by Janel Schroeder*

Members of the Security Council vote on a resolution extending the mandate of UNFICYP until 31 December 1994. *Credit: UN Photo 185392 / J. Bu*

Former President Bill Clinton (left) of the United States, President Jean-Bertrand Aristide (center) of Haiti, and Boutros-Ghali are seen waving to the crowds. *Credit: UN/DPI Photo / E. Schneider*

Boutros-Ghali places a flower wreath next to a shed in which lie the remains of Rwandan civilians that had been massacred.
Credit: UN/DPI Photo / C. Dufka

Boutros-Ghali greets Pope John Paul II on his arrival at the United Nations. Credit: UN/DPI Photo / E. Schneider

Brigadier-General Jose Rodriguez, Chief Military Observer, presenting a Unidad Revoluncionaria Nacional Guatemalteca (UNRG) member his certificate of completion of the demobilization process during closing ceremonies at Finca Sacol, Guatemala. *Credit: UN/DPI Photo by John Olsson*

paved the way for the creation of a permanent International Criminal Court, which may serve as another major guardian of human rights.

Cairo, 1994

The Conference on Population and Development proved to be one of the most interesting of the mega-conferences for two reasons. First, the conference endorsed a major change of course for population policies and programs. Instead of governments attempting to achieve demographic targets, the emphasis would be placed on the empowerment of women, the education of girls, and primary health care for mothers and their children. All three measures had been proven to reduce birth rates. Second, the Vatican and Islamic states mounted a fierce counteroffensive against abortion, artificial contraception, and feminism, which caught the attention of the media. This led to clashes with delegations from the United States and Europe and with NGOs. It also paved the way for further confrontation at the Fourth World Conference on Women in September 1995.

Population issues were not a major concern for the UN until the 1960s. In fact, during the 1950s, many countries focused on lowering child mortality, thereby increasing population growth rates. It was only as a result of successive famines in the 1960s, particularly in South Asia, that exponential population growth rates and the specter of resource exhaustion and environmental degradation became a major concern. The realization quickly grew that global population could more than triple to well over ten billion within half a century. At the same time in the West, the revolution in artificial contraception made family-planning easier. The rise of NGOs, such as Planned Parenthood, sought to make family planning instruments available worldwide. The population management movement found allies in the feminist and environmental movements. However, the task of convincing socially conservative governments in the South was daunting. Until the famines of the 1950s and 1960s, few states saw the need for any form of population management program. After the famines and as demographers began to raise warning flags, a struggle began to put the population issue on the international agenda. In 1969, the United Nations Fund for Population Activities (UNFPA) was established to assist developing countries with population programs. After the 1972 Stockholm Conference on the Environment had raised issues of depleted and degraded resources, the door was opened to a population conference.

The World Population Conference was held in 1974. The UN chose Bucharest, Romania, to be the location. Choosing Romania for a population conference was as unfortunate as selecting Iran to host a human rights conference, because the neo-Stalinist Ceaucescu dictatorship favored unlimited population growth and suppressed family planning. At the conference, the international community adopted a World Population Plan of Action, which the UN subsequently reviewed and modified every five years and which provided guidance for population policies for the UN and for member states. The Plan of Action outlined three principles. The first was that population policy was the sovereign right of each nation. The second was that couples and individuals had the right to decide the number and spacing of their children and should have the information, education, and the means to do so. The third was that development and the reduction of poverty were vital for population management. At Bucharest, little mention was made of the central role of women in the family planning process.[27]

In 1984, the International Conference on Population in Mexico City adopted a declaration and recommendations for improving the 1974 Plan of Action. Greater emphasis was placed on the need to improve the status of women and on universal access to family planning information and services. At the beginning of 1993, preparations for the International Conference on Population and Development (ICPD) commenced, with the blessing of the General Assembly. The 1984 revised Plan of Action served as the basis for the negotiations around the Programme of Action in Cairo in 1994. In addition, the Programme built on Agenda 21 from the Earth Summit and Rio Declaration, as well as the agreements reached at the 1990 Children's Summit and the 1993 Vienna Human Rights Conference.

During the process leading up to the conference, consensus was reached on many issues. However, debates continued on other issues, especially abortion. Egypt was chosen as the venue for the conference, because of the perceived need to have a Middle East country to hold one of the mega-conferences and because Egypt was Boutros-Ghali's homeland. However, Egypt in the 1990s was in the midst of a wave of conservatism, with women's rights under particularly severe attack. Also, the widespread practice of female genital mutilation in Egypt attracted criticism. Consequently, Cairo was not the most hospitable location for a conference that would attempt to stress the empowerment of women.[28]

The conference opened in September 1994, with a parallel NGO forum nearby of over fifteen hundred NGOS and four thousand individuals.
From the beginning, the Vatican and the Islamic states launched high-
profile attacks on the right to abortion and artificial contraception, as well
as women's rights. The controversial debates attracted world attention to
the Cairo conference and led to unusually intense media coverage over
the course of the next two weeks.[29]

After several days of debate on the right to abortion, the conference
managed to agree that unsafe abortion should be treated as a public health
issue and that expanded family planning services would reduce the
recourse to abortion. During the second week of the conference, a compromise was reached on abortion and women's rights. Another compromise was reached between the South, which insisted on the link between
development and population management, and the North, which was
concerned with limiting population growth in order to conserve resources
and the environment.[30]

The final text of the conference rejected the promotion of abortion as a
method of family planning. It continued, "in circumstances in which
abortion is not against the law, such abortion should be safe. In all cases
women should have access to quality services for the management of
complications arising from abortion."[31] The text called on countries to
review legislation that punished women who underwent illegal abortions.
Another pivotal compromise affirmed "the right of men and women to be
informed and to have access to safe, effective, affordable, and acceptable
methods of family planning of their choice, as well as other methods of
their choice for the regulation of fertility, which are not against the
law."[32] Finally, the conference called for the empowerment of women
and the guarantee of reproductive rights, including the right to determine
the number of children.

The Programme of Action, adopted by the conference, was intended to
guide population policies until 2014. It endorsed the new strategy, which
focused on the empowerment of women and the needs of families, rather
than on governments and demographic targets. The programme contended that ensuring women's reproductive rights and health was a key to
empowerment and advancement. It sought to enable people to exercise
their reproductive rights, including the right to determine the number and
spacing of children, through the provision of family planning and reproductive health care programs. The programme stressed efforts to increase
access to education, especially for girls, and to improve primary health
care delivery systems. It recognized that efforts to slow population

growth, eliminate gender inequality, and reduce poverty, as well as to achieve economic progress and protect the environment were mutually reinforcing. The programme emphasized that adolescents needed access to reproductive health services and that men needed to be involved in helping to manage those services. It emphasized that NGOs should help to formulate and implement reproductive programs, as well as monitor them. The programme made recommendations on increasing HIV/AIDS prevention, as well as on migration and patterns of consumption that were unsustainable.

The conference agreed to targets for assistance, based on estimates of what was required to enable every country to make reproductive health and family planning accessible to all individuals by 2015. Achieving this goal would require an estimated $17 billion for the year 2000 and more than $21 billion per year by 2015. One-third of the requirements, it was agreed, had to come from the international community. The figures represented more than a threefold increase above 1994 assistance levels.[33]

Thanks to media coverage of the abortion controversy, the Cairo conference raised popular awareness concerning population issues. The pronouncement that was most noted worldwide was that of empowering women and girls and providing them expanded access to education and health services and employment opportunities. Another noteworthy goal was making family planning universally available by 2015. China's "one-family, one child" policy and other coercive approaches to family planning were rejected, and the conference reaffirmed that voluntary family-planning decisions were a basic human right.

The Cairo conference advocated a new and more integrated approach, in which family planning information and services were to be provided as part of a comprehensive approach to reproductive health care. The approach included prenatal, safe delivery, and post-natal care. It involved the prevention of abortion and management of the consequences of unsafe abortions. It included the prevention of sexually transmitted diseases and HIV/AIDS. The new approach involved the prevention of infertility, screening for reproductive tract infections and cervical and breast cancer. It included active discouragement of harmful practices, such as female genital mutilation. The Cairo conference generated a commitment to integrate population concerns into sustainable development programs and policies.

The UNFPA took the lead in following up the Cairo conference and overseeing the implementation of the Programme of Action. After Cairo, UNFPA reoriented its program focus and operational strategies toward reproductive health, including family planning and sexual health. It also linked population and development strategies more closely. After Cairo, UNFPA worked with the donor community to secure resources for population programs and with developing countries to enhance their allocation of resources. Since the conference, a number of donor countries announced their intentions to increase funds for population-related activities. Japan, Germany, and the United Kingdom, as well as the Netherlands, Denmark, and the European Union made significant increases in their support.[34]

After Cairo, countries drew up national plans of action. Workshops were held at the national level to operationalize the "reproductive health approach." In many countries, women played an active role in designing and implementing reproductive health programs. In addition, a number of governments and NGOs worked together to address the reproductive health needs of adolescents and to reduce teen pregnancy.

After Cairo, the General Assembly oversaw the review of the Programme of Action and its implementation. ECOSOC provided coordination within the UN system for population policy formulation, development cooperation and resource mobilization. In March 1995, the Commission on Population and Development was given responsibility for monitoring, reviewing and assessing the implementation of the Programme of Action and considered five sets of country reports annually. Each report focused on the theme of the year. For example, the theme for 1996 was reproductive rights and reproductive health, including population information, education, and communication.[35]

Subsequent mega-conferences, including the World Summit for Social Development and the Fourth World Conference on Women, were influenced by the Cairo conference's emphasis on meeting individual needs and empowering women. All of the mega-conferences, Rio, Vienna, Cairo, Copenhagen, and Beijing, affirmed that desired development and demographic trends were interrelated. The Cairo debates on reproductive rights and health paved the way for women's movements to push for the inclusion of a strong section in the Platform for Action of the Beijing Women's Conference in Beijing, which was in the initial stages of formulation in late 1994.

Copenhagen, 1995

The 1995 World Summit for Social Development (WSSD) brought together over 180 heads of state and government at Copenhagen in

March 1995, and they committed themselves to the eradication of poverty, the expansion of employment, and the promotion of social integration. The most notable product of the summit was a most ambitious commitment to end absolute poverty in ten years (by 2005). The agenda of the Social Summit came partly from the Group of 77 (G-77), stressed the right to economic and social development and aid from the North to combat poverty. Another side of the agenda came from European social welfare states that sought government-led solutions to rising unemployment that did not involve cuts in generous social benefits. The social integration side came from those in the human rights community who were concerned with the rights of disadvantaged and excluded groups. For the countries of the South, the Social Summit was the centerpiece in the series of mega-conferences, from Rio to Beijing. For the South, socio-economic development was a necessary condition for environmental protection and human rights.

The founders of the UN were aware that the Nazis had come to power in Germany because of poor social conditions in the 1920s and 1930s. The Nazis then mobilized Germans in starting the Second World War. Therefore, from 1945 onward, the UN endorsed policies that balanced social and economic development. However, the tendency of developing countries, as well as the World Bank and the International Monetary Fund (IMF), has been to promote economic development first and then pursue social development. The "New International Economic Order," espoused by the G-77 in the 1960s and 1970s, took such an approach. In contrast, advocates for poverty alleviation arose in the 1960s, especially in development NGOs, and focused on "basic needs" strategies for the approximately one billion poor people and on aiding the "least developed countries." In the 1970s, the World Bank turned to a basic needs strategy and began to target the "poorest of the poor." The bank was joined in this strategy by the UNDP, UNFPA, and UN specialized agencies, including ILO, UNICEF, and the World Health Organization (WHO).

The decision to hold the World Summit for Social Development was spurred by concerns among member states and the UN that problems of social development had been neglected and, in some cases, had become unmanageable. It was recognized that widespread poverty, mass unemployment, and social disintegration were causing social conflict and insecurity and causing crises in different parts of the world. A recent example was the 1994 Rwandan genocide, which was partly caused by severe social underdevelopment and high population density. At the international level, despite the end to Cold War rivalries and slowing military expenditures, the gap between North and South was growing and causing resentment in the South.

In preparing for the Copenhagen Summit, the UN was joined from 1993 onward by hundreds of NGOs and interested member states. In March 1995, the heads of state and government of over 180 countries attended the summit. Conspicuous in his absence was U.S. President Clinton, who was busy coping with a sudden rightward and anti-UN swing in the U.S. Congress. In addition, the U.S. position on development and job creation, which focused on the private sector, did not gain widespread acceptance at the summit. Subsequently, the Copenhagen Summit focused on a more "statist" approach to job creation and on calls for greater development assistance.

At the end of the summit, the leaders endorsed the Copenhagen Declaration on Social Development and Programme of Action and its commitments. The leaders generated the largest international consensus ever on social development priorities. The leaders pledged to devise strategies and allocate resources to eliminate poverty. They agreed to quickly ensure that poor people could gain access to productive resources, including credit, land, education and training, as well as technology, knowledge and information, and public services. A concrete example of poverty eradication that featured at the Summit was the Grameen Bank in Bangladesh, which promoted micro-credit and micro-enterprises, particularly among impoverished women.[36]

At the end of the summit, a declaration cited ten commitments and recommendations for action. The eradication of absolute poverty by 2005 was the most notable commitment. High priority was given to the rights and needs of women, children, and vulnerable and disadvantaged groups. Gender equality was endorsed. The goal of full employment was supported. Social integration was urged through the acceptance of cultural, ethnic, and religious diversity and the promotion of human rights for all. Universal and equitable access to quality education and health care was supported. The problems of Africa and the least developed countries were highlighted. Concerns were raised about IMF and World Bank structural adjustment programs, and a call was made to modify programs to include social development goals.[37]

Poverty-eradication strategies included national poverty mapping and assessments, with attention to the gender dimensions of poverty and involved the setting of national goals and targets for poverty elimination. The strategies included an emphasis on social mobilization, participation, and partnerships, with private sector and community-based organization involvement and with the decentralization of decision making.[38]

The Social Summit's Programme of Action recognized the role of the UN system in social development and gave UNDP, with its network of country offices and "resident representatives", the mandate to organize UN system efforts toward capacity-building and program implementation. UNDP changed its focus to poverty eradication and reoriented its programming activities, including gender equity, job creation, sustainable livelihoods, environmental preservation, and governance to revolve around this focus. The Commission for Social Development, under ECOSOC, assumed the primary responsibility for follow-up and review. The commission adapted its mandate and agenda in an effort to ensure an integrated approach to social development. Donor countries, the IMF, World Bank, and the UN system intensified their partnership with developing countries, while respecting their sovereignty and priorities. However, dramatic increases in development assistance were not forthcoming. The UN provided technical and financial assistance to strengthen capacities for carrying out research, for designing and implementing anti-poverty strategies and monitoring the eradication of absolute poverty and reduction of overall poverty. In conclusion, the Social Summit was not as momentous or controversial as the other mega-conferences, but it did provide a needed focus on the poorest of the poor.

Beijing, 1995

The Fourth World Conference on Women was held in Beijing, China, in September 1995. The conference marked the culmination of decades of struggle within the UN to raise the issue of women and their rights to the same level as that of the environment or human rights. Between 1945 and 1975, the UN paid relatively little attention to the issue of women and gender equality. Women's movements were relatively weak until the 1960s and exerted little pressure on their governments, much less the UN. By the late 1960s, the feminist revolution was sweeping the North and was led by increasingly powerful women's movements that pressed for government intervention to fight discrimination and secure equal rights. Women's movements and some governments from the North pressed for women's rights to be taken up by the UN. As a result, the General Assembly approved the first UN women's conference, which was held in Mexico City in 1975.

At the first UN women's conference, a divide developed between delegations from the North, which tended to advocate equal rights, and more conservative delegations from the South. In spite of these differences, the conference declared 1976-85 as the United Nations Decade for the Advancement of Women, which brought resources and focus to the issue of women and their rights. Also, the conference promoted the signing and ratification of CEDAW. Most significantly, the convention recognized violence against women as a human rights problem. In 1980, the second UN conference on women was held in Copenhagen and, in 1985, the third was held in Nairobi. Each conference pushed women's rights a step forward. The 1985 conference approved the "Nairobi Forward-Looking Strategies for the Advancement of Women by the Year 2000." The "Strategies" were most ambitious in promoting women's rights and gender equality.

A number of UN bodies were established under ECOSOC, which focused on women's issues. There were plenary bodies, CEDAW and the Commission on the Status of Women (CSW). The CEDAW and CSW met annually and issued reports to ECOSOC, which assisted in coordinating work within the UN system on the advancement of women. Other bodies included the Division for the Advancement of Women (DAW), the International Research and Training Institute for the Advancement of Women (INSTRAW), and the UN Development Fund for Women (UNIFEM). Based within the UN Secretariat, DAW monitored the advancement of women and provided services for annual meetings of the CSW and the CEDAW. INSTRAW collected and analyzed data on the condition of women. UNIFEM worked under the UNDP umbrella, helping to mount development projects for women.[39]

Four years after Nairobi, the perception grew within UN women's agencies and among women's movements that implementation of the Forward-Looking Strategies was unsatisfactory. Commitments that had been made to ensure greater equality for women, reduce and prevent violence against women, and advance participation in decision making were not being fulfilled. Consequently, a proposal for a fourth women's conference in 1995 was presented to the General Assembly, which gave its approval.

Women's movements and issues greatly influenced the 1990s cycle of mega-conferences. Consequently, the 1990 Children's Summit in New York emphasized the special needs of the girl-child. At Rio, the Earth Summit articulated women's central role in sustainable development. In Vienna, special emphasis was put on the equal rights of women and that women's rights were part and parcel of human rights. At Cairo, the empowerment of women was identified as the key to successful population management. Copenhagen underscored the central role that women have to play in combating poverty. These conferences prepared the way for the Beijing Conference and gave women's movements the opportunity to advance the struggle for equal rights and a larger role in decision making. After Beijing, at the 1996 Habitat Conference in Istanbul, women's rights to control decisions affecting their health, families, and homes were affirmed.

Beijing was chosen as the site for the conference because Asia was due to hold one of the mega-conferences and no other Asian country stepped forward and offered to host it. For most Asian countries, the advancement of women was not a top priority issue and the prospect of 50,000 foreigners, many of them politically active women, descending on them was not enticing. China offered to host the conference as a way of restoring its reputation after the 1989 Tien An Men massacre. Until 1993, China was in the running for the 2000 Olympic Games, and leaders believed that agreeing to host a UN conference might enhance China's chances. The UN chose China with the knowledge that the conference would face political restrictions and logistical difficulties. In preparations for the conference during the first half of 1995, China vetoed the participation of Taiwanese and Tibetan women's groups and made entry into the country difficult for a number of NGOs, which were trying to gain authorization to attend. The Chinese government decided that the NGO forum would not take place in Beijing, but at the town of Huairou, well north of the capital. This was the Chinese way of ensuring that no demonstrations would take place in Beijing, which might embarrass the government. Once underway, the NGO forum and the main conference featured regular interference by the Chinese hosts. Many conference delegates were kept under surveillance, and their bags were searched.

In late August 1995, the NGO forum commenced in Huairou, with more than thirty thousand participants and thousands of NGOs in a vibrant atmosphere, in spite of Chinese efforts. As the main conference began on September 3, more than two thousand NGOs and more than five thousand representatives converged on Beijing. All told, the Beijing conference brought together more than forty thousand women and men. The dynamic of the conference was, in some ways, similar to that of the Cairo conference. The Vatican and Islamic states once again raised the issue of women's reproductive rights and, particularly, abortion rights. However, the preponderance of women shifted the balance of power and prevented the Vatican and Islamic states from paralyzing the Beijing conference, as they had at Cairo a year earlier.[40]

The conference centerpiece was advocacy of the conscious use of a gender perspective to analyze a range of issues, including equality, development, politics, and conflict resolution. The conference delegates called for the "mainstreaming" of a gender perspective in all policies and programs. They reaffirmed that such a perspective was necessary to ensure sustainable development and that the advancement of women would bring progress to each nation's society. The delegates took the concept of mainstreaming back to their home countries, where a number of governments adopted a gender perspective in formulating their budgets, policies, and programs.

The Beijing Declaration and the Platform for Action were adopted by consensus on September 15. The platform identified measures for action for the advancement of women over five years until the 2000 review conference. The platform aimed to enhance the empowerment of women and help improve their health and access to education and promote their reproductive rights. The platform demanded concrete actions in health, education, decision making, and legal reforms by certain dates.

In 1979, CEDAW recognized violence against women as a human rights problem. In 1995, the platform went further in indicating that all member states affirmed that women's rights were human rights and agreed that violence against women was one of the most important of all the human rights problems. The platform asserted the right of women to have control over their sexual and reproductive health, free of coercion, discrimination, and violence. On this issue, the platform went further than the Cairo Programme of Action. Reviewing laws on illegal abortion, the platform asked nations to "consider reviewing laws containing punitive measures against women who have undergone illegal abortion."[41] This represented a major advance on the Cairo conference's language on women and abortion rights.

Women's right to inherit was promoted by the platform. It inveighed against traditional legal structures that discriminated against women and, especially rural women, in inheriting land and property. The platform called for legislation ensuring women's rights to inherit and the enforcement of those rights. In a compromise with more conservative forces, the platform pointed out the importance of the family as the basic unit of society. It recognized the "social significance of maternity, motherhood, and the role of parents in the family and in the upbringing of children." On a more progressive note, the platform stressed that maternity should not impede the full participation of women in society. For the first time, rape was recognized by UN member states as a war crime, punishable under international law. According to the platform, rape was a war crime, and in some cases, such as in Bosnia and Rwanda, an act of genocide. Those guilty of such a crime, according to the platform, "must be punished" whenever possible.[42]

An overarching message of the Beijing conference was that the issues addressed were global and universal. The delegates rejected multiculturalism and cultural relativism and recognized that changes in values, attitudes, practices, and priorities were necessary to overcome inequality and discrimination against women. In a bold statement rejecting cultural relativism, the platform found that traditional interpretations of religious texts often marginalized the role of women in society. Balancing this statement, the platform stated that religion could "contribute to fulfilling women's and men's moral, ethical, and spiritual needs and to realizing their potential in society."[43]

The platform stressed that rapid action and accountability were essential, if its targets were to be met by the 2000 review conference. Governments were called upon to prepare national action plans by the end of 1996, with support from NGOs and civil society. The platform gave the UN system the central role in monitoring of implementation, and it expected the UN to change its policies and programs in order to do so. Most countries did respond quickly by preparing plans of action for review.

When Boutros-Ghali became secretary-general in 1992, he promised to bring about gender equality within the UN Secretariat. However, he fell far short of that promise, and men continued to dominate the most important UN positions. The Beijing conference and the Platform for Action called on the UN system to lead the way in gender equality and in mainstreaming a gender perspective in all its work. After Beijing, the UN Office of Human Resources Management was established as a "focal point" to promote improvement in the status of women inside the UN. Promises of equality continued to be made, with slow fulfillment.

The Beijing conference called for greater interaction between UN bodies under ECOSOC that focus on women's issues. These included CSW, and CEDAW, as well as DAW, INSTRAW, and UNIFEM. In 1997, ECOSOC devoted the segment on the coordination of development activities in the UN system to the mainstreaming of gender perspectives into all plans, policies and programs. Secretary-General Boutros-Ghali assumed responsibility for coordination of UN policy for the implementation of the Platform for Action and established an inter-agency committee on women and gender equality in April 1996. This committee became part of arrangements for the follow-up to the UN mega-conferences of the 1990s. The secretary-general also designated an assistant secretary-general in his office as his special gender advisor to ensure system-wide implementation of the Platform for Action.[44]

DAW played the coordinating role for agencies in the UN system for the advancement of women and the implementation of the Platform for Action, mandates, and recommendations of the other mega-conferences. This role required indicators on the informal sector, political and economic decision making, and unremunerated work, as well as on poverty, the girl-child, and violence against women. It also required the provision of technical assistance in developing countries.[45]

After Beijing, UNIFEM focused on women's economic and political empowerment out in the field, supporting women's organizations to increase leadership opportunities for decision making, and advocacy for women. INSTRAW continued to identify types of research and methodologies to be given priority and strengthen the capacity to carry out research on women, the girl-child, and gender. It helped develop networks of research institutions to do this work. The IMF and World Bank and regional development banks allocated loans and grants to help the platform's implementation in Africa, the least developed countries, and other developing countries. The IMF, the World Trade Organization, the World Bank, and UN system agencies assisted former communist countries to design and implement policies and programs for the advancement of women.

The UN pushed governments to establish "national machineries" for the advancement of women at the highest political level, preferably at the presidential or prime ministerial level. The UN also advocated gender mainstreaming and the integration of gender analysis into policies and programs. In June 2000, the five-year review conference was held at the UN in New York. Progress had been made in establishing national machineries and in mainstreaming gender in many countries. However, much work needed to be done in regard to women's rights and gender equality.

Conclusion

Planning for the mega-conferences was initiated in the late 1980s and early 1990s, when optimism about a much-enlarged role for the United

Nations was on the rise. In assessing the most effective conference, one must assess the types of problems that each of them dealt with and the solutions that were proposed. Clearly, global warming, deforestation, and the extinction of species posed the greatest danger to all of humankind, and the solutions proposed at Rio were visionary and bold. The follow-up at Kyoto and in New York demonstrated that the struggle to fulfill the commitments made at Rio was continuing. Beijing and Vienna were also impressive, especially in extending human rights into the household and recognizing that women's rights were one of the most important forms of human rights. With vigilant NGOs and increasingly committed states, the human rights and gender equality regimes made great progress in the 1990s.

By the time the conferences concluded, the UN was falling deeply into debt and euphoria was fading. The mega-conferences became the target of critics of the UN system, both for their extravagance and for the ideas that they were promoting. The critics scoffed at the idea of cutting carbon dioxide emissions to curb global warming, the right to development, and foreign aid. They raised the alarm about the surrender of sovereignty to the UN. This challenge to the UN is analyzed in the next chapter.

In the face of criticism and a burgeoning debt, the UN did not plan for any new mega-conferences. However, the UN did not retreat from the principles and plans that were agreed upon at previous conferences. The UN, in cooperation with NGOs and progressive states, led the way in action on the environment, human rights, gender equality, and development. Regimes had been established in those areas over several decades, and the UN and its partners extended those regimes and the commitment to globalism. Twenty years from now, the mega-conferences will still be remembered as seminal events.

Notes

1. Werner J. Feld, et al., *International Organizations: A Comparative Approach* (Westport, Conn.: Praeger, 1994), 141-42.

2. Karen A. Mingst and Margaret P. Karns. *The United Nations in the Post-Cold War Era*, 2nd ed. (Boulder: Colo.: Lynne Rienner, 2000), 146-47.

3. Thomas G. Weiss, et.al. *The United Nations and Changing World Politics*, 2nd ed. (Boulder: Colo.: Westview, 1997), 211.

4. Michael Weisskopf, "Climate Treaty Offers View of President's Role in Complex Policy," *Washington Post,* October 31, 1992, A01.

5. Mingst, 151.

6. Tom Kenworthy, "Treaty on Biological Diversity Offers Possibility of Breakthrough," *Washington Post*, June 1, 1992, A15.

7. Mingst, 149, 152.

8. *Basic Facts about the United Nations* (New York: United Nations Department of Public Information, 1997), 195-96.

9. Weiss, 211.

10. *UN Briefing Papers, The World Conferences: Developing Priorities for the 21st Century* (New York: United Nations Department of Public Information, 1997), 23.

11. *World Conferences*, 27.

12. Weiss, 203.

13. *World Conferences*, 21.

14. *World Conferences*, 26.

15. Derek Osborn and Tom Bigg, *Earth Summit II: Outcomes and Analysis* (London: Earthscan, 1998), 95.

16. Osborn, 56.

17. *World Conferences*, 27.

18. David B. Ottaway, "Rights Assembly Demands Action on Bosnia 'Genocide,'" *Washington Post*, June 25, 1993, A31.

19. Felice D. Gaer, "Human Rights Nongovernmental Organizations and the UN," in *NGOs, the UN, and Global Governance*, Thomas G. Weiss and Leon Gordenker, eds. (Boulder, Colo.: Lynne Rienner, 1996), 58-59

20. David B. Ottaway, "Universality of Rights Defended by U.S.: Protest over Dalai Lama Mars Vienna Talks," *Washington Post*, June 15, 1993, A15.

21. Gaer, 59.

22. *World Conferences*, 31.

23. *Basic Facts*, 230. The vulnerable groups included women, children, indigenous people, and refugees, as well as disabled people, detainees, and enforced disappearance victims, and migrant workers and their families.

24. *World Conferences*, 34.

25. *World Conferences*, 35. A human rights presence was established in the former Yugoslavian republics of Bosnia, Croatia, and the Federal Republic of Yugoslavia and in the central African states of Burundi, Rwanda, Zaire (since 1998, the Democratic Republic of the Congo), and Malawi.

26. *Basic Facts*, 227.

27. *World Conferences*, 40.

28. John Lancaster, "Population Conference Tests Egypt's Rulers: Mubarak Seeks to Show Country's Stability, But Islamic Groups Threaten Protests, Attacks," *Washington Post*, September 3, 1994, A13.

29. Boyce Rensberger and John Lancaster, "Vatican Abortion Stance Riles Many at Forum," *Washington Post*, September 8, 1994, A30.

30. John Lancaster, "Vatican Supports Abortion Wording: Population Debate Moves Ahead, But Issue Could Resurface," *Washington Post,* September 10, 1994, A16.

31. *World Conferences*, 40.

32. *World Conferences*, 41.

33. *World Conferences*, 41.

34. *Basic Facts*, 177-78.

35. *World Conferences*, 42.

36. William Drodziak, "Rich, Poor Meet at Summit, and then Go Their Separate Ways," *Washington Post,* March 12, 1995.

37. *Basic Facts*, 158.

38. *World Conferences*, 52.

39. *Basic Facts*, 179-80. The author's worked in DAW, 1994-98, which provided personal insights into the division and its work.

40. Steven Mufson, "Vatican Will Not Contest Language on Abortion," *Washington Post*, September 8, 1995, A28.

41. *World Conferences*, 58.

42. *World Conferences*, 58.

43. *World Conferences,* 58.

44. *Basic Facts*, 180.

45. *World Conferences*, 60.

8

The United States Turns Away from the UN

Starting with the events in Somalia in October 1993, the United Nations under Boutros Boutros-Ghali declined in importance as a peace and security body. At the same time, the United States lost enthusiasm for the "new world order" and for the UN as an instrument for maintaining global peace and security. By 1995, the UN was experiencing a severe financial crisis, which threatened to paralyze the organization. The decline of the UN and mistakes attributed to Boutros Boutros-Ghali led to his removal as secretary-general in the last half of 1996.

The UN's decline and Boutros-Ghali's fall from power can be explained in terms of factors that are both internal and external to the UN. Internal factors, particularly failures in peacemaking and peacekeeping, have been examined in the preceding chapters. A secondary factor was the conduct of the secretary-general, who was too assertive and unapologetic, particularly for U.S. policymakers. In chapters 3 and 4, the failures of the UN in terms of armed peacemaking (or peace enforcement) were described and explained. The most dramatic failures occurred in Somalia in October 1993 and in Rwanda in April-May 1994. They starkly illustrated the inadequacies of the UN, the United States, and other states. The failure in Bosnia was sustained over a three-year period, which slowly eroded the credibility of the UN, the secretary-general, and the Security Council, as well as of European states and the United States. As the most powerful state, the United States was able to shift blame from itself and onto the "unapologetic" secretary-general. Thus, it appeared that the United States was reverting to a long-established pattern of criticizing the UN and using it as a scapegoat.

By far the most important external factor was the reversal of U.S. government attitudes toward the UN. The Clinton administration's abandonment of "assertive multilateralism" in October 1993 and, especially, the November 1994 "Republican revolution" in Congress contributed to a dramatic turnaround. A Republican-dominated Congress brought demands for UN reform, which had been downplayed since the 1980s, to the fore. The withholding of back payments of UN dues by Congress helped to precipitate and aggravate the organization's budget crisis. President Clinton's desire to appear "centrist" in time for the November 1996 elections led to his adoption of Republican positions, including criticism of the secretary-general, and to his announcement that the United States would veto the reelection of Boutros-Ghali to a second term.

The United States and the United Nations

In order to understand how the U.S. position could change so quickly, it is necessary to understand the development of U.S. foreign policy, relations with the UN, and the international system since 1945. The United States led in founding the UN, envisioning it as the organizational embodiment of the 1942-45 "United Nations alliance" against the aggressive Axis powers. In 1945 and after, the United States saw itself as the leader of the UN organization, just as it had been the head of the UN alliance. From 1945 through the mid-1960s, the United States was able to use the UN to its advantage in Korea and in peacemaking and peacekeeping in the Middle East, the Congo, and in other locations in the South. The United States, along with its European partners, was able to promote its agenda in the areas of human rights and development. The United States valued the UN so much that it initially paid 40 percent of the budget and helped the UN out of its first financial crisis during the early 1960s.[1]

In contrast to the enthusiasm of the executive branch and a majority in Congress, a sizable minority in Congress opposed the UN from the 1940s onward. While the executive branch helped to push for a number of UN conventions, the oppositional minority in the Senate blocked the two-thirds majority required to ratify them. For example, the Senate failed to ratify the 1948 Genocide Convention until the late 1980s. In blocking ratification, the minority argued that international law should not supersede U.S. law.

During the 1960s, U.S. support for the UN eroded, as the balance of power in the organization shifted toward the South and the East. In 1964, states from the South formed the Group of 77 and pressed for a New International Order, rejecting U.S. positions on human rights and development. The first secretary-general from the South, U Thant of Burma (Myanmar), questioned U.S. involvement in Vietnam and the Dominican Republic. In the early 1970s, the South joined with the East and inflicted a series of defeats on the United States and its interests, including the admission of the People's Republic of China, the suspension of South Africa from the General Assembly, and the "Zionism is racism" resolution. At the same time, the General Assembly continued to approve expansion of the UN budget, programs and personnel to largely meet the needs of the South. As a result, American leaders increasingly felt that the investment that the United States had made in the UN had been overly generous. The growing U.S. ambivalence toward the UN was shared both by the executive branch and a growing proportion in Congress.

After 1978 Republican gains in congressional elections, the first efforts to withhold funds from the UN began. During the 1979 appropriations debate, an amendment was attached to the FY 1979 Appropriations Bill, stipulating that the UN could not use funds for "technical assistance." The Carter administration contended that the amendment was illegal, violating the U.S. treaty obligation to the UN, and struggled with Congress to restore the funds.[2] In 1981, the conservative Reagan administration came to office with a deep distrust of the UN, resentment against the South and East's dominance of the General Assembly and frustration with the continued deadlock in the Security Council, especially over the Soviet intervention in Afghanistan. With the appointment of Jeanne Kirkpatrick as UN Ambassador and the staffing of the U.S. Mission to the UN with staunch anti-communists from the Heritage Foundation, U.S. relations with the UN plunged to their nadir from 1981 to 1986.[3] During this period, the United States threatened to withhold payment of its full annual assessment because of UN inefficiency and actions by the General Assembly and UN specialized agencies, which conflicted with U.S. interests. At the end of 1981, the Reagan administration supported the reelection of Kurt Waldheim for a third term. Waldheim was preferred to Salim Ahmed Salim of Tanzania, who was rejected as too anti-American. Finally, the

United States accepted Javier Pérez de Cuéllar as a compromise candidate. As a consequence of U.S. hostility toward the UN, Pérez de Cuéllar spent much of his first term dealing with Group of 77 issues, such as the debt crisis, and not with peace and security issues.[4] By 1984, members of the Reagan administration were letting it be known that the UN could leave New York, if it did not appreciate U.S. policy and comply with demands for dramatic reductions in the UN bureaucracy and for the introduction of weighted voting in the General Assembly.[5]

Following the lead of the Reagan administration, Republican Senator Nancy Kassebaum submitted an amendment in 1985 against perceived waste in the UN. The Kassebaum Amendment sought to downsize the UN bureaucracy and programs and introduce a weighted voting system in the General Assembly. If these goals were not achieved, a 20 percent cut in the annual assessment of the United States would occur from 1986 through 1989. The Kassebaum Amendment led to U.S. arrears in payments to the UN, which set the stage for the budget crisis of the mid-1990s. Even after Operation Desert Storm, the United States continued to lead campaigns for control of the UN budget and bureaucracy, albeit in a lower-key fashion.[6] Until 1989, the prevailing U.S. government attitude toward the UN was one of diminishing enthusiasm and increasing hostility. The underlying hostility or skepticism persisted among congressional Republicans, even as the Bush and Clinton administrations became very supportive toward the UN, with the Gulf War and the revived utility of the Security Council.

Bush's New World Order and Clinton's Assertive Multilateralism

In preceding chapters, the increased utility of the UN for the United States, during the three years after the Gulf War, has been described. Bush's perception of renewed U.S. leadership of the UN led to his call for a "new world order." The U.S. attitude toward the UN improved dramatically, as the United States reasserted leadership in the Security Council and even began to regain influence in the General Assembly, especially with the overturning of the anti-Israel "Zionism is racism" resolution. The Bush administration continued to press for reform at the UN, but did not publicize the issue and pledged that the United States would resolve the back dues problem. As the peacekeeping budget mushroomed, from $230 million in 1988 to $3.61 billion in 1994, the Bush and Clinton administrations remained willing to continue to pay over 30 percent of a fast-rising sum.[7]

In 1992, Clinton campaigned against Bush on a platform that included an "assertive multilateralism" plank, calling for even greater uses of the UN in peacemaking and enforcement. Clinton sharply criticized Bush for forsaking his "new world order" by failing to act in Bosnia, as ethnic cleansing escalated in the summer of 1992. When Clinton assumed the presidency in January 1993, assertive multilateralism became the guiding principle for the first nine months of his foreign policy. As demonstrated in chapter 3, the principle was implemented with the conversion of UNITAF into UNOSOM II in March 1993. However, the Clinton team was less assertive in proposing the "lift-and-strike" plan for Bosnia to its European allies. In regard to the back dues problem, the Clinton administration was making strides, in league with the Democrat-controlled Congress, in resolving the issue, while continuing to quietly raise concerns about institutional reform. As Germany and Japan assumed larger shares of the regular and peacekeeping budgets, the United States also began to push for the two states to be rewarded with permanent seats on the Security Council.

Disputes between the United States and Boutros-Ghali

In 1992, at the beginning of his term, Boutros-Ghali was already being characterized as "independent" and "outspoken," as well as "arrogant" and "heavy-handed."[8] His outspokenness was initially accepted by the Bush and Clinton administrations for two reasons. First, given their multilateralist foreign policies, both administrations expected a somewhat more outspoken and energetic secretary-general. President Bush wanted to revive the UN, promised to fully repay U.S. back dues in three years, and looked for an assertive secretary-general to lead the UN. Second, since Boutros-Ghali promised that he would only serve one term, both administrations were not concerned that he acted independently, since he would be replaced after five years. On the other hand, the Bush administration had initially opposed Boutros-Ghali's candidacy for secretary-general and only abstained, when he promised that he would leave after one term. If the Bush administration had known that Boutros-Ghali would break his promise and stand for a second term, the United States probably would have vetoed his candidacy. In late 1991, the United States was concerned about his outspokenness, his age, and doubts that his diplomatic career had given him the political and management experience to be effective in the post. Finally, tradition could not be discounted. Customarily, the United

States and the other permanent members of the UN Security Council preferred a secretary-general who was more a servant, rather than a leader. Boutros-Ghali saw himself as a leader and not as a servant.

When Boutros-Ghali took office, he stated that his priorities were streamlining the bureaucracy and fighting corruption. Initially, he succeeded in cutting a number of high level positions, including several assistant secretaries-general. However, the General Assembly, which was dominated by the G-77 states, blocked other reform proposals. In addition, the UN's growing number of peacekeeping and humanitarian missions and *An Agenda for Peace* soon demanded most of his attention. In response, Congress, as well as the Bush and Clinton administrations, began to raise concerns that the secretary-general had forgotten that UN reform was his top priority. Furthermore, Boutros-Ghali was asserting himself in the Security Council to a greater extent than his predecessors, which surprised U.S. officials. He did not merely make destabilizing situations known to the Security Council; he made recommendations as to what the UN must do about them, frequently telling them what they should and should not do. With *An Agenda for Peace,* Boutros-Ghali proclaimed his intention to make the UN more powerful and assertive than during the Cold War era.

As the Bosnian conflict intensified in the summer of 1992, Boutros-Ghali characterized it as a "rich people's war" and complained that the attention given to Bosnia was not being given to African conflicts. "The Europeans care more about the Bosnian disaster in Europe than about equally great or greater disasters in the non-European worlds."[9] He contradicted the American position that the Bosnian Serbs were to blame. He commented that the conflict was "between Side A and Side B" and that "no party in Bosnia was free of at least some of the blame."[10] Boutros-Ghali criticized the Security Council for a lack of realism in adopting resolutions on Bosnia without providing the means to implement them. And when visiting Bosnia at Christmas 1992, he told the people he met, "You have a situation that is better than ten other places in the world. I can give you a list."[11]

The October 1993 deaths of the eighteen U.S. Army Rangers in Somalia caused U.S. attitudes toward the UN to revert back toward the hostility of the 1980s. While Congress was especially critical, the Clinton administration also blamed the UN and Boutros-Ghali for the Somalia failure. However, both Congress and the administration neglected to admit that the Rangers were under the command of U.S. officers on a mission to capture General Aideed, of which the UN had not been apprised. The administration blamed the UN regardless, since U.S. troops were in the country under UN mandate. The administration also failed to acknowledge that the U.S. Ambassador to the UN, Madeleine Albright, had demanded the arrest of Aideed. The Rangers would not have been on a mission to attack the stronghold of Aideed in the first place had Albright not called for his arrest.

As has been demonstrated, Boutros-Ghali could be blamed for bias against Aideed and other warlords based on past involvement, as Egyptian envoy, in Somalian politics. He could also be blamed for removing Special Representative Sahnoun and pushing for nation building and a peace agreement that excluded the warlords. His support for the deposed dictator, Siad Barre, led to great suspicion among Aideed and other warlords. When Aideed and other warlords attacked the peace process, Boutros-Ghali's prejudice helped push him toward a policy of pursuing and capturing the warlord. However, Madeleine Albright concurred with Boutros-Ghali, which started the UN and the United States down the road toward defeat.

The ongoing Bosnian conflict further soured relations between the Clinton administration and Boutros-Ghali. In 1994, Boutros-Ghali insisted on having a decisive input in the ordering of NATO air strikes against Bosnian Serb artillery positions that might put UN troops on the ground in harm's way. The United States blamed his insistence and subsequent caution for blocking decisive action by NATO warplanes against Bosnian Serb gunners. As French, British, and other UN peacekeepers suffered persistent casualties, claims of helplessness on the part of the UN and Boutros-Ghali escalated. The United States led these claims, and congressional and administration leaders called for a "lift-and-strike" option. This was easy for American policy makers to do, since there were no U.S. troops on the ground. In July 1995, when Bosnian Serbs captured the UN-designated safe haven of Srebenica, Boutros-Ghali drew criticism for proceeding with a trip to Africa. He replied by repeating that he would not be paralyzed by what he referred to as the "rich people's war" in Europe.

During the Bosnian conflict, Boutros-Ghali and several non-permanent members of the Security Council pressed the United States, France, and the United Kingdom to take decisive action. When the three permanent members passed resolutions and then failed to follow up, Boutros-Ghali criticized the Security Council for a lack of credible response. He accused the council of "using phrases and making de-mands that it knows cannot be implemented, in order to please public opinion" and of "using the United Nations as a substitute for making their own hard decisions and allocating adequate resources."[12] After the Bosnian conflict ended in 1995, Boutros-Ghali conceded that it was the outstanding example of UN failure under his tenure as secretary-general. He attributed the UN involvement in the conflict as fatally eroding the "key principles of international behavior: no acquisition of territory by force; no genocide; and guarantees of the integrity and existence of UN member states."[13]

In 1994, Boutros-Ghali also criticized the United States for its conduct during the Rwandan genocide, especially after the United States effectively blocked reinforcements of the UNAMIR forces already there. The lack of intervention prior to the genocide was deemed the UN's failure. However, as Kofi Annan later explained, the UN had little choice but to stay aloof, given the resistance of the United States and other powers to any type of intervention. In May 1994, the United States vetoed the plan to send 5,500 African peacekeepers to Rwanda because it would have to pay 30 percent of the bill. Later, Boutros-Ghali commented that "the genocide in Rwanda is 100 percent American responsibility."[14] He neglected to mention that warnings of genocide had come in January 1994. He also failed to mention that he had recommended the withdrawal of most of the UN blue helmets in April 1994.[15]

The cases of Somalia, Bosnia, and Rwanda were UN failures due to a lack of will and resources. However, the most important factor was the UN's inherent incapacity to enforce peace. Over several decades, the United States helped to ensure that the UN was ill suited to undertake armed peacemaking or peace enforcement missions, failing to provide the UN with a standing military that could train for those sorts of missions. In spite of the UN's lack of capacity, it was the UN and the secretary-general whose credibility and reputation were tarnished, while the United States remained relatively unscathed.

By the middle of his term, Boutros-Ghali had gained a reputation as arrogant, aloof, impatient, imperious, and unapproachable. "His management style is high-handed and sometimes indecisive. . . . It's no secret that other senior diplomats agree that morale at UN headquarters has been affected by (his) sometimes imperial style."[16] When Melissa Wells, Under-Secretary-General for Management and Administration, resigned her post with the UN after only a few months, she sent him a note, which her staff leaked to the press, criticizing his management style. "While many have varying degrees of individual contact with you, I have not once during my tenure here experienced that sense of in-house collegial spirit under your leadership." Furthermore, Wells found Boutros-Ghali's reform efforts inadequate, writing that the Secretariat was "almost totally lacking in effective means to deal with fraud, waste, and abuse by staff members."[17] Thus, Boutros-Ghali had made himself vulnerable to growing criticism over the UN reform issue. In May 1994, the accountant, Joseph Connor, became the Under-Secretary-General for Management. Connor began to push forward the process of reform. Nevertheless, public criticism of the UN and Boutros-Ghali over reform and peace and security issues by Congress and the Clinton administration grew during 1994. Criticism sharpened considerably after the "Republican revolution" of November 1994 and set the stage for the removal of Boutros-Ghali as secretary-general.

The 1994 Republican Revolution

In the campaign for the November 1994 congressional elections, Representative and House Minority Leader Newt Gingrich rallied Republican candidates to sign the "contract with America" and helped lead the Republican Party to victory. Part of the Republican platform was a rejection of assertive multilateralism and the UN and the reassertion of "virile" unilateralism in support of U.S. national interests. Election day ended with a political tsunami, by which the Democrats were swept from power in both the Senate (after eight years) and the House of Representatives (after forty years) and which produced the "Republican revolution." The party that triumphed was not the Republican Party of George Bush and the "new world order." This was the party of Republican unilateralists, including Gingrich and Jesse Helms. Like the Reagan administration, they were opposed to the UN as an obstacle to U.S. sovereignty. One of the more extreme Republican candidates who was elected to the House, Helen Chenoweth of Idaho, even gave credence to members of local "militias" who claimed that "black helicopters" from the UN were over-flying the United States as a prelude to a takeover by international forces.

In January 1995, the Republican Party was installed as the majority in both the Senate and the House of Representatives of the U.S. Congress and assumed leadership of congressional committees. The new Senate Majority Leader, Bob Dole, presented the Peace Powers Act to the Senate, which unilaterally reduced U.S. contributions to peacekeeping operations from 31 percent to 25 percent of the budget.

In the House, the National Security Revitalization Act was passed, which also reduced U.S. contributions to the UN and forbade the United States from sending soldiers to peacekeeping operations, if they were to be commanded by non-U.S. officers in UN blue helmets.

In January 1995, the most significant change for the UN was the ascension of Jesse Helms to become chairman of the Senate Foreign Relations Committee. Helms had been a staunch anti-communist for decades, and he viewed the UN as an ideological adversary. He had even spoken about the possibility of the United States leaving the UN altogether. In 1995, Helms led the charge against the UN, demanding dramatic downsizing, before he would consent to any payment of back dues. Helms quashed ongoing efforts by the Clinton administration to resolve the back dues problem. As a result, the financial crisis at the UN became even more severe. Helms attacked the UN's failures to reform and to be more selective in authorizing peacekeeping missions. Finally, Helms continued to brandish the ultimate weapon, as he and his colleagues periodically threatened to pull the United States out of the UN completely.[18]

Boutros-Ghali earned the wrath of Jesse Helms and other Republican revolutionaries in Congress. They believed that he was slow to reduce the UN bureaucracy and that he was campaigning for the independence of the UN and the secretary-general, a standing, on call military force, and tax collection by the UN. In response to criticism that he was strangling the UN, Helms stated that the UN did not have a revenue problem; it had a spending problem that Boutros-Ghali had failed to end. In 1995 and 1996, the Republicans used Secretary-General Boutros-Ghali as the target for their hostility to the UN. For more than a year, the Republican presidential candidate, Senator Bob Dole derided "Boo-outros Boo-outros" on the campaign trail and attacked the UN's failures in Bosnia and Somalia. Attacking Boutros-Ghali on Bosnia, Dole strongly advocated that the United States unilaterally "lift" the arms embargo against the Bosnian government and "strike" Bosnian Serb positions with U.S. air power.

On the fiftieth anniversary of the signing of the United Nations Charter, June 25, 1995, Boutros-Ghali sought, with little success, to placate the increasingly negative mood in Washington toward the UN by calling for a reduction of U.S. dues to 15 percent. The hostility of Republican leaders was evident, as none attended the fiftieth anniversary ceremonies in San Francisco. In spite of the implacability of

Republicans in Congress, a majority of U.S. public opinion remained supportive of the UN and U.S. participation.[19] On October 24, the UN celebrated the fiftieth anniversary of the ratification of the UN Charter. At the celebration, President Clinton praised Boutros-Ghali for the last time.

In 1995, reports emerged that Warren Christopher would step down as secretary of state and that Madeleine Albright was one of several candidates to replace him.[20] However, Albright could not become secretary of state unless President Clinton could recover from the political disaster caused by the Republican revolution. In an effort to resume U.S. funding of the UN, Madeleine Albright began cultivating Senator Helms, the new Chair of the Foreign Relations Committee. Albright acknowledged his criticisms of the UN and Boutros-Ghali's failure to dramatically reform the Secretariat. Consequently, Helms came to "think very highly of her."[21]

As 1995 progressed, President Clinton's reaction to the Republican revolution included vetoing legislation deemed to be extreme and, in October 1995, confronting the Republicans in a budget battle. In November 1995 and January 1996, the Republican Congress responded by causing government "shutdowns." In reaction, public opinion blamed the Congress and supported Clinton. Suddenly, the chances for Clinton's reelection and Albright becoming secretary of state improved dramatically. In the second half of 1995, President Clinton adopted a strategy of "triangulation" in order to enhance his chances for reelection in November 1996, and the Clinton campaign placed a number of effective ads against Dole, Gingrich, and the Republican revolutionaries. Clinton's centrist strategy entailed the adoption many Republican positions. One such position involved distancing the administration from the UN and Boutros-Ghali. Domestic American politics helped to make Boutros-Ghali and the UN expendable in Clinton's own quest for reelection.

The United States Turns Away from the UN

In January 1995, President Menem of Argentina called for a second Security Council summit, three years after the summit that had led to *An Agenda for Peace,* and Boutros-Ghali submitted an updated version of *An Agenda for Peace.* By 1995, however, robust peacekeeping and peace enforcement had become very controversial subjects for the United States and other permanent members of the Council. So, the

Clinton administration, along with the United Kingdom, France, Russia, and China, rejected the idea. The rejection demonstrated how far the United States had distanced itself, in just fifteen months, away from assertive multilateralism.

In the first half of 1995, the UN and Boutros-Ghali continued to lose credibility over Bosnia. The Christmas 1994 cease-fire, negotiated by former U.S. president, Jimmy Carter, collapsed in January 1995. On May 25, NATO air strikes led the Bosnian Serbs to capture and hold UNPROFOR hostages. In July, Srebenica fell and thousands of Bosnian Muslims were massacred, shattering the UN's credibility as a guarantor of "safe havens" and opening the door to the American "lift and strike" option. From August 30 to September 20, the Croatian army, supplied with American weapons, conducted an offensive, striking at both Krajina and Bosnian Serb forces and communities, driving them into retreat. NATO aircraft struck at Bosnian Serb positions. Bosnian government forces attacked, leading to the conditional surrender of Bosnian Serb forces, which paved the way for the Dayton Peace Accords and the NATO Implementation Force (IFOR).

In Bosnia, a regional organization had proved to be more capable than the UN of mounting an armed peacemaking effort. A similar situation had occurred in West Africa. Nigeria had led the Economic Community of West African States Cease-fire Monitoring Group (ECOMOG) in armed peacemaking actions in Liberia from 1990 onward and in Sierra Leone from 1991 onward. ECOMOG action in Liberia prevented the rebel leader, Charles Taylor, from seizing power and from exacting further retribution and paved the way for protracted peacemaking efforts. ECOMOG intervention in Sierra Leone prevented another rebel leader, Foday Sankoh of the Revolutionary United Front (RUF), from seizing power. The United States noted the qualified successes of ECOMOG and began to look at regional organizations and powers as alternatives to the relatively weak UN in enforcing peace and preventing or stopping another Rwanda or another Bosnia.

At the end of November 1995, the Dayton Accords were signed. While NATO assumed responsibility for enforcing the Dayton Accords in Bosnia, the United States and NATO relegated the UN to a secondary role in the former Yugoslavia. The Clinton administration requested the UN to oversee the transfer of authority in Eastern Slavonia, as the province was in transition from Yugoslavian occupation to Croatian sovereignty. Boutros-Ghali was upset that NATO had wrested responsibility for Bosnia away from the UN, and he proclaimed his reluctance to commit peacekeeping troops to Eastern Slavonia. Albright's spokesperson and aide, James Rubin, criticized Boutros-Ghali's position and the U.S. mission to the UN protested. The secretary-general reacted strongly to Rubin's criticism and denounced the "vulgarity" of Albright's language.[22] In fighting the United States over the relatively minor issue of Eastern Slavonia, Boutros-Ghali further antagonized Albright and the Clinton administration, jeopardizing his chances for a second term.

As a result of the Eastern Slavonian episode, Albright and Rubin concluded that Boutros-Ghali had to be removed as secretary-general.[23] He was obstructing Clinton administration policies on UN reform and the former Yugoslavia and was seen by the Republican-dominated Congress as the personification of everything that was wrong with the UN. There seemed to be little chance that Congress would pay more than one billion dollars in withheld UN dues as long as Boutros-Ghali remained as secretary-general. Albright and Rubin decided that making a deal with the Congress and paying back the UN were more important than keeping Boutros-Ghali as secretary-general. In the first salvo of the anti-Boutros-Ghali campaign, stories began to leak to the press about Albright confronting the secretary-general.[24]

At the same time as the Clinton administration was mobilizing against Boutros-Ghali, Under-Secretary-General Kofi Annan was working with U.S. leaders in the process of managing the transition from UNPROFOR to IFOR in Bosnia. There was speculation in UN circles that the secretary-general had sent Annan to Bosnia in 1995 to remove a potential competitor. In the meantime, Boutros-Ghali began to lobby for a second term. However, Annan's performance in Bosnia impressed U.S. leaders. Therefore, Rubin and Albright began to see Annan as an alternative to Boutros-Ghali. In particular, the election of Annan would satisfy African demands for a second term for an African in the secretary-general's position.

Boutros-Ghali's Bid for Reelection and the U.S. Veto

In January 1996, Boutros-Ghali made a speech at Oxford University, in which he spoke of the importance of the secretary-general's independence. During his speech, he mentioned a number of controversial proposals, including a levy on airfares to support the UN through financial crises. His speech came at a time in which the UN continued to slide toward bankruptcy and in which a 10 percent cut of the nearly

10,000 staff at UN headquarters was under way. In reaction to the speech, more than forty members of Congress, including Senator Helms, registered their protests. The media and political leaders interpreted Boutros-Ghali's speech as an informal declaration of his intention to stand for reelection to a second term. In March 1996, his speech was published in *Foreign Affairs*, laying out a vision for the UN and expounding his views on the future role of the secretary-general.[25] Again, the media interpreted the article as a thinly veiled declaration of intent and reported that Boutros-Ghali was reneging on his commitment, made at the end of 1991, not to stand for a second term.[26]

Reports of Boutros-Ghali's intention to seek a second term came as a surprise to the Clinton administration, which had held out hope that the secretary-general would keep his pledge to step down after one term. In March 1996, Rubin presented to President Clinton and Ambassador Albright his plan to oust Boutros-Ghali and replace with him with Kofi Annan. President Clinton approved the plan. In arguing in favor of the change, Rubin commented that many Secretariat staff members had come to equate Secretary-General Boutros-Ghali's interest with the UN interest, which was unhealthy for the organization.[27] On April 14, Secretary of State Christopher sent a note to Boutros-Ghali, informing him that the United States would veto his candidacy for a second term and, on April 22, Christopher phoned to verbally confirm the veto plan. Boutros-Ghali was upset. In spite of his differences with the United States, he thought that his relations with the Clinton administration were still relatively good. Furthermore, Boutros-Ghali had been lining up support with a large number of countries and was increasingly sure of his reelection chances. He remained confident that Clinton would change his mind after his reelection in November 1996. Therefore, Boutros-Ghali decided to postpone the official announcement of his candidacy until after the U.S. presidential election.[28]

In April and May 1996, Boutros-Ghali had disputes with the Clinton administration over the Middle East and Russia, which added to the increasingly bad feelings between the two former partners. The most important dispute was over Israeli retaliatory bombing in Lebanon, which had killed a large number of civilians. The Clinton administration wanted no Security Council action against Israel, which might threaten the chances of Shimon Peres and the Labor Party in the May 1996 Israeli elections. Other council members and Boutros-Ghali insisted that a resolution condemning Israel had to be passed. In addition, there were disputes over the oil-for-food program with Iraq and Boutros-Ghali's visit to the Commonwealth of Independent States (CIS). The Clinton administration did not believe that the CIS was a legitimate regional organization, like NATO or the European Union, and that a Boutros-Ghali trip would give unwarranted credibility to the CIS.[29]

On May 3, the *Wall Street Journal* leaked the Clinton administration's decision to veto Boutros-Ghali's bid for a second term. The report enabled the Clinton administration to begin to counteract the Dole campaign's efforts to make Boutros-Ghali an election issue. The report also came as a surprise to a large number of states that were leaning toward reelecting Boutros-Ghali. After the leak, a number of newspapers and television commentators in the United States launched attacks on Boutros-Ghali over his reform performance and proposal for UN taxes, as well as on Somalia and Bosnia. Some even held Boutros-Ghali responsible for U.S. dues arrears. Only a few newspapers, such as *The Washington Post*, came to the defense of the secretary-general.[30] However, *The New York Times* editorial board recommended that Boutros-Ghali give way to a more dynamic secretary-general.[31]

On May 13, Christopher met with Boutros-Ghali and personally confirmed the U.S. intention to veto a second term and urged Boutros-Ghali to reconsider his decision to stand. On June 5, Christopher visited Boutros-Ghali again and urged Boutros-Ghali to drop out before the Organization of African Unity Summit in Cameroon and an Arab League meeting in July 1996. On June 6, the United States offered Boutros-Ghali an extra year as secretary-general, if he would agree to leave office in December 1997. Boutros-Ghali refused the U.S. offer and pointed out that most states wanted him to serve a second term. The African states were stressing that they deserved two terms in the secretary-general position. Presidents Mandela and Mubarak were the most prominent African supporters of Boutros-Ghali. Once the offer of a one-year extension was rejected, the Clinton administration proceeded to confirm the leaked report, announcing that it would veto a second term for Boutros-Ghali. In response, Boutros-Ghali announced that he was standing for a second term, thereby dropping plans to wait until after the U.S. elections.

In late June 1996, the United States launched a campaign to convince states to reject a second term for Boutros-Ghali. The United States stressed that if Boutros-Ghali were removed, subsequent UN reform would prompt Congress to authorize payment of UN arrears. At the end of June, the Group of Seven (G-7) meeting in Lyons featured a struggle between the United States and France over Boutros-Ghali.

France and five other G-7 nations did not blame Boutros-Ghali for the UN's problems in Somalia and Bosnia and for the slow pace of UN reforms. In fact, other G-7 members thought that Boutros-Ghali had done relatively well at reforms in the face of Group of 77 opposition in the General Assembly. In July, the United States attempted to persuade the Organization of African Unity (OAU) and offered to support another African to succeed Boutros-Ghali. While some African leaders considered the American proposal, in the end, the OAU unanimously endorsed Boutros-Ghali. Following their African counterparts, Arab leaders met and endorsed him. Subsequently, Russia and China also announced their support for Boutros-Ghali.

While the Clinton administration failed on the diplomatic front, the Clinton reelection campaign continued to benefit from its opposition to Boutros-Ghali. While Bob Dole continued his derisory attacks on Boutros-Ghali, Clinton's opposition to reelection deflected the issue. Furthermore, Albright and Rubin stepped up their attacks on Boutros-Ghali. Ambassador Albright, who had once been the strongest proponent of assertive multilateralism and who had been in accord with Boutros-Ghali, worked vigorously during the last half of 1996 to block his quest for a second term. Her outspoken criticism of Boutros-Ghali's UN reform efforts and his management of the Bosnian and Somalian missions continued to impress President Clinton and Congress, including Senator Helms. Albright had solidified her position as the leading candidate for secretary of state, in February 1996, when she appeared before a packed stadium in Miami and denounced Castro for a lack of *cajones,* over the shooting down of two Cuban-American planes that had deliberately flown into Cuban airspace. Her efforts at unseating Boutros-Ghali were further aiding her campaign to become the first female secretary of state.

In their campaign against Boutros-Ghali, Albright and the U.S. mission to the UN alienated other members of the UN, including states on the Security Council. Some saw Albright's moves as self-promotion in her campaign to become secretary of state. Most member states were not persuaded by American arguments. They did not blame him for the shortcomings of the UN in the way that the United States did. They were generally satisfied at the pace of reform and did not hold Boutros-Ghali accountable for the failures in Bosnia, Rwanda and Somalia. Many were indignant at being told what to do by the biggest non-payer of UN dues. Even the closest U.S. allies, including the British, came to criticize American behavior.

On November 5, President Clinton was reelected for a second term. Boutros-Ghali launched his campaign for reelection and hoped that Clinton would change his mind about the veto. However, Clinton had made a campaign promise, which he felt compelled to fulfill. In addition, Albright's credibility and campaign to become secretary of state were at stake. Consequently, Clinton and Albright proceeded with the plan to veto Boutros-Ghali and replace him with another African candidate. Two weeks after the election, from November 19-20, the Security Council met to consider Boutros-Ghali's bid for a second term. Fourteen states voted in favor of Boutros-Ghali, thereby rejecting the U.S. campaign against him. In the face of unanimous opposition, Albright proceeded to cast the veto. The U.S. veto had done its work, ending Boutros-Ghali's tenure as secretary-general.[32]

For twelve days, until December 1, support for Boutros-Ghali held firm. However, Albright and Rubin continued to attack Boutros-Ghali and urged that the Security Council select another African candidate. On December 1, Ghana began to support its native son, Kofi Annan. At the same time, President Biya of Cameroon, the Chairman of the OAU from 1996-97, issued a letter putting forward other Africans, including Annan, as candidates. On December 5, President Clinton nominated Albright as secretary of state. Her nomination meant that the United States would not reverse its veto against Boutros-Ghali. Albright had been elevated to a more powerful position and was treated with greater deference at the UN. On December, five Africans, including Annan, were nominated for consideration by the Security Council. On December 10, the council cast votes on the African candidates. Kofi Annan tallied ten votes in favor, the highest number of votes of the five candidates. However, France and the three African members of the council voted against Annan, because the United States had vetoed their candidate, Boutros-Ghali, and because Annan was perceived as the U.S. candidate. As the end of the General Assembly session approached, pressure intensified for a decision. Finally, the three African states, including Egypt, decided to drop their opposition to Annan. On December 13, France relented, after the African states had dropped their opposition, and cast its vote for Annan. His candidacy then went to the General Assembly, where on December 17, he was elected as the seventh secretary-general.

On January 1, 1997, Boutros-Ghali left office. Before he departed, Boutros-Ghali issued *An Agenda for Democratization,* which stressed the principle of personal sovereignty as a focal point for democratization. In August 1995, he had presented *An Agenda for Democratization* to the General Assembly staff, but they had rejected it as too controversial.[33] However, in December 1996, Boutros-Ghali had nothing to lose and issued the document. Though little noticed, *An Agenda for Democratization* capped four remarkable years, in which human rights, women's rights, and democracy were promoted more than ever before by the UN, by progressive states and by NGOs. Thus, the three agendas, for peace, development, and democratization, became part of Boutros-Ghali's legacy as he departed for a new life, as the secretary-general of the French-speaking commonwealth, the *Francophonie*.[34]

Kofi Annan Replaces Boutros-Ghali

On December 17, 1996, Kofi Annan, a career UN staff member from Ghana, began the transition process to become Boutros-Ghali's successor. With a background in two high-profile issues on the UN agenda, Annan seemed to be the ideal choice to manage the UN out of its financial and peacekeeping crises. An expert on UN administration and finances, Annan came to the job from the post of Under-Secretary-General for Peacekeeping. He had managed to be an honest broker among the United States and the other major powers involved in Bosnia, even when they disagreed. Also, in his peacekeeping position, he was credited with creating the mechanism that introduced cost efficiency to UN troop deployments.

Soon after he took up his new position, Annan stated that he would make the UN more effective, and would try to rebuild the UN-U.S. relationship. Also, he commented on how his style of operation would differ from Boutros-Ghali's. "I have never believed that you have to be contentious to demonstrate your independence." It soon became obvious that Annan's demeanor and management style were very different from Boutros-Ghali's. "He has an elegance that comes less from dress than from *equipoise*. He barely moves when he speaks, and he never hurries either a gesture or a word."[35] In contrast to Boutros-Ghali, Annan was not an abstract thinker. Instead, his gifts were "kindness, attentiveness, self-possession, clarity, an utter lack of pretense arising from an impulse of protection."[36] He had distinguished himself by his tactfulness throughout his career at the UN. He also became known for his efficiency and his "mysterious powers of persuasion."[37]

On December 17, 1996, Annan addressed the UN. He said that member states and the UN Secretariat should "embark on a time of healing" and that the UN could not function without the political and material support of states. He called for a healing of "wounded morale and ideals within the Secretariat whose dedicated staff deserves our thanks and encouragement." He went on to say, "Applaud us when we prevail; correct us when we fail; but, above all, do not let this indispensable, irreplaceable institution wither, languish, or perish as a result of Member State indifference, inattention, or financial starvation."[38] Annan's comments were obviously directed partly at the United States. Although he started on good terms with the Clinton administration and began to cultivate cordial relations with Congress, Annan also remained critical of the United States and its unilateralist approach to the UN. Annan soon proved to be a more competent secretary-general than Boutros-Ghali and began to restore the UN's credibility, especially in the eyes of U.S. policymakers. Even so, Annan faced a struggle in persuading the United States to pay its dues.

Conclusion

The UN and Boutros-Ghali incurred the blame for the failed missions in Bosnia, Somalia, and Rwanda and for the slow pace of reform. The caustic, public criticisms that Boutros-Ghali heaped on the UN Security Council and the United States eventually turned the Clinton administration against him and led to the U.S. campaign to oust him after one term. In particular, the personal relationship between Boutros-Ghali and Madeleine Albright deteriorated. More important than factors internal to the UN were external factors, the Republican revolution, and President Clinton's quest for reelection.

The dispute between Boutros-Ghali and the United States can be traced to the Cold War and its aftermath. As the only remaining superpower, the United States possessed an innate desire to remake the world in its own self-image and with minimum expense. From 1990 to 1993, this desire was manifested in the new world order, of which the UN was an integral part. However, when using the UN proved to be costly, voices of unilateralism prevailed. Domestically, American voters and their representatives became more conservative. Within the UN, other states continued to support multilateralism, despite its costs, and its proponent, Boutros-Ghali. American unilateralism damaged the consensus that had existed on the Security Council. Russia and China moved away from American positions, and the struggle over Boutros-Ghali helped to distance France from the United States as well. Thus, the seeds of multipolarity had been planted in the Security Council.

Notes

1. A. Leroy Bennett, *International Organizations: Principles and Issues,* 4th ed.(Englewood Cliffs, N.J.: Prentice Hall, 1988), 93-96.
2. Robert W. Gregg, *About Face? The United Nations and the United States* (Boulder, Colo.: Lynne Rienner, 1993), 64-66.
3. Gregg, *About Face?* 68.
4. During the first term of Secretary-General Pérez de Cuéllar (1982-87), the UN failed to become involved in conflict management in the following conflicts: Central America, Lebanon, Southern Africa, the Horn of Africa, Afghanistan, Cambodia-Vietnam-China, Iran-Iraq, and Argentina-United Kingdom.
5. Bennett, *International Organizations,* 96-97.
6. Gregg, *About Face?* 67.
7. Figures collected by the author at briefing at the United Nations, January 1995.
8. Boutros Boutros-Ghali, *Unvanquished: A U.S.-UN Saga* (New York: Random House, 1999), 45.
9. Boutros-Ghali, *Unvanquished,* 44.
10. Boutros-Ghali, *Unvanquished,* 42.
11. Boutros-Ghali, *Unvanquished,* 53.
12. Ian Williams, "Boutros-Ghali Bites Back," *Nation* June 14, 1999, 63.
13. Williams, "Boutros-Ghali," 63.
14. "Remembering Rwanda," *Christian Science Monitor,* May 12, 1998, 12.
15. Michael Dobbs, *Madeleine Albright: A Twentieth-Century Odyssey* (New York: Henry Holt Company, 1999), 357.
16. Peter Grier, "U.S. Feud with UN Runs Deep," *Christian Science Monitor,* November 21, 1996, 1.
17. "Highest Ranking U.S. Official at the UN Resigns," *Africa Report* March/April 1994, 10-11.
18. Jesse Helms, "Boutros Boutros-Ghali Dreams of UN Sovereignty," *Human Events,* March 15, 1996, 14.
19. William Branigin, "UN: 50 Years Fending off WWIII," *Washington Post,* June 25, 1995, A1.
20. Al Kamen, "Resurrection," *Washington Post,* September 6, 1995, A19.
21. Dobbs, *Madeleine Albright,* 366.
22. John M. Goshko, "UN's Normal Decorous Diplomatic Discourse Takes

Beating in Dispute," *Washington Post,* December 16, 1995, A30.

23. Dobbs, *Madeleine Albright,* 364.

24. Dobbs, *Madeleine Albright,* 365.

25. Boutros Boutros-Ghali, "Global Leadership after the Cold War," *Foreign Affairs* 75, 2, March/April 1996, 86-98.

26. Boutros-Ghali, *Unvanquished,* 4.

27. Dobbs, *Madeleine Albright,* 366.

28. Boutros-Ghali, *Unvanquished,* 5; Dobbs, *Madeleine Albright,* 366.

29. Boutros-Ghali, *Unvanquished,* 264, 267.

30. Thomas W. Lippman, "UN Decision Cuts 2 Ways for Clinton: Boutros-Ghali Retains Much Support Abroad," *Washington Post,* June 21, 1996, A25.

31. "Finding a New UN Chief," *New York Times,* June 23, 1996, A30.

32. "The Scapegoat," *Economist,* November 23, 1996, 47.

33. Boutros-Ghali, *Unvanquished,* 320.

34. Boutros-Ghali, *Unvanquished,* 334.

35. James Traub, "Kofi Annan's Next Test," *New York Times Magazine* March 29, 1998, 48.

36. Traub, "Kofi Annan's," 49-50.

37. Traub, "Kofi Annan's," 46-47.

38. Kofi Annan, "From the Secretary-General: Let Us Embark on a Time of Healing," *UN Chronicle* Vol. 33, Issue 3, 1996, 2.

9

Conclusion: The UN Redefined

The United Nations under Boutros Boutros-Ghali proved to be the most eventful and active period in the organization's half-century of existence. More than ten major peace operations and five mega-conferences were mounted in the span of only five years, 1992-97. In this period, the UN was given, for the first time in its history, the freedom to fully demonstrate what it could accomplish, particularly in the realm of peace and security. The UN scored some significant successes. It helped to bring peace and a semblance of democracy to Cambodia, Mozambique, Haiti, South Africa, El Salvador, and Guatemala, and it partially disarmed one of the world's most aggressive states, Saddam Hussein's Iraq. Through the mega-conferences, the UN advanced regimes in the areas of the environment, human rights, and women's rights. At the end of an intense five years, the UN was redefined as an organization that could perform multiple functions in peacekeeping operations and that embraced sustainable development and largely accepted democratic governance and human rights. On the negative side, the UN was redefined by severe budgetary constraints, caused primarily by the United States, and by failure to enforce peace in Bosnia, Somalia, and Rwanda. In this concluding chapter, the events and trends of the Boutros-Ghali years will be recapitulated and an assessment will be made concerning where the UN stood in 1997 and the direction that the UN was heading as the new millennium dawned.

Redefining a Peace and Security Regime

In the area of peace and security, the future role of the post-Cold War
UN was made clearer by the experiences of the 1992-97 period. With
the Security Council finally free to commit the UN to resolve almost
any type of conflict, it became clear what the UN was capable of doing
and what were its limitations. As demonstrated in chapter 1, Boutros-
Ghali's 1992 *An Agenda for Peace* laid out an ambitious blueprint for
the UN and, in this concluding section, the document serves as a
starting point, as the failures and successes of the UN in peace and
security are analyzed.

A question that arises from the UN's experiences during the 1990s
is whether or not a "regime" that guided the behavior of states was
revived in the realm of peace and security, much like the human rights
regime or the environmental regime. From the late 1940s to the mid-
1960s, a modest peace and security regime, centered on the UN,
operated relatively effectively in the moderation of conflicts, as wars in
the Middle East and Kashmir and civil wars in the Congo and Yemen,
were effectively managed. The original peace and security regime was
not based on collective security, as the drafters of the UN Charter had
intended but on peacemaking and the innovation of peacekeeping,
guided by Chapter VI of the Charter. The fundamental features of the
peace and security regime were energetic diplomacy by the secretary-
general and his representatives that often circumvented the Security
Council and peacekeeping by troops from "middle powers," such as
Canada, India, and the Nordic states. The United States was able to use
the peace and security regime to manage conflicts where the stakes
were low enough to preclude direct military intervention but high
enough where interests of the United States and the West were at stake.
The regime declined during the 1960s, as the United States and the
West lost control over UN institutions and as the Group of 77 gained
influence over the General Assembly and the UN Secretariat.

The end of the Cold War, the activation of the Security Council under U.S. leadership, and the opening of conflicts to peacemaking led
toward a revival of the peace and security regime, as confirmed by the
1988 award of the Nobel Peace Prize to the UN blue helmets. From
1992-97, the UN and Boutros-Ghali struggled to define a renewed
regime. While middle powers, such as the Nordic states, advocated
caution in regenerating the regime, Boutros-Ghali and the United States
in 1992-93 were committed to a more expansive and powerful UN.

In 1992-93, the United States was still in a paramount position in the Security Council and was enthusiastic about the UN, the victory over Iraq, and the "new world order" and "assertive multilateralism." Therefore, the United States envisioned a peace and security regime that included collective security and peace enforcement. President Bush implemented the American vision for the UN and the new world order by sending U.S. troops to Somalia. For the United States, Iraq's defeat, disarmament, and containment were the most important manifestations of the more "muscular" peace and security regime, which included collective security. However, after the Gulf War, UN peace operations shifted from interstate to intrastate conflicts, which presented greater challenges for the emerging regime.

From 1992-94, the importance of the United States as the leader of the UN peace and security regime was evident. In Somalia, Haiti, and elsewhere, the United States led the operations and contributed the bulk of the resources, including logistics, for a rapidly expanding set of missions. The reemergence of the peace and security regime in the 1990s demonstrated that cooperation by the UN with the United States remained a necessary condition for effective UN conflict management.

Boutros-Ghali's *An Agenda for Peace* proposed expanding the peace and security regime to include armed peacemaking. With his insistence, the UN attempted to implement his armed peacemaking proposals in Somalia. Subsequently, the October 1993 Mogadishu killings extinguished U.S. enthusiasm for assertive multilateralism, a more vigorous peace and security regime, and Boutros-Ghali as secretary-general. The failure of UNOSOM II exposed Boutros-Ghali's lack of judgment in a major UN operation, spelled the end to his vision of armed peacemaking, and helped cause the U.S. Congress to return to a position of resentment and, for some, hostility against the UN.

The Somalia fiasco minimized the possibility of future UN peace enforcement operations. Furthermore, in failing to stop genocide in Rwanda and Bosnia, the UN demonstrated that it did not have the political will or the capacity to be effective in peace enforcement. Genocide created renewed demand for peace enforcement, which the UN was unable to supply. The inability of the UN to mount peace enforcement operations has remained a central issue in the area of peace and security. Since 1994, the United States and other powers have looked outside the UN to regional powers and organizations for the additional supply of security that might halt further episodes of genocide and other man-made disasters.

On the positive side, UN successes in Cambodia, Mozambique, and elsewhere demonstrated that the UN could prevail in complex, multi-dimensional peacekeeping operations where the danger of resumed hostilities persisted. Cooperation between military peacekeepers and civilian personnel, including police and a significant number of women, became a hallmark of UN peacekeeping. Multi-dimensional peacekeeping represented a significant expansion of the peace and security regime. In the Former Yugoslav Republic of Macedonia (FYROM), the UN demonstrated that preventive deployment could deter conflict from spreading. However, preventive deployment has yet to be employed outside of the FYROM.

For the final three years of Boutros-Ghali's term of office, 1994-97, a struggle developed to define the peace and security regime, which centered on the issues of Bosnia and Iraq. The struggle led to fissures in the cooperative relationship among the Permanent Five members of the Security Council that had developed between 1987 and 1993.

In Bosnia, the Europeans reacted to ethnic cleansing and war by devising a strategy of humanitarian intervention in 1992, which included consolidating safe havens and facilitating the delivery of food and medical supplies. Subsequently, humanitarian relief and safe havens became part of the lexicon of the peace and security regime. In contrast, the United States advocated assertive self-defense by the Bosnian government, aided by NATO, which was embodied in the "lift-and-strike" option. The split between the United States and the Europeans, especially France, condemned the UN to ineffectiveness in Bosnia for three excruciating years and led to contention between the United States and France. In particular, Russia, Serbia's ally, moved away from cooperation with the United States.

Escalating conflict in Bosnia in June and July 1995 led to the inno-vation of "wider peacekeeping" rules of engagement. In response to the seizure of UN peacekeepers as hostages and the Srebenica massacre, the British innovated rules, which enabled UNPROFOR to conduct more robust peacekeeping activities. The British also took the lead in reorganizing UNPROFOR and establishing a rapid reaction force to defend remaining safe havens and prevent UN blue helmets from being taken hostage. Since 1995, the United Kingdom and Australia have sent rapid reaction forces to Sierra Leone and East Timor respectively, and wider peacekeeping has been employed, thereby strengthening the peace and security regime.

If UNAMIR had been armed with a wider peacekeeping mandate in 1993-94, the operation would have been robust enough to defend innocent civilians against genocide in Rwanda. Similarly, a UN rapid reaction force could have intervened and stopped genocide. Thanks to the United Kingdom, wider peacekeeping has become part of the UN peace and security regime. However, a rapid reaction force remains a proposal that will not be realized any time soon.

The United States and other powers rebuffed Boutros-Ghali's call, in the 1995 update to *An Agenda for Peace,* for a UN rapid reaction force, which would create a stronger peace and security regime and provide the UN with the capacity to respond to genocide and other man-made humanitarian disasters. The Netherlands was the only state to support the proposal. The prospect of greater military power in the hands of the UN was unacceptable, particularly in the United States, and especially after the 1994 Republican revolution.

Another struggle to define the peace and security regime centered on Iraq and Chapter VII collective security and enforcement powers. While the United States retreated from assertive multilateralism after Somalia, it still insisted on using the UN to control Iraq. Russia, China and France drew away from U.S. leadership, particularly in regard to collective security and the sanctions regime against Iraq. All three states desired an end to sanctions against Iraq, so that they could resume commercial activities, including arms sales.

In assessing the strength of the peace and security regime, it is useful to ask if Iraq invaded Kuwait in 1996, would the Security Council have authorized a collective security operation as in 1990? The United States and its coalition partners may not receive the same sweeping approval to use sanctions and force. Russia and China might have insisted on restrictions to Security Council resolutions, which, in turn, would have forced the United States and the coalition to bend the resolutions and perhaps act outside of the UN, as during the 1999 Kosovo operation, Allied Force.

In the mid-1990s, regionalism was a trend that came to partly define the peace and security regime. Regional powers and regional organizations played the leading role in peace enforcement, because they possessed the salience and cohesion to act effectively and with sufficient force. In Bosnia (and Kosovo in 1999), NATO took the lead role in enforcing the peace, while ECOMOG did the same in Liberia and Sierra Leone. After the 1994 Rwandan genocide, the United States, the United Kingdom, and France and other powers switched their focus toward building African peacekeeping and peace enforcement capacity on a regional basis. Therefore, regional powers and organizations, with the salience and the capacity to subdue warring parties, have been left with the task of responding to intractable conflicts caused by insurgencies and by collapsed states. There will be no more Somalias for the UN.

The greatest obstacles to the consolidation of the new peace and security regime were the 1993 Somalia fiasco and the 1994 Republican revolution. Subsequently, the United States took a much harder line regarding its own sovereignty in relation to the UN, participation in peace operations, the UN peacekeeping budget, and a UN rapid reaction force. The 1994-97 period demonstrated that U.S. leadership and an expanded peace and security regime could recede as quickly as it had resumed in the late 1980s. However, by 1997, a peace and security regime still existed. It was more modest than envisaged by Boutros-Ghali and *An Agenda for Peace*. However, the regime was more robust and expansive than the regime that was effective during the 1950s and 1960s. For instance, in 1996, the United States still saw the UN as a useful tool in Eastern Slavonia for peacekeeping and would continue to do so in other situations. Thus, it is highly likely that the peace and security regime will persist and could even experience resurgence over time.

Reforming and Redefining the UN

Another central feature of the UN under Boutros-Ghali was reform. With the end of the Cold War and with calls for a "new world order," it appeared that the UN was ripe for reform, not only in regard to peacekeeping and the bureaucracy and budget, but in other areas as well. Most significantly, plans were announced to expand the Security Council and to give Germany and Japan permanent seats on the Security Council in recognition of their contributions to the UN budget and programs. The Economic and Social Council (ECOSOC) was to be made more effective. The UN Secretariat would have greater authority to coordinate activities by the specialized agencies, such as UNHCR and WHO. However, by 1997, there was still little prospect for Security Council reform, due to the difficulty of deciding on permanent members and enlargement, and only marginal changes in ECOSOC and the specialized agencies.

In bringing real reform to the UN system, the 1992-95 mega-conferences accomplished perhaps more than any other initiative. The promotion of regimes in the areas of sustainable development, human rights, and women's rights redefined the UN mission and led to reorganization within the UN system in order to adequately address the problems confronting each of the regimes.

Under Boutros-Ghali, the agenda for organizational and budgetary reform was far-reaching, including reducing administrative costs and using savings for development activities. UN work programs were reorganized into core areas, namely peace and security; development, economic, and social affairs; and humanitarian affairs, with human rights as a crosscutting issue. Other initiatives included creating the position of deputy secretary-general to oversee day-to-day work within the UN and coordinate UN reform efforts, as well as consolidating the work of the UN Secretariat in economic and social affairs into one department. Other reforms included combining programs on human rights into a single office and consolidating programs on fighting crime, drug trafficking, money laundering, and terrorism.

Although the UN under Boutros-Ghali achieved success in reorganization, the results did not significantly cut the UN budget and bureaucracy and, therefore, did not impress U.S. officials and other reform advocates. Since Boutros-Ghali's achievements were not as impressive as those of his successor, Kofi Annan, one must concur with the observation that Boutros-Ghali spent too much effort on conflict management and not enough time on the budget and bureaucracy and other areas of concern to the United States. Also, procedures for reform within the UN were cumbersome, making change difficult, and as an outsider, Boutros-Ghali, as opposed to Annan, did not know how the UN system worked. Boutros-Ghali's inability to bring sweeping reform was one of the factors that ended his hopes for a second term.

When Boutros-Ghali arrived at the UN, reform was viewed as a positive initiative that was achievable. By 1995, reform had become a weapon in the hands of anti-UN forces in the U.S. Congress. President Clinton believed in the obligation to pay UN dues, as well as the necessity of pushing for reform. However, the 1994 Republican revolution shifted power over UN affairs to Congress. In the 1980s, Republicans in Congress had made reform a major issue, and they did so again after the Republican revolution and anti-UN sentiment after Somalia. Similarly, in the 1980s, the precedent had been set of withholding UN dues, a practice that was repeated after 1994. Republicans in Congress held the UN in low esteem as inefficient, with little relevance to U.S. interests and foreign policy, and which squandered taxpayer dollars. For most Republicans, the reforms set out by the UN were not happening fast enough.

The position was coupled with the belief that expenditures in foreign assistance and development programs were exorbitant and that unilateralism was often preferable to multilateralism. Some Republicans were seeking to recapture the UN as an organization under U.S. control, while a minority did not care if the UN survived.

Under the UN Charter, states that failed to make contributions for two years lost their vote in the General Assembly. However, many in Congress did not care if the United States lost its vote. They pointed out that the real diplomatic work in the UN took place in the Security Council where the United States could not lose its vote. Opinions like this infuriated many states, which then became less willing to support the United States on a range of issues. Furthermore, the Clinton administration pointed out that, without a General Assembly vote, the United States would lose the ability to influence the battle to restrain the growth of the UN, which was the major reform initiative.

The Clinton administration had little choice but to engage Senator Helms and the Republicans in negotiations to arrive at a compromise position that would allow UN dues to be repaid. As a result, the debate became a bipartisan effort linking UN reform to paying the U.S. debt, which supposedly would result in a lighter, leaner UN. In addition to sweeping reform, the Congress insisted on decreasing the U.S. regular assessment from 25 to 20 percent and the peacekeeping budget from more than 30 to 25 percent, which the Clinton administration had to take into account in negotiating a compromise.[1]

In spite of pressures to reform and cut the size of the UN and the U.S.-induced financial crisis of the mid to late 1990s, the UN would survive and would go on to accomplish much after Boutros-Ghali left office.

Boutros-Ghali as a UN Secretary-General

The primary measure of a secretary-general's performance is in the area of peace and security, especially peacemaking and the coordination of peacekeeping activities. Boutros-Ghali's vision of UN peacemaking, including coercive diplomacy, coordination of complex missions, and introduction of preventive diplomacy, broadened the definition of effective conflict management by secretaries-general and the UN peace and security regime. Only Dag Hammarskjöld, 1953-61, could claim a similar achievement, with the innovation of traditional peacekeeping in the

Middle East and peace enforcement in the Congo in 1960-61. Therefore, Boutros-Ghali must be given high marks for his vision.

In the area of peacemaking, Boutros-Ghali was relatively rigid as the UN's chief diplomat and consequently less successful, as demonstrated by his failures in Somalia and Bosnia. In contrast, the more assertive, persuasive Hammarskjöld was successful in the Middle East and elsewhere (with U.S. backing), and the more tactful Pérez de Cuéllar was able to negotiate an end to the Iran-Iraq war. U Thant did not have great diplomatic skills, but he was flexible enough to call on the services of U.S. envoys, particularly Ralph Bunche and Ellsworth Bunker, to assist him in the early 1960s in resolving conflicts in eastern Indonesia and elsewhere. The only secretary-general who was less successful diplomatically than Boutros-Ghali was the passive and malleable Kurt Waldheim. For example, in Somalia, Boutros-Ghali would not budge from his position of circumventing the warlords, and he mistakenly sought to use the UN to force a settlement. In Bosnia, he erroneously thought that he could persuade the Bosnian Serbs to compromise, when they still had the upper hand.

Boutros-Ghali erred in not cultivating the United States to a greater extent than he did. While Hammarskjöld proved to be a skillful and inventive secretary-general, he could not have been effective without backing by the United States. In the late 1980s and early 1990s, Pérez de Cuéllar worked with the United States, which helped him to become diplomatically successful. His ineffectiveness in the early 1980s is related to the alienation of the United States from the UN. Boutros-Ghali insisted on autonomy from the United States and other powers. However, he might have found greater success by working with the United States, especially the Republican Congress after 1994.

With the end of the cold war and with unipolarity, the United States used the Security Council to great effect, with the secretary-general in a supporting role rather than a leading role. In the mid-1990s, with fissures growing in the Security Council, Boutros-Ghali may have been more successful if he had moved closer to the United States, rather than maintaining his distance. With the use of the Security Council becoming more difficult, the United States began to circumvent the Security Council. In the 1950s and 1960s, the United States turned to the secretary-general for assistance in conflict management and could have done the same in the 1990s, if Boutros-Ghali had been more cooperative. If secretaries-general, such as Boutros-Ghali, insist on autonomy from the United States, a cooperative partnership may not be possible.

Epilogue: The UN after Boutros-Ghali (1997-2001)

As Boutros-Ghali departed and Kofi Annan rose to the position of secretary-general, in January 1997, the UN was in turmoil, after the former's struggle with the United States. Boutros-Ghali's parting criticisms of the United States were not helpful in regard to the deterioration in the UN-U.S. relationship. The relationship between old allies, the United States and France had suffered. Annan began to repair the damage and took actions to prepare the UN to move into the twenty-first century, particularly through the consolidation of the peace and security regime and the achievement of significant reform. In contrast to his predecessor, Annan sought to avoid being dragged into a confrontation with the United States. Instead, he sought to cultivate the United States and, in particular, Senator Helms and the Republican-dominated Congress.

In regard to the peace and security regime, Annan scored a major peacemaking success and gained the trust of the United States and other powers, with his February 1998 negotiations in Iraq, which saved UNSCOM. Annan used powers of persuasion to convince Saddam Hussein to end his standoff with the UN weapons inspection teams. Without a UN Security Council mandate and only agreed advice by the council, Annan was able to convince Hussein to allow unlimited access to the eight so-called "presidential sites," previously designated as off-limits to inspectors.[2] At the time, the Clinton administration and the UNSCOM head, Richard Butler, were concerned that Annan would capitulate to Iraq and diminish UNSCOM's role. However, the agreement, reached by Annan, included everything the UN and the United States wanted. After the negotiations, Butler, President Clinton and others praised Annan's success.[3] Annan's success did much to restore the credibility of the UN that had been damaged under Boutros-Ghali.

Saddam Hussein complied with the terms of the UNSCOM agreement for less than a year, leading to the bombing of Iraq in Operation Desert Fox in December 1998. UN control over Iraq's weapons of mass destruction and the sanctions regime continued to deteriorate. Subsequently, Annan assisted the Security Council in evaluating how to revamp the sanctions regime and resume arms inspections. In 2001, the administration of President George W. Bush and the government of Prime Minister Tony Blair worked to bridge the gap with France, Russia, and China over Iraq by introducing a proposal for targeted sanctions.

In 1998, the Security Council, in considering the Kosovo crisis, deplored massive human rights abuses by the Serbian government under

Milosevic. However, the council stopped short of granting NATO Chapter VII enforcement powers to stop ethnic cleansing. In March 1999, without Security Council authorization, NATO attacked Serbia, after Milosevic rejected the Rambouillet Accords and continued to order massive ethnic cleansing. In May 1999, the UN Tribunal for the Former Yugoslavia indicted Milosevic for crimes against humanity in Kosovo, and he was handed over by the democratically elected government of Serbia to the UN in 2001. After Milosevic capitulated to NATO in June 1999, the Security Council established a peacekeeping mission, supervised by UN Chief of Mission Bernard Kouchner and with NATO at its core in the Kosovo Enforcement Force (KFOR).

Under Annan, there were no peace and security disasters, like those in Somalia, Bosnia, and Rwanda, though genocide continued to threaten in Burundi. The one surprise that threatened to turn into a disaster was in Sierra Leone in May 2000, when hundreds of UN peacekeepers were taken hostage by the Revolutionary United Front (RUF). However, thanks to quick enforcement action by the United Kingdom, which deployed paratroopers, the blue helmets were freed. On the positive side, the UN became involved in successful peace operations in East Timor, and the Central African Republic. In East Timor, Australia intervened with force to stop Indonesian militias from slaughtering any more of the local population and was followed by a UN peacekeeping force. With the July 1999 Lusaka Peace Accords, the UN was tasked with a major peacekeeping operation (MONUC) in the Democratic Republic of the Congo where fighting had escalated since August 1998. Eighteen months later, after the assassination of President Laurent Kabila in January 2001, the way was cleared for the warring parties to disengage and MONUC to deploy. In the Congo, Sierra Leone, and other conflict situations, Annan played a constructive peacemaking role.

A significant milestone occurred in August 2000, with the release of the Brahimi Report on UN Peace Operations.[4] At the time, the UN was dealing with major missions in East Timor, Sierra Leone, Congo, Bosnia, and Kosovo. The report called for more resources for the Department of Peacekeeping Operations (DPKO), which would enable it to plan, execute, and manage several operations at one time. In comparison to such a vital department as DPKO, the Department of Public Information (DPI) had more personnel and resources. The report also proposed extensive restructuring of DPKO; a new information and strategic analysis unit to service all UN departments concerned with peace and security; an integrated task force at UN Headquarters to plan and support each peacekeeping mission from its inception; and more systematic use of information technology. The report called for on-call units from states to be prepared for more rapid deployment. To what extent the Brahimi Report will be implemented remains to be seen.

Regimes in the areas of peace and security, environment, human rights, and women's rights were sustained after Boutros-Ghali's departure. Important additions to the peace and security regime included the International Criminal Court and the Comprehensive Test Ban Treaty (CTBT). However, the United States rejected both measures. In strengthening the environmental regime, the 1997 Kyoto Protocol and the 2000 Hague Conference on Global Warming (and the reduction of carbon dioxide omissions) were highlights. However, the new Bush administration rejected the Kyoto Protocol in March 2001. Five-year review conferences for the Rio, Vienna, and Beijing conferences were held at the UN between 1997 and 2000, and plans for conferences outside the UN in the coming decade (2001-10) were planned.

Reform remained a major challenge for the UN after Boutros-Ghali and was the principal reason why the Clinton administration selected Kofi Annan. In July 1997, Annan delivered a speech, laying out his much-anticipated reform program, in which he proposed a cut of 1,000 staff and a one-thirds budget reduction. In carrying out the reform process, the deputy secretary-general, Canadian Louise Frechette, assisted him. By March 1998, most of Annan's proposals were implemented, including the appointing of an Under-Secretary for Internal Oversight Services, reducing operating expenses, and cutting high-level posts, as well as eliminating more than 1,000 positions and saving more than $100 million. The eliminated jobs comprised a considerable chunk of the UN workforce, especially considering that the UN workload, including several new peacekeeping and humanitarian missions, increased in the late 1990s. Therefore, the Clinton administration's faith in Annan proved to be justified, as he proved to be a better manager of the UN than Boutros-Ghali and kept his reform promises. After 1998, Annan continued reform efforts, which would continue to improve UN efficiency.

From January 1997 until December 2000, Annan and the Clinton administration worked to induce Congress to release the back dues the United States owed the UN on terms acceptable to the UN General Assembly. In his January 1997 State of the Union Address, President Clinton made the opening remark in the campaign by commenting that, if America was to continue to lead the world, U.S. leaders simply had to find the will to pay America's way.[5]

In February 1997, the Senate Foreign Relations Committee, chaired by Jesse Helms, confirmed Secretary of State Madeleine Albright. Helms and Albright started a working relationship to reach a compromise on the UN dues and reform issues. With his July 1997 reform speech, Annan joined the lobbying process, making several trips to Washington to meet with Congress and the Clinton administration.

In 1997, the first bill authorizing payment of the back dues made its way through the Congress. However, in October 1997, President Clinton vetoed the bills because of an amendment by Representative Christopher Smith, which tied repayment to the United States withholding money from any organization that provided information to foreign governments on abortion.

By March 1998, Annan had completed his promised reforms and had helped to restore the credibility of the UN through his negotiations in Iraq. However, some members of Congress were not satisfied with the reforms and thought that the process was not going far enough. Distrust in the UN and belief that it did nothing for U.S. interests and foreign policy ran deep in some members of Congress. In responding to Congress, Albright and other Clinton officials argued that the UN was valuable to the United States in a number of ways. The largest positive effects were in the area of counterproliferation. The United States was depending on the UN to induce "states of concern," like Iraq and North Korea to roll back their weapons programs. The United States was continuing to depend on the UN to keep peace in places like East Timor, Sierra Leone, and Kosovo where the United States did not want to make a large commitment. Also, U.S. companies were consistently the largest sellers of good and services to the UN, securing more than half of the procurement done by UN Headquarters in New York, amounting to almost $200 million per annum. Annan argued to Congress that U.S. leadership had been compromised by the nonpayment of dues and that nonpayment had provoked America's friends and foes alike.[6]

As a result of Annan's efforts and Albright's lobbying, Senator Helms co-sponsored a 1998 bill to repay some of the outstanding U.S. debt. However, Helms inserted the condition that the U.S. General Accounting Office (GAO) be allowed to go over the UN books, which was totally unacceptable to Annan and the UN.[7] In addition, Helms called for the elimination of 4,500 jobs, far more than the 1,000 or so that Annan cut. After considerable changes, the bill made its way to

President Clinton's desk in October 1998 where he vetoed it because of another anti-abortion amendment by Representative Smith.

By December 2000, the parties finally solved the back dues issue to everyone's general satisfaction. In October 1999, Congress passed a bill to pay back dues, which Clinton signed, even though the bill had mild anti-abortion provisions and other conditions attached. For most of 2000, Ambassador Richard Holbrooke focused on negotiating with the UN and Congress to resolve the dues issue. Finally in December 2000, Holbrooke gained the support of the General Assembly for compromising with U.S. conditions. Ted Turner provided $34 million to enable the United States to reduce its regular assessment to 22 percent from 25 percent and its peacekeeping contribution to 27 percent from 31 percent.

In April 2001, UN members, who were upset at U.S. nonpayment of dues and the Bush administration's veto of the Kyoto Protocol, punished the United States by helping to vote it off the Human Rights Commission for a year. In reaction, Congress voted to withhold part of the back dues repayment until the U.S. position was restored.

The terrorist attacks of September 11, 2001 changed the Bush administration's somewhat distant attitude toward the UN. In order to build an international coalition against terrorism, the administration found the UN to be a very useful institution.

Kofi Annan appeared to have learned from Boutros-Ghali's mistakes and led the UN in a positive direction. In recognition of his efforts, Annan was rewarded with a second term. This was a major achievement, since Africa's two terms in the secretary-general's position were due to expire in December 2001 and Asia's time to have the secretary-general's position was due to run from 2002-12. Part of the recipe for Annan's success was the fact that, in contrast to Boutros-Ghali, he had forged a close relationship with the United States, including the Congress.

The UN bounced back from failures in Bosnia, Somalia, and Rwanda and became a modest, though effective part of the peace and security regime. Boutros-Ghali led the UN through the momentous mid-1990s and established a road map through much trial and error that laid the groundwork for the successes of the Annan era. The UN has adjusted to the end of the Cold War and is working to maintain peace and security and to guarantee sustainable development, as well as human rights and women's rights. The relevance of the UN is now greater than it has ever been.

Notes

1. "Foreign Policy Coup," *Washington Post,* May 24, 1995, A24.

2. James Traub, "Kofi Annan's Next Test," *New York Times Magazine,* March 29, 1998, 46, 49.

3. Traub, "Kofi Annan's," 74.

4. *Report of the Panel on United Nations Peace Operations,* UN Document A/55/305, S/2000/89, August 17, 2000.

5. *The 1997 State of the Union Address of President William J. Clinton, February 4, 1997,* The University of Oklahoma Law Center, <http://www.law.ou.edu/hist/state97.html>.

6. "Clinton Gives Annan 'Credit' for Iraqi Deal: UN Chief Presses U.S. to Pay $1.2 Billion in Dues it Owes," *Washington Post,* March 12, 1998, A23.

7. Traub, "Kofi Annan's," 74.

Appendix A

United Nations Members

1945 Argentina, Australia, Belarus (Byelorussia), Belgium, Bolivia, Brazil, Canada, Chile, China, Colombia, Costa Rica, Cuba, Czechoslovakia,* Denmark, Dominican Republic, Ecuador, Egypt,† El Salvador, Ethiopia, France, Greece, Guatemala, Haiti, Honduras, India, Iran, Iraq, Lebanon, Liberia, Luxembourg, Mexico, Netherlands, New Zealand, Nicaragua, Norway, Panama, Paraguay, Peru, Philippines, Poland, Russian Federation,‡ Saudi Arabia, South Africa, Syrian Arab Republic,† Turkey, Ukraine, United Kingdom of Great Britain and Northern Ireland, United States of America, Uruguay, Venezuela, Socialist Federal Republic of Yugoslavia§

1946 Afghanistan, Iceland, Sweden, Thailand

1947 Pakistan, Yemen"

1948 Myanmar

1949 Israel

1950 Indonesia

1955 Albania, Austria, Bulgaria, Cambodia, Finland, Hungary, Ireland, Italy, Jordan, Lao People's Democratic Republic, Libyan Arab Jamahiriya, Nepal, Portugal, Romania, Spain, Sri Lanka

1956 Japan, Morocco, Sudan, Tunisia

1957 Ghana, Federation of Malaya (Malaysia)#

1958 Guinea

1960 Benin, Burkina Faso, Cameroon, Central African Republic, Chad, Congo, Côte d'Ivoire, Cyprus, Democratic Republic of the Congo, Gabon, Madagascar, Mali, Niger, Nigeria, Senegal, Somalia, Togo

1961 Mauritania, Mongolia, Sierra Leone, Tanganyika (United Republic of Tanzania)**

1962 Algeria, Burundi, Jamaica, Rwanda, Trinidad and Tobago, Uganda

1963 Kenya, Kuwait, Zanzibar (United Republic of Tanzania)**

1964 Malawi, Malta, Zambia

1965 Gambia, Maldives, Singapore#

1966 Barbados, Guyana, Lesotho

1967 Democratic Yemen"

1968 Equatorial Guinea, Mauritius, Swaziland
1970 Fiji
1971 Bahrain, Bhutan, Oman, Qatar, United Arab Emirates
1973 Bahamas, German Democratic Republic and Federal Republic of Germany (Germany)
1974 Bangladesh, Grenada, Guinea-Bissau
1975 Cape Verde, Comoros, Mozambique, Papua New Guinea, Sao Tome and Principe, Suriname
1976 Angola, Samoa, Seychelles
1977 Djibouti, Vietnam
1978 Dominica, Solomon Islands
1979 Saint Lucia
1980 Saint Vincent and the Grenadines, Zimbabwe
1981 Antigua and Barbuda, Belize, Vanuatu
1983 Saint Kitts and Nevis
1984 Brunei Darussalam
1990 Liechtenstein, Namibia
1991 Democratic People's Republic of Korea, Estonia, Federated States of Micronesia, Latvia, Lithuania, Marshall Islands, Republic of Korea
1992 Armenia, Azerbaijan, Bosnia and Herzegovina,§ Croatia,§ Georgia, Kazakhstan, Kyrgyzstan, Republic of Moldova, San Marino, Slovenia,§ Tajikistan, Turkmenistan, Uzbekistan
1993 Andorra, Czech Republic,* Eritrea, Monaco, Slovak Republic,* The former Yugoslav Republic of Macedonia§
1994 Palau
1999 Kiribati, Nauru, Tonga
2000 Tuvalu, Federal Republic of Yugoslavia§

* Czechoslovakia dissolved (1992) to create two independent member states: Czech Republic and Slovak Republic.
† Egypt and Syria were original members under the union, United Arab Republic. Syria assumed its independent status in 1961. In 1971 the United Arab Republic changed its name to the Arab Republic of Egypt.
‡ Union of Soviet Socialist Republics dissolved to into eleven member countries,most of which became UN member states.
§ The Socialist Federal Republic of Yugoslavia dissolved to create independent member states, Bosnia and Herzegovina, Croatia, Slovenia, former Yugoslav Republic of Macedonia, and Federal Republic of Yugoslavia.
* Yemen and Democratic Yemen merged in 1990 and represent a unified state in the UN under the name "Yemen."
# Formerly part of the Federation of Malaya, Singapore became an independent state as well as a member of the UN.
** Tanganyika and Zanzibar united to create the United Republic of Tanganyika and Zanzibar and became UN member under the new name (1964); now United Republic of Tanzania.

Appendix B

Excerpt from the Charter of the United Nations

Chapter XV

Article 97

The Secretariat shall comprise a Secretary-General and such staff as the Organization may require. The Secretary-General shall be appointed by the General Assembly upon the recommendation of the Security Council. He shall be the chief administrative officer of the Organization.

Article 98

The Secretary-General shall act in that capacity in all meetings of the General Assembly, of the Security Council, of the Economic and Social Council, and of the Trusteeship Council, and shall perform such other functions as are entrusted to him by these organs. The Secretary-General shall make an annual report to the General Assembly on the work of the Organization.

Article 99

The Secretary-General may bring to the attention of the Security Council any matter which in his opinion may threaten the maintenance of international peace and security.

Article 100

1.   In the performance of their duties the Secretary-General and the staff shall not seek or receive instructions from any government or from any other authority external to the Organization. They shall refrain from any action which might reflect on their position as international officials responsible only to the Organization.

2.   Each member of the United Nations undertakes to respect the exclusively international character of the responsibilities of the Secretary-General and the staff and not to seek to influence them in the discharge of their responsibilities.

Article 101

1.   The staff shall be appointed by the Secretary-General under regulations established by the General Assembly.

2.   Appropriate staffs shall be permanently assigned to the Economic and Social council, the Trusteeship Council, and, as required, to other organs of the United Nations. These staffs shall form a part of the Secretariat.

3.   The paramount consideration in the employment of the staff and in the determination of the conditions of service shall be the necessity of securing the highest standards of efficiency, competence, and integrity. Due regard shall be paid to the importance of recruiting the staff on as wide a geographical basis as possible.

From the *Charter of the United Nations and Statute of the International Court of Justice*, Department of Public Information, United Nations, 2000.

Chronology

1991

January 16 U.S. President George Bush, in announcing the start of hostilities with Iraq, proclaims "a new world order . . . in which a credible United Nations can use its peacekeeping role to fulfill the promise and the vision of the UN's founders."

January 17 Operation Desert Storm is launched against Iraq in accordance with United Nations Security Council Resolution 678, authorizing "all means necessary" to force Iraqi compliance.

March 2 Security Council Resolution 686 (1991) orders cessation of combat, providing that Iraq complies with Security Council resolutions.

April 3 Security Council Resolution 687 ends the Gulf War. The Security Council proceeds to establish UNIKOM (on the Iraq-Kuwait frontier) and UNSCOM (arms control).

May 20 ONUSAL created to implement El Salvador peace agreement.

May 31 Bicesse Accords for Angola signed; leads to UNAVEM II.

December 3 Boutros-Ghali elected UN Secretary-General.

1992

January 1 Boutros-Ghali starts five-year term as secretary-general.

January 8 Security Council endorses immediate dispatch to Yugoslavia of a group of fifty military liaison officers to help maintain the cease-fire brokered by Cyrus Vance between Yugoslavia and Croatia.

January 14 ONUSAL mandate is extended until October 31, 1992, adding military and police components to the human rights mission.

January 16 Government of El Salvador and the *Frente Farabundo Marti para la Liberacion Nacional* (FMLN) sign a peace treaty in Mexico City, ending a twelve-year civil war after twenty-one months of UN-sponsored negotiations.

January 23 Security Council imposes an arms embargo on Somalia in response to civil war and famine.

January 27-30 UNSCOM mission is sent to Iraq to oversee implementation of Security Council Resolutions 707 (1991) and 715 (1991) regarding Iraq's disclosure of information on its biological and chemical weapons programs and ballistic missile program.

January 31 Heads of State or Government Security Council summit meeting requests the secretary-general to prepare a report that will become *An Agenda for Peace*. They agree that Iraq must uphold Security Council resolutions and improve the condition of its citizens.

February 4 UN High Commissioner for Refugees declares that Somali refugees are streaming into Kenya at a rate of 700 per day.

February 21 Security Council establishes UNPROFOR (UN Protection Force) to create conditions for peace and security required for negotiation of an overall settlement of the Yugoslav crisis.

February 28 Security Council authorizes the establishment of UNTAC in Cambodia, a $1.9 billion peacekeeping mission, involving more than 22,000 personnel, to oversee elections and the transition to a new government for the country.

March 2 Twelve new states join the UN, in the wake of the break-up of the Soviet Union and Yugoslavia. The total number of states is 179.

March 3 Warring factions in Somalia agree to a cease-fire following UN negotiations and a Security Council arms embargo on Somalia, which leads to the establishment of UNOSOM I. However, the cease-fire does not hold.

March 3 Independence of Bosnia-Herzegovina declared, after a referendum in which 99 percent of the voters choose full independence and Bosnian Serbs boycott. Shelling of Sarajevo and "ethnic cleansing" by Serbs follows.

March 10 Boutros-Ghali appeals for voluntary contributions to finance the long running UNFICYP peacekeeping mission in Cyprus, citing a $196 million deficit.

March 18 Boutros-Ghali welcomes the "positive results" of the March 17 "whites only" referendum in South Africa on ending apartheid.

March 19 Boutros-Ghali calls for an end to the "human tragedy" caused by Afghanistan's ongoing civil war.

March 24 UNAVEM II mandate enlarged to include observation and verification of Angolan elections.

April 10 UNSCOM chairman discloses to the Security Council that Iraq has threatened UNSCOM aircraft and personnel.

April 15 Arms and air embargo is imposed against Libya for suspected role in December 1988 terrorist bombing of Pan Am Flight 103 over Lockerbie, Scotland.

April 24 Security Council establishes UNOSOM I to help end hostilities and maintain a cease-fire in Somalia.

May 30 Security Council imposes an arms embargo against Yugoslavia, Croatia, and Bosnia-Herzegovina, among others, to force an end to the conflict in Bosnia-Herzegovina.

June 3-14 Earth Summit (UN Conference on the Environment and Development) in Rio de Janeiro. Agenda 21 adopted to reshape activities toward the environment and create a global partnership for sustainable growth. The United States is pressured to sign conventions on global warming and biodiversity.

June 8 Mandate for UNPROFOR is enlarged and further deployments are authorized to help reopen the Sarajevo airport for humanitarian deliveries.

July 6-29 In its first of many confrontations with the Iraqi government, an UNSCOM team is denied access to the Ministry of Agriculture building.

July 22 UNSCOM team withdraws from outside Iraq's Ministry of Agriculture building following an attack against a member of the team.

July 28-29 After negotiations and Security Council pressure, the UNSCOM team is granted access to the Ministry of Agriculture building. Suspected arms evidence has been moved.

August 12 According to custom, UNFICYP (Cyprus) is extended for six months, in spite of mounting debt.

August 17 Security Council authorizes Boutros-Ghali to deploy UN observers in South Africa (UNOMSA) to help end the cycle of violence and to monitor the human rights situation.

August 28 Security Council authorizes additional deployment for UNOSOM I, bringing the total to 4,219. However, only 500 peacekeepers are on the ground in Mogadishu, Somalia.

September 15 Opening of the forty-seventh session of the General Assembly, introducing Boutros-Ghali's *An Agenda for Peace*.

September 19 Yugoslavia barred from participating in the work of the General Assembly because of aggression against Croatia and Bosnia-Herzegovina.

September 29-30 Angola's first multi-party and parliamentary elections, as well as presidential elections, held under UNAVEM II supervision. Voter turnout is 91 percent. MPLA wins a parliamentary majority, and a run-off for president is declared necessary between President dos Santos and Jonas Savimbi of UNITA.

October 2 Security Council assumes control of Iraqi assets frozen outside the country to compensate victims of Iraqi invasion of Kuwait and to defray costs of UN activities related to Iraq.

October 4 In Rome, a General Peace Agreement for Mozambique is signed between the government and RENAMO. The UN is invited to monitor the agreement, leading to ONUMOZ.

October 17 UN declares Angolan elections "free and fair." UNITA leader, Jonas Savimbi, rejects the results, and the civil war resumes.

November 29 As the famine worsens in Somalia, the Security Council and secretary-general agree to a U.S. proposal to send a large force to ensure humanitarian deliveries.

December 10 After Security Council authorization, UNITAF ("Operation Restore Hope"), a U.S.-led operation, arrives in Somalia to ensure the delivery of humanitarian assistance.

December 16 Security Council resolution authorizes ONUMOZ in Mozambique to monitor the withdrawal of foreign forces, administer elections, and deliver humanitarian assistance.

December 31 Boutros-Ghali visits Sarajevo, meets with leaders of Bosnia-Herzegovina and the Bosnian Serbs, inspects UNPROFOR troops, and tours hospitals.

1993

January 11 Iraq condemned for violating Security Council resolutions.

January 19 After separating, Czech Republic and Slovak Republic join the UN, bringing the total number of member states to 180.

February 5 Security Council responds to continuous Iraqi challenges to the UN imposed cease-fire by authorizing an enlarged and militarized UN presence in the region. UNIKOM is transformed from an observer mission to an armed peacekeeping force.

February 9 UN troops from Italy arrive in Mozambique as the first contingent of UNOMOZ.

February 22 Security Council votes to establish an international tribunal to prosecute people responsible for serious violations of international humanitarian law in the former Yugoslavia. This is the first time the UN has established an international court with power to prosecute crimes committed during armed conflict.

February 22 The Rwandan government announces a cease-fire. Uganda and Rwanda request observers along their border.

March 21 A joint deployment of 100 OAS/UN human rights and relief workers arrives in Haiti.

March 26 UNOSOM II is established and replaces UNITAF. The UN presence in Somalia is expanded, with 30,000 troops and civilians (the largest peacekeeping force in UN history).

May 20 Boutros-Ghali proposes the creation of UNOMUR to observe the Uganda-Rwanda frontier.

May 23-28 Elections held in Cambodia under UNTAC supervision.

May 28 In a letter to Prince Sihanouk of Cambodia, Boutros-Ghali congratulates Cambodians for participating in the elections.

May 29 The Special Representative to Cambodia declares the elections "free and fair."

May 31 Prince Sihanouk thanks UNTAC for the successful maintenance of the cease-fire and the holding of elections.

June 5 "Warlord" forces of Mohamed Farah Aideed kill twenty-four Pakistani peacekeepers in Somalia. Leads to UNOSOM II hunt for Aideed and escalation of conflict Aideed.

June 10 In Cambodia, the royalist FUNCINPEC party is proclaimed the winner of the elections. Both major parties agree to create a government of national unity and one national army.

June 14-25 World Conference on Human Rights held in Vienna.

June 18 Security Council announces its support of UNSCOM attempts to install missile-test-monitoring equipment in Iraq.

July 3 Governor's Island Agreement calls for the return of President Aristide to power in Haiti and the removal of coup leaders.

July 15-19 UNSCOM's executive chairman announces that Iraq has complied with Security Council resolutions to destroy precursor chemicals and chemical weapons producing equipment.

July 25 The UN Security Council recognizes ECOWAS as the primary peacemaking entity in Liberia, through the Cotonou Agreement, and ECOMOG as the primary peacekeeping force.

August 4 The Government of Rwanda and the Rwandan Patriotic Front (RPF) sign the Arusha Accords, calling for a broad-based, transitional unity government for two years before elections, for the RPF to join a reduced Rwandan army, and for an international peacekeeping force (UNAMIR) to monitor implementation.

August 18 An agreement between Bosnian Serbs and the Bosnian Government make Srebenica a demilitarized zone and a UN "safe haven" for refugees.

August 24 Security Council establishes the first UN peacekeeping mission in the former USSR, the UN Observer Mission in Georgia (UNOMIG).

August 24 Boutros-Ghali requests that UNAMIR be established to implement the Arusha Accords and suggests that the UN Observer Mission on the Ugandan-Rwandan border (UNOMUR) forces join the operation, which consists of two infantry battalions and 2,500 personnel.

September 9 Israeli-Palestinian peace agreement, negotiated in Oslo, signed at the White House.

September 22 UNOMIL (Liberia) established by Security Council Resolution 866 (1993) to assist ECOMOG in monitoring the cease-fire and observing elections scheduled for 1994.

September 23 UNMIH in Haiti established to provide guidance and training to the police in order to reduce human rights abuses.

September 24 UNTAC mandate ends. Government of national unity is in place in Cambodia.

October 3 Eighteen U.S. Army Rangers killed in Somalia, leading to the end of UNOSOM II and to a decline in UN peacekeeping activities.

October 4 UNPROFOR mandate extended in Bosnia and Croatia.

October 5 UNAMIR is established in Rwanda to monitor implementation of peace agreement between the government and the RPF. Only one infantry battalion is assigned to the mission.

October 8 General Assembly ends a thirty-one-year ban on economic and other ties with South Africa and its nationals in areas of trade, investment, finance, travel and transportation in recognition of the end of apartheid.

October 13 UN threatens to reapply sanctions on Haiti if the military dictator, Cedras, does not resign by October 15.

October 21 A failed coup d'etat in Burundi results in the slaying of President Melchior Ndadaye and escalating tensions in Burundi and Rwanda.

October 25 Security Council condemns attempted coup in Burundi.

October 28 Deposed President Aristide addresses the General Assembly, calling for military operations or a blockade to restore him to power. In Haiti, Cedras calls for an amnesty for those involved in the coup.

November 5 ONUMOZ mandate renewed, as the operation in Mozambique proceeds.

November 11 New sanctions imposed on Libya by the Security Council, widening the air and arms embargo in place since April 1992.

November 16 Security Council Resolution 885 authorizes a Commission of Inquiry to investigate armed attacks on UNOSOM II personnel.

November 16 The UN Convention on the Law of the Sea comes into effect, after Guyana becomes the sixtieth state to ratify.

November 17 Start of International Tribunal for War Crimes in the former Yugoslavia, at The Hague, The Netherlands.

November 18 UNOSOM II mandate renewed until May 31, 1994, as the operation winds down.

November 30 ONUSAL mandate extended for six months, until May 31, 1994, as the operation in El Salvador proceeds.

December 15 UNAVEM II mandate extended three months, as the fighting in Angola continues.

December 15 UNIFICYP is extended in Cyprus until June 15, 1994, in spite of financial difficulties.

December 15 Palau is admitted to the UN as the 185th member state.

December 20 UNOMUR mandate extended on the Uganda-Rwanda border between the warring parties.

December 29 Creation of the post of UN Commissioner for Human Rights.

1994

January 6 Security Council approves early deployment of the second battalion for UNAMIR, as the security situation worsens.

January 11 UNAMIR Commander, General Romeo Dallaire, telegraphs UN headquarters, warning of impending genocide and requesting permission to confiscate an arms cache, but receives no authorization.

January 12 The Special Representative of the Secretary-General in Rwanda informs President Habyarimana that UNAMIR is aware of the genocide plot and the arms cache.

January 26 OAS and UN MICIVIH observers resume Haitian human rights monitoring.

February 4 UNOSOM II mandate revised to include nation-building activities, at the same time as the operation is winding down.

February 5 Mortar attack in Sarajevo kills sixty-eight civilians and leads to the threat of NATO air strikes against Bosnian Serb positions.

February 14 Jose Ayalo Lasso of Ecuador appointed first Commissioner for Human Rights.

February 21 UN and NATO deadline for Serb withdrawal from Sarajevo passes without compliance. NATO threatens air strikes.

March 4 All parties involved in Bosnian conflict called upon by the Security Council to cooperate with UNPROFOR in the consolidation of a cease-fire. However, the war continues.

March 7 Under the supervision of ECOMOG and UNOMIL, a Liberian National Transitional Government is installed, led by the former rebel leader, Charles Taylor.

March 16 UNAVEM II extended until May 31, 1994. The civil war in Angola continues.

March 19 Fact finding mission sent to Burundi to investigate the 1993 coup.

March 20 Runoff election in El Salvador brings an ARENA Party victory. ONUSAL declares elections "free and fair," with some discrepancies.

March 25 UNOMIG mandate extended in Georgia.

March 29 The Government of Guatemala and rebel URNG sign the Comprehensive Agreement, which recognizes the mandate of MINUGUA mission.

March 31 UNPROFOR mandate extended until September 30, 1994, with the addition of 3,500 troops, bringing the total to 28,000.

April 4 Quadripartite Agreement provides for the safety of refugees returning to their homeland in Caucasus countries.

April 5 UNAMIR mandate extended until July 29, 1994, because of the deterioration of the security situation.

April 6 Presidents of Rwanda (Juvenal Habyarimana) and Burundi (Cyprien Ntaryamira) are killed when their plane is shot down by Hutu extremists. The incident provides the signal for the genocide to begin.

April 7 Hutu extremists begin their organized campaign of killing Tutsi and moderate Hutu civilians. UNAMIR peacekeepers comply with their mandate and do not intervene. Prime Minister Agathe Uwilingiyimana and ten Belgian peacekeepers are captured, tortured, and killed.

April 8 The killings continue in Rwanda. UNAMIR does not intervene but attempts to protect its personnel, provide humanitarian aid, and work with the parties to the Arusha Accords to maintain the cease-fire. RPF troops in southern Rwanda move north to join forces around Kigali, but the RPF is unable to stop the killings.

April 15 As the genocide unfolds, the Belgian foreign minister campaigns to withdraw UNAMIR, and Boutros-Ghali proposes that the Security Council reduce the existing forces or completely withdraw or reinforce UNAMIR and expand its mandate.

April 21 As the genocide continues, the Security Council decides to reduce existing UNAMIR forces from 2,500 to 250 in Rwanda.

April 27 Seven thousand troops are added to the UNPROFOR mission in Bosnia, bringing the total to 35,000, the largest force in UN history.

April 30 The Security Council ends eight hours of discussion on Rwanda with a decision not to call the events "genocide." Therefore, parties to the 1948 Genocide Convention are not obligated to intervene. Two hundred and fifty thousand Hutu, including extremists, flee from advancing RPF forces in Rwanda and enter Tanzania. This is one of the largest single-day border crossings in history.

April 30-May 17 The Security Council debates Rwanda.

May 3 U.S. Presidential Defense Directive 25 is issued, placing limits on the types of peacekeeping operations that the United States would be willing to support and rejecting enforcement missions, such as UNOSOM II.

May 4 Israel and the PLO sign the Cairo Agreement that provides for Palestinian self-rule in the Gaza Strip and Jericho.

May 5 ONUMOZ mandate in Mozambique is extended until November 15, 1994, as election preparations are made.

May 6 Sanctions against Haiti are expanded to include a comprehensive trade embargo and are conditional on the removal of Cedras and other coup leaders.

May 10 Nelson Mandela is inaugurated as the South African president following the first non-racial and democratic elections held that UNOMSA declares to be "free and fair."

May 17 Security Council agrees in principle to a new UNAMIR with 5,500 peacekeepers (mainly from Africa) and a new mandate to provide humanitarian aid, protect civilians and refugees, and aid relief efforts. The council places an arms embargo on Rwanda. The genocide continues.

May 26 ONUSAL mandate is extended for six months in El Salvador.

May 31 UNOSOM II mandate renewed until September 30, 1994, stressing the humanitarian aspect of the mission.

June 8 UNAMIR is extended to December 9, 1994. The genocide has been largely completed.

June 8 One-month cease-fire between the Bosnian government and Serbs initiated by UNPROFOR.

June 15 UNFICYP in Cyprus is extended until December 31, 1994.

June 18 Cease-fire in Bosnia is ended by Bosnian Serbs after ten days.

June 22 Operation Turquoise initiated by France in Rwanda, with UN approval, to create "humanitarian protection zones" for fleeing Hutu refugees and former government officials in southwestern Rwanda.

June 23 South Africa regains its seat in the General Assembly after thirty-one years.

June 29 UNAVEM II is extended in Angola until September 30, with threats of further sanctions against UNITA and the government for noncompliance with Security Council resolutions.

July 4 The RPF captures, Kigali, the capital of Rwanda.

July 18 The RPF unilaterally declares a cease-fire, after winning the civil war in Rwanda and ending the genocide.

July 19 As the RPF takes power, a broad-based government of national unity is formed.

July 20 The United States announces that Haitian refugees will no longer be eligible for asylum but will be held at Guantanamo Bay and other countries.

July 26 Israel and Jordan sign the Washington Declaration, setting the stage for a peace treaty between the two states.

July 31 Security Council Resolution 940 (1994) creates a twenty-seven state multi-national force (MNF) for Haiti, led by the United States.

August 29 Security Council's evaluation of ONUMOZ is favorable, as demobilization of forces, reintegration of soldiers into society, and the registration of voters continue in Mozambique.

September 12 Akosomobo Agreement is signed in Ghana, supplementing the Cotonou Agreement for Liberia. The civil war ends in mid-1996.

September 14 ICFY observer mission is deployed after a cease-fire in Yemen.

September 19 A U.S. led multinational force (MNF) is sent to Haiti and threatens to invade. President Clinton demands that the military regime turn power over to President Aristide and sends Senator Sam Nunn, President Jimmy Carter, and General Colin Powell to Haiti to negotiate with the coup leaders

September 19 MINUGUA established by General Assembly Resolution 48/267 for Guatemala.

September 23 Security Council calls for more sanctions against Bosnian Serbs.

September 29 After Cedras, other coup leaders, and police chief Michel Francois leave Haiti, the MNF succeeds in securing Haiti, and the Security Council lifts sanctions. Haiti's elected parliament meets and passes a limited amnesty for political but not other criminals.

September 29 UNAVEM II is extended until October 30, 1994, in Angola as the civil war continues.

September 30 UNOSOM II is extended until October 31, 1994, in Somalia, as the mission draws to a close.

September 30 UNPROFOR is extended for six months, as the fighting in Bosnia continues.

October 4 Joint declaration signed by the government of El Salvador and FMLN to implement peace accords.

October 6 Iraqi troops mass on the border of Kuwait, while Saddam Hussein threatens to cease cooperation with UNSCOM and the IAEA.

October 8 Security Council declares Iraq's defiance as unacceptable and requests that UNIKOM monitor Iraqi actions to document compliance with Security Council resolutions.

October 15 President Aristide returns to Haiti.

October 21 UNOMIL is extended in Liberia until January 13, 1995, as the civil war continues.

October 26 Jordan and Israel sign a peace treaty, ending a forty-seven-year state of war.

October 27 Boutros-Ghali declares that Mozambique's elections will proceed after RENAMO is persuaded to abandon a boycott. Voting begins at 7,244 UN monitored polling places.

October 31 UNOSOM II is extended until November 4, 1994, while the Security Council considers any further extension.

November 3 General Assembly Resolution 49/10 urges the Security Council to ease the arms embargo against the Bosnian government so that it might defend itself against the Bosnian Serbs.

November 4 UNOSOM II is extended until the final withdrawal date of March 31, 1995.

November 4 Security Council Resolution 954 ends UNOSOM II.

November 8 Security Council Resolution 955 (1994) creates an international tribunal to prosecute humanitarian law violations in Rwanda.

November 19 Joaquim Chissano wins the presidential and FRELIMO the parliamentary elections in Mozambique. Elections are declared "free and fair."

November 20 The Government of Angola and UNITA sign the Lusaka Protocol and again promise to end the civil war.

November 23 ONUSAL is extended until April 30, 1995. Security Council urges the government of El Salvador and the FMLN to work together to implement the final parts of the peace agreement.

November 29 UNDOF, the observer mission between Israel and Syria for twenty years, is extended until May 31, 1995.

November 30 In the wake of the genocide and RPF assumption of power, UNAMIR is extended until June 9, 1995.

December 8 UNAVEM II is extended until February 8, 1995, as renewed peace efforts strive to implement the Lusaka Protocols and end the Angolan Civil War.

December 16 UNMOT in Tajikistan begins to monitor a cease-fire between the government and rebel forces, investigate cease-fire violations, and support deployment of UN humanitarian personnel and aid deliveries.

December 21 Liberia's warring factions ratify the Accra Agreement, calling for previous peace agreements to be implemented.

December 23 President Alija Izetbegovic of Bosnia and Radovan Karadzic of the Bosnian Serbs sign a cease-fire to take effect on December 24.

December 23 Boutros-Ghali congratulates President Chissano and the new Assembly of Mozambique as they are inaugurated.

December 29 *Operation Retour* begins in Zaire as a UN project to guard against violence in refugee camps and assist in repatriation of Hutu refugees to Rwanda. The operation makes little progress.

December 31 Bosnian President Izetbegovic and Bosnian Serb leader Karadzic sign a complete cessation of hostilities agreement to take effect on January 1, 1995. Eventually, the agreement fails and fighting resumes.

1995

January 1 World Trade Organization (WTO) is formally established.

January 12 UNOMIG is extended in Georgia until May 15, 1995.

January 13 UN Mission for the Referendum in Western Sahara (MINURSO) is extended in Western Sahara until May 31, 1995. Efforts are stalled to hold a UN-monitored referendum in accordance with Security Council Resolution 658 of June 1990 to determine whether citizens want independence or annexation by Morocco.

January 25 Boutros-Ghali issues report S/1995/65 that estimates Hutu refugees in Burundi, Tanzania, and Zaire at two million.

January 25 Boutros-Ghali welcomes Iraq's official recognition of Kuwait, fulfilling a condition of Security Council Resolution 833.

January 25 Supplement to *An Agenda for Peace* is released. Calls for UN command of peacekeepers and a rapid reaction force.

January 27 UNHCR and Zaire agree to cooperate in the repatriation of Hutu refugees through the efforts of 1,500 Zairian troops and UN observers. The agreement produces minimal results.

January 30 UNIFIL extended in south of Lebanon until July 31, 1995.

February 1 Boutros-Ghali asks Security Council for a larger operation to replace UNAVEM II in Angola.

February 6 Boutros-Ghali asks Security Council to authorize a small team of UN officials to remain in El Salvador to verify the peace agreement once UNOSAL leaves.

February 8 Security Council Resolution 976 (1995) establishes UNAVEM III with a mandate to help implement the Lusaka Protocols and to begin on August 8, 1995. UNAVEM III is given a larger mandate and more troops than UNAVEM II.

February 10 Security Council issues S/PRST/1995/7, condemning Rwandan Hutu leaders who were preventing the efforts of the UN and Zaire to repatriate Hutu refugees. Security Council decides to add thirty more troops to support the ninety person UNAMIR force in Rwanda, as cross-border raids by Hutu extremist guerrillas intensify.

February 22 Security Council selects Arusha, Tanzania, as the site of the international tribunal for Rwanda.

27 UN Commission on Human Rights in Geneva announces a cease-fire in Chechnya. However, fighting resumes for another year.

March 6 UNMOT in Tajikistan is extended until April 26, 1995.

March 6-13 World Summit for Social Development takes place in Copenhagen, Denmark.

March 20 UNPROFOR forces now number 38,599.

March 29 Security Council declares that it will consider intervention in Burundi to prevent waves of killings from intensifying into a Rwanda-like genocide.

March 30 Boutros-Ghali arrives in Haiti as part of ceremony in which UNMIH replaces the MNF.

March 30 Security Council Resolution 748 (1992) continues sanctions against Libya for harboring the Lockerbie bombing suspects.

March 31 General Assembly renews MINUGUA for six months.

March 31 Security Council Resolution 981 (1995) creates UN Confidence Restoration Operation (UNCRO) in Croatia. Security Council

Resolution 982 (1995) extends UNPROFOR in Bosnia until November 30, 1995. Security Council Resolution 983 (1995) renames UNPRFOR in the FYR Macedonia as UNPREDEP, a preventive deployment force.

March 31-April 6 Conference on Disarmament in Geneva includes discussion of Comprehensive Nuclear Test Ban Treaty.

April 6-7 UNSCOM reports that Iraq has an undeclared, functioning biological weapons program.

April 10 UNIKOM in Kuwait is extended until October 1995. UNSCOM reports on its monitoring and verification regime in Iraq.

April 10-15 A Special Committee on Peacekeeping Operations discusses the proposal for a rapid reaction force as suggested in the *Supplement to An Agenda for Peace.*

April 13 UNOMIL mandate ends. ECOMOG remains in Liberia.

April 14 Security Council Resolution 986 (1995) allows states to import a maximum of $1 billion worth of Iraqi oil in a ninety-day period.

April 17-May 12 Non-Proliferation Treaty (NPT) Review and Extension Conference takes place at the UN and results in indefinite extension of the NPT.

April 18 Boutros-Ghali creates a small political office in Somalia to replace formal UN representation.

April 21 Security Council Resolution 988 (1995) calls for the continuation of sanctions against the former Republic of Yugoslavia until July 1995.

April 22 At the refugee camp in Kibeho, Rwanda, the combination of Rwandan Patriotic Army suppression of suspected Hutu extremists, intra-camp attacks, and a chaotic flight of refugees from the camp leads to several hundred reported deaths.

May 8-10 Boutros-Ghali visits Moscow for talks with Russian President Boris Yeltsin.

May 11 The Review and Extension Conference of the Parties to the NPT decides to renew the treaty indefinitely.

May 12 UNOMIG is extended in Georgia until January 12, 1996. Armenia and Azerbaijan agree to cease-fire in war over Nagorno-Karabakh. Organization for Security and Cooperation in Europe (OSCE) is requested to monitor the cease-fire.

May 26 The last nuclear device is destroyed at Semipalatinsk, Kazakhstan, in accordance with the Strategic Arms Reduction Treaty I between the United States and the former Soviet Union.

May 30 UNDOF is extended until November 30, 1995, on the Golan Heights.

June 1-July 6 Conference on Disarmament held in Geneva resumes discussion of the Comprehensive Nuclear Test Ban Treaty.

June 9 Security Council Resolution 997 (1995) extends UNAMIR until December 8, 1995, while reducing troop strength over the following months from 5,500 to 2,330 to 1,800.

June 16 Security Council calls for an increase of up to 12,500 troops for UNPROFOR for a total of more than 50,000. Security Council Resolution 998 (1995) calls for Bosnian Serbs to release UN personnel.

June 16 UNMOT is extended in Tajikistan until December 15, 1995.

June 23 UNFICYP is extended in Cyprus until December 31, 1995.

June 25 Haiti holds local and legislative elections.

June 26 UN celebrates its fiftieth anniversary in San Francisco, California.

June 26-30 First plenary session of the International Criminal Tribunal for Rwanda.

June 30 MINURSO is extended in Western Sahara until September 30, 1995.

July 11 Bosnian Serbs attack the Srebenica "safe area" in Bosnia. Thousands of Bosnian Muslim men are taken away and killed. The massacre leads to NATO air strikes and Dayton peace talks.

July 14-16 Boutros-Ghali visits Angola and inspects the transition from UNAVEM II to UNAVEM III.

July 25 Bosnian Serbs attack Zepa, another UN "safe haven" in Bosnia.

July 28 UNIFIL is extended in Lebanon until January 31, 1996.

August 7 UNAVEM III is extended in Angola until February 8, 1996.

August 16 Security Council permits the sale of weapons to Rwanda through UN monitored checkpoints.

August 17 A cease-fire is signed in Tajikistan between President Emomali Rakhmonov and opposition leader Abdullo Nuri.

August 17 Iraq admits it has produced biological weapons, attempted to build a nuclear weapons program, and been successful with a "home-grown" program of producing VX nerve gas and ballistic missiles.

August 19 Abuja Agreement orders a cease-fire and the creation of a Council of State for Liberia.

August 20 UNSCOM and the IAEA receive videos, microfilm, microfiche, disks, and other documentation on Iraq's weapons programs.

August 22 UNHCR condemns the forcible repatriation of Rwandan refugees by the Zairian government.

August 23 Security Council asks Zaire to end its campaign of forcible repatriation of Rwandan refugees.

August 28 Security Council sets up a body to investigate the 1993 assassination and coup attempt in Burundi.

August 30-September 8 1995 NGO Forum on Women in takes place in Huairou, China, north of Beijing.

September 1 Council of State for Liberia is appointed, headed by the rebel, Charles Taylor.

September 4-15 Fourth World Conference on Women held in Beijing, China.

September 7 Security Council sets up an International Commission of Inquiry to investigate the military training of Rwandan government forces before the genocide.

September 8 Geneva Statement and Agreements on principles to negotiate an end to the war in Bosnia.

September 13 Interim Accord between Greece and the Former Yugoslav Republic of Macedonia (FYROM) states that the FYROM will no longer be subjected to the 1994 Greek trade embargo and the FYROM will no longer use its national flag.

September 14 The Bosnian Serbs agree to the plan for cessation of hostilities within the Sarajevo Temporary Exclusion Zone.

September 15 Sanctions against Yugoslavia are renewed until March 18, 1996.

September 15 The Beijing Declaration and Platform for Action are adopted at the conclusion of the Fourth World Conference on Women.

September 19 Fiftieth Anniversary Session of the General Assembly is opened.

September 22 MINURSO is extended in Western Sahara until January 31, 1996, though there is no sign that a referendum will be held.

September 22 International Court of Justice (ICJ) dismisses New Zealand's complaint against France for a nuclear test in the Pacific.

September 28 Yitzhak Rabin and Yasir Arafat sign a peace agreement that provides for Palestinian self-rule on the West Bank.

September 30 Major General Chris Garuba if Nigeria is replaced by Major General Phillip Sibanda of Zimbabwe as the Force Commander of UNAVEM III.

October 22-24 Special Commemorative Meeting of the General Assembly is held on the Fiftieth Anniversary of the UN.

November 15 Boutros-Ghali visits Haiti to inspect UNMIH operations, as presidential elections approach.

November 21 Dayton Accords initialed, after Bosnian peace agreement is reached.

December 14 Dayton Accords signed in Paris. NATO Implementation Force (IFOR) begins to deploy to Bosnia, replacing UNPROFOR.

1996

January 3 Boutros-Ghali reports misgivings about the inquiry into the 1993 assassination of President Ndadaye of Burundi.

January 5 Security Council condemns all that were responsible for the genocide in Burundi.

January 7 Alvaro Arzu takes office in Guatemala after winning in the second round of presidential elections, fulfilling part of the December peace agreement.

January 7-8 UNHCR investigates the possible use of security forces in eastern Zaire refugee camps against Hutu extremists.

January 8 UNAVEM III is extended until May 8, 1996 in Angola.

January 12 Organization of African Unity joins UN investigation into assassination and attempted coup in Burundi.

January 15 Madeline Albright, the U.S. Permanent Representative to the UN, addresses the General Assembly about ways to make the UN more efficient.

January 16 Boutros-Ghali informs the Security Council about the deterioration of security throughout Burundi.

January 18 As killings intensify, Burundi's Permanent Representative to the UN rejects the use of UN guards to protect officials.

January 19 The Security Council approves the dispatch of a technical security team to Burundi.

January 25 Italy announces to the UN that the European Union (EU) would increase its contributions to the UN to ease the budget crisis.

January 25 The Security Council calls for Somali factions to negotiate the establishment of a national unity government.

January 25 UN agencies urge donor governments to increase humanitarian aid contributions in order to alleviate the deteriorating conditions in Iraq.

January 26 The UN announces that it is in arrears because of the inconsistent payments by member states, especially the United States.

January 27-February 3 Technical security team looks into enhancing security in Burundi.

January 29 Boutros-Ghali urges the Security Council to consider preventive measures in order to stop the conflict in Burundi from spreading to its neighbors.

January 31 Thirty-one countries sign the Global Treaty on Fisheries to regulate high seas fishing.

February 5 Under-Secretary for Administration and Management Joseph E. Conner warns the UN that it is nearing bankruptcy.

February 7 Rene Preval becomes President of Haiti, replacing Aristide. UNMIH prepares to reduce its presence.

February 13 Burundi government officials claim that they have begun talks on deterring all extremist and factional groups that were undermining peace.

February 15 The UN condemns the fighting in Afghanistan between the Taliban and the government because of its effect on regional stability, drug trafficking, and terrorism.

February 16 Boutros-Ghali urges the Security Council to set up a stand-by-multinational force of up to 25,000 soldiers to provide for a quick response to humanitarian emergencies.

February 29 UNMIH is extended with a mandate to increase stability and help train the Haitian police.

February 29 While visiting Brazil, Boutros-Ghali states that UN support for democracy extends beyond ensuring free and fair elections.

March 4 Boutros-Ghali declares that terrorist bombings in Israel are harmful to the peace process.

March 8 Mandate for UNAMIR ends at the request of the Rwandan government.

March 8 Second round of reform meetings for strengthening the UN and Security Council, as well as implementing *An Agenda for Development* and *An Agenda for Peace*.

March 9-15 UNSCOM is denied access to inspection sites in Iraq.

March 13 At the Summit for Peacemakers, Boutros-Ghali labels terrorism as a "global phenomenon."

March 15 The Security Council reviews the aftermath of UNOSOM II, one year after withdrawing.

March 15 Boutros-Ghali launches a ten-year, $25 billion plan for African development, involving the UN, the World Bank, UNDP, and other UN specialized agencies.

March 19 Boutros-Ghali asks the Conference on Disarmament to continue its work on nuclear disarmament.

March 19 The Security Council demands that Iraq cooperate with UNSCOM and allow full access to all suspected weapons sites.

March 21 Boutros-Ghali expresses satisfaction that the URNG has suspended military attacks in Guatemala.

March 25 The World Health Organization (WHO) announces that malnutrition, disease, and mortality rates are increasing in Iraq.

March 27 An import-export mechanism is installed to monitor Iraq's attempts to build a nuclear weapons program.

March 28 Draft of the Comprehensive Nuclear Test Ban Treaty (CTBT) is presented to the UN Conference on Disarmament.

April 3 The General Assembly renews the MINUGUA peace agreement in order to encourage peace in Guatemala.

April 4 The Security Council demands that all of the parties in the Bosnia peace process work to fully implement the peace agreement and create security measures beneficial to each party.

April 11 UNSCOM announces that the Iraqi government is again interfering with its mission.

April 12 Continued factional fighting in Monrovia, Liberia causes thousands to become internally displaced and seek refuge in embassies. Boutros-Ghali condemns factional fighting in Liberia, as well as in Lebanon.

April 18 UNAMIR ends as the last of the peacekeepers withdraw.

April 18 The Commission on Human Rights discusses child exploitation in the world.

April 18 Israel attacks a UN compound in Lebanon, inflicting civilian casualties.

April 18 IFOR assumes the authority of UNPROFOR in the former Yugoslavia. IFOR is composed of approximately 55,000 personnel from sixteen NATO and sixteen non-NATO states.

April 28 Boutros-Ghali meets with the executive directors of the UN programs and organizations to plan a new initiative on Africa.

April 30 UNAVEM III reports that the Lusaka Protocol is being implemented slowly in Angola.

May 6 The Security Council demands that the factions in Liberia end their fighting.

May 6 Boutros-Ghali declares that peace in Guatemala is strengthening.

May 20 The UN and Iraq establish an "oil-for-food" program after more than four years of negotiation.

May 5-23 UN-sponsored symposium in Cairo to discuss the Palestinian economy and international assistance to the area.

May 29 Security Council approves Boutros-Ghali's suggestion of a 20 percent reduction of UN forces operating in Western Sahara.

June 3-14 Second UN Conference on Human Settlements (Habitat II) takes place in Istanbul, Turkey. World leaders at Habitat II commit to providing assistance to ensure adequate living standards and development aid for all people.

June 20 UNSCOM announces that Iraq's former biological weapons facility, Al Hakam, has been destroyed.

June 24-26 NGO Symposium in New York discusses Palestinian economy and state building.

June 25 Boutros-Ghali requests the resumption of talks between Turkey, Greece, and Cyprus.

June 28 UN support mission in Haiti is launched to assist the Haitian government and "professionalize" the police force.

July 8-26 Human Rights Committee calls for the restoration of democracy in Nigeria and an end to human rights violations in Brazil and Peru.

July 18 Representatives from over 150 states call for a lowering of greenhouse gas emissions in accordance with the Global Warming Convention.

July 19 Boutros-Ghali denounces attacks on Sudanese refugees in Uganda.

July 30 The Security Council reiterates its support of Lebanon as an independent state.

July 31 The UN runs out of the funds needed to pay its bills for the third time in 1996. Over 100 of the 185 UN member states owe $3 billion in arrears.

July 31 Concern is raised about the effect of sanctions on the Iraqi people. Food prices in Iraq are increased between 50 to 100 percent, crop production drops 30 percent, unemployment rises, and hyperinflation occurs.

August 14 Boutros-Ghali deplores the clashes that occurred in the UN "buffer zone" on Cyprus.

August 14 Sudan is given ninety days to extradite three Egyptian suspects wanted for the 1995 assassination attempt on Egyptian President Hosni Mubarak in Ethiopia. The Security Council threatens sanctions if Sudan does not comply.

August 14 Liberian warring factions reconcile, ending the conflict.

August 19 A UN press release states that the budget for the next year (1997) will be $178 million or 6.9 percent lower than the previous year, due to the reduction of positions.

August 20 Boutros-Ghali appeals to the parties in the peace negotiations over Western Sahara to become more flexible.

August 29 The Stockholm Declaration is adopted by a World Congress to stop the sexual exploitation of children.

August 30 Boutros-Ghali proposes a better system for providing information concerning the effects of sanctions.

August 31 Cease-fire in Liberia takes hold. Fighting does not resume.

September 10 UN adopts the Comprehensive Nuclear Test Ban treaty (CTBT), although India and Pakistan reject it.

September 16 World Solar Summit ends with over 100 states exploring clean renewable energy in improving the quality of life.

September 23 The International Labor Organization (ILO) reports that there are 1.1 billion agricultural workers worldwide, many of whom are on the lowest rung of the wage earning scale.

September 26 Boutros-Ghali expresses concern over conflict in the West Bank and Gaza Strip.

September 27 The UN appeals for $40 million to help the most vulnerable Iraqis for the next three months.

September 28 Security Council calls for a halt to all acts escalating conflict and threatening the Middle East peace process.

September 28 Security Council denounces actions taken by the Taliban in Afghanistan, especially the murder of former President Najibullah.

October 1 Security Council finds that Yugoslavia has met the conditions of the 1995 Dayton Accords and lifts sanctions.

October 10 UNIDO launches an initiative to integrate the private sector into the promotion of global industrialization.

October 24 The International Convention on Nuclear Safety begins a discussion of nuclear power plant safety worldwide.

November 5 President Clinton is reelected for a second term, and Boutros-Ghali launches his campaign for reelection.

November 13-17 The World Food Summit in Rome convenes and agrees to a "food for all" proposal.

November 29 The World Youth Forum proposes that every member state have a forum for persons under twenty-five years of age in a youth organization.

December 9 The UN "oil-for-food" program is authorized to allow Iraq to sell up to $2 billion in petroleum and related products over six months in order to earn revenue to purchase humanitarian supplies for Iraqi civilians.

December 17 After the United States vetoes a second term for Boutros Boutros-Ghali, the Security Council unanimously elects Kofi Annan as the next secretary-general of the UN.

December 17 Boutros-Ghali issues *An Agenda for Democratization.*

December 26 UN launches a campaign against desertification.

1997

January 1 Kofi Annan succeeds Boutros-Ghali as secretary-general.

Bibliography

Books

Adelman, Howard and Astri Suhrke, eds. *The Path of a Genocide: The Rwanda Crisis from Uganda to Zaire*. New Brunswick, N.J.: Transaction Publishers, 1999. Explores the Rwandan genocide from the different vantage points, including historical analysis and the perspectives of different actors.

Anstee, Margaret Joan. *Orphan of the Cold War: The Inside Story of the Collapse of the Angolan Peace Process, 1992-3*. New York: St. Martin's Press, 1996. The author's experiences as the head of UNAVEM II and challenges as a woman in charge of a most difficult and conflict-filled operation. Anstee analyzes decision-making inside UNAVEM II and implementation of this post-Cold War mission. UNAVEM II failed because of the mission's complex relationship with the warring factions, with NGOs, and with the UN machinery, as well as the structure of the Bicesse Accords and the lack of world interest in Angola.

Bailey, Kathleen C. *The UN Inspections in Iraq: Lessons for On-Site Verification*. Boulder, Colo.: Westview Press, 1995. Examines the success of UNSCOM as a model for future inspection missions. Looks at the difficulties weapons inspectors face when searching in a sovereign state. Chapters are organized to examine the inspection of chemical weapons, biological weapons, nuclear weapons, missiles, and the ability of states to proliferate weapons. Describes Iraq's methods of concealment, and what future inspectors should learn.

Ballard, John R. *Upholding Democracy: The United States Military Campaign in Haiti, 1994-1997*. Westport, Conn.: Praeger, 1998. Historical analysis of Haiti's political problems, including chapters on international involvement following 1991 coup. Concludes that UNMIH was successful because of early planning and long-term focus, but stresses the continued need for international support for democracy. Includes maps, appendices, and a glossary.

Basic Facts about the United Nations. New York: United Nations Department of Public Information, 1998. Periodic compendium of information about the activities of the UN.

Beigbeder, Yves. *Judging War Criminals: The Politics of International Justice.* London: MacMillan, 1999. Examines war crimes tribunals from the Nuremberg trials to the former Yugoslavia and Rwanda tribunals.

Belgrad, Eric A. and Nitza Nachmias (editors). *The Politics of International Humanitarian Aid Operations.* Westport, Conn.: Praeger, 1997. Describes and explains the post-Cold War increase of humanitarian aid missions, despite their non-strategic status. Case studies in Rwanda, Cambodia, the former Yugoslavia, and Somalia analyze the challenges faced by humanitarian missions.

Bennett, A. Leroy. *International Organizations: Principles and Issues.* 6th ed. Englewood Cliffs, N.J.: Prentice Hall, 1995. Examines UN and other international organizations.

Bennett, Christopher. *Yugoslavia's Bloody Collapse: Causes, Course and Consequences.* New York: New York University Press, 1995. Examines Yugoslavia from its creation to its dissolution in 1992 and the difficulties in maintaining stability. Later chapters discuss the buildup to war, the secession of Yugoslav states, and the international community's involvement (including the UN's) that is criticized as a model of post-Cold War irresponsibility toward conflict prevention and resolution.

Blackman, Ann. *Seasons of Her Life: A Biography of Madeline Korbel Albright.* New York: Scribner Books, 1998. A largely positive biography of the former U.S. Ambassador to the UN. Albright's role in opposing the reelection of Boutros-Ghali is treated as a defining event that impressed President Clinton and helped lead him to choose Albright as the first female secretary of state.

Bourantonis, Dimitris and Marios Evriviades. *A United Nations for the Twenty-First Century.* The Hague: Kluwer Law International, 1996. Chapters focus on the UN role in diplomacy, security, peacekeeping, disarmament and arms control, and economic development. A finding is that the UN has experienced difficulties in adapting to the changing international setting and addressing post-Cold War crises, because its structure has been too inflexible to deal with non-state actors and intrastate problems. Reforms are advocated that would make the UN more able to combat these new crises.

The Blue Helmets: A Review of United Nations Peacekeeping 3rd ed. New York: United Nations Department of Public Information, 1996. Peacekeeping analyzed as a UN tool, with descriptions of all missions from 1948-1996. Comprehensive descriptions of UNAVEM II, UNOMOZ, UNAMIR, MINURSO, UNIKOM, ONUSAL, UNPROFOR, UNTAC, UNOSOM II, UNMIH, UNOMIL, UNOMIG, UNMOT, UNASOG, and UNOMUR; including maps, charts, and participant lists.

Boutros-Ghali, Boutros. *An Agenda for Peace: Preventative Diplomacy, Peacemaking, and Peacekeeping.* New York: United Nations Department of Public Information, 1995. Proposes innovative approaches to maintain peace in the post-Cold War era. Contains resolutions of the General Assembly and of the Security Council, reports and correspondence of Boutros-Ghali, speeches and declarations; of special note is the 1992 report to the Security Council and General Assembly, "An Agenda for Peace." The foreword and index are thoroughly cross-referenced into other documents. Operations in Somalia and Cambodia are cited often, while Angola, Bosnia, Rwanda, Haiti, and Mozambique are referred to briefly. Advocates involvement in the earliest stages of a conflict (preventive deployment) to deter the use of military force; a rapid reaction force under UN command; persistent efforts to preserve peace; preparedness to use peacekeeping on any or all occasions; and the easing of tensions before, during and after war.

———. *Building Peace and Development 1994.* New York: United Nations Department of Public Information, 1994. Boutros-Ghali's evaluation of the crucial issues that the UN faced in the key years, 1993-4, review of the "Agenda for Peace," and claim that a lack of resources was making difficult the implementation of conflict resolution, development, and human rights programs.

———. *Unvanquished: A U.S.-UN Saga.* New York: Random House, 1999. Boutros-Ghali's version of the chain of events that led to the Clinton administration rejecting him for a second term. Presents his vision for the UN and his perception of UN failures in Bosnia, Somalia, and Rwanda.

Boyle, Francis A. *The Bosnian People Charge Genocide: Proceedings at the International Court of Justice Concerning Bosnia v. Serbia on the Prevention and Punishment of the Crime of Genocide.* Amherst, Mass.: Alethia Press, 1996. Using papers from ICJ proceedings, the author presents the case of genocide against Serbia, portrays the failure of the international community, and describes the scale of atrocities that occurred in Bosnia, starting in 1992. The author is also critical of the international community, because it did not act in the way that was outlined in international agreements on genocide.

Childers, Erskine, ed. *Challenges to the United Nations: Building a Safer World*. New York: St. Martin's Press, 1994. Focuses on the post-Cold War era and the increased role of UN bodies in human rights issues and peacekeeping. Case studies on the Gulf War, Somalia, Haiti, Rwanda, Western Sahara, Angola, Cambodia, El Salvador, and Mozambique; discusses the relationship between UN bodies and NGOs; calls on member states to invest more commitment and resources to strengthen the UN system.

Cigar, Norman L. *Genocide in Bosnia: The Policy of "Ethnic Cleansing."* College Station: Texas A&M University Press, 1995. Intensive analysis of the origins and strategy of ethnic cleansing by Serb leaders in Bosnia.

Cimbala, Stephen J. *Collective Insecurity: U.S. Defense Policy and the New World Disorder*. Westport, Conn.: Greenwood Press, 1995. Describes several post-Cold War conflicts and ramifications for U.S. policymakers.

The Commission on Global Governance. *Our Global Neighbourhood*. Oxford: Oxford University Press, 1995. The report discusses the changing international climate in the post-Cold War period. Sections on reform provide an overview of UN bodies, address the problems that these bodies suffer, and suggest ways of making the UN a more substantial actor in world affairs. States the need to reform the current UN system, including changing membership of the Security Council, increasing organizational support and resources for the General Assembly, eliminating UNCTAD, ECOSOC, and other bodies, promoting regional organizations, and making the Secretariat more efficient.

Cordesman, Anthony H. and Ahmed S. Hashim. *Iraq: Sanctions and Beyond*. Boulder, Colo.: Westview Press, 1997. Discusses the effect that UN sanctions have had on Iraq's economy and power structure. Stresses the need for aggressive diplomacy, instead of UN sanctions, as a tool to bring change to Iraq.

Cox, David. *Exploring An Agenda for Peace: Issues Arising from the Report of the Secretary-General*. Ottawa: Canadian Centre for Global Security, 1993. A comprehensive analysis of the process of developing and debating the report. Focuses on the contradiction between Boutros-Ghali's advocacy of peace enforcement and defenders of traditional peacekeeping. Foreshadows the Somalia debacle.

Curtis, Grant. *Cambodia Reborn? The Transition to Democracy and Development.* Washington, D.C.: Brookings Institution Press, 1998. Studies Cambodia's rebuilding period following twenty years of civil war. Examines the degree to which UNTAC has facilitated the rebuilding, and the efforts to rebuild that have taken place since UNTAC's mandate ended.

Diehl, Paul F. *International Peacekeeping.* Baltimore, Md.: Johns Hopkins University Press, 1993. History and analysis of international peacekeeping, with particular attention to how international norms function. Cambodia and Somalia are discussed briefly, while the operations in Angola, Yugoslavia, and Iraq are covered in more detail. Views the current peacekeeping paradigm as ineffective, and explains alternatives that would more effectively achieve the purpose of current peacekeeping missions.

Diehl, Paul F., ed. *The Politics of Global Governance,* 2nd ed. Boulder, Colo., Lynne Rienner, 2001. Analyzes a range of international organizations, especially the UN, and how they work together or fail to cooperate to provide global public goods.

Dobbs, Michael. *Madeleine Albright: A Twentieth-Century Odyssey.* New York: Henry Holt Company, 1999. Includes description of Albright's confrontation with Boutros-Ghali.

Donia, Robert J. and John V.A. Fine, Jr. *Bosnia and Herzegovina: A Tradition Betrayed.* New York: Columbia University Press, 1994. A history of Bosnia, which emphasizes the role that historical factors and perceptions of the Balkans have played in influencing modern crises. Later chapters describe the factors that led to the breakdown of the Yugoslav state, the wars, and the diplomacy of the United States, UN, and the EU. Includes a chronology and glossary.

Doyle, Michael W. *UN Peacekeeping: UNTAC's Civil Mandate* Boulder, Colo.: Lynne Rienner, 1995. Focuses on the first large-scale attempt by a UN mission and, particularly, a large contingent of civilian bureaucrats and police to administer a conflict in transition from war to peace.

Doyle, Michael W., Ian Johnstone, and Robert C. Orr, eds. *Keeping the Peace: Multidimensional UN Operations in Cambodia and El Salvador.* Cambridge: Cambridge University Press, 1997. Comparisons of the various functions of two different operations.

Dupuy, Alex. *Haiti in the New World Order: The Limits of the Democratic Revolution.* Boulder, Colo.: Westview Press, 1997. Describes the emergence of Haiti's democracy in the 1980s and the threat that the 1991 coup posed. Describes U.S. pressures to restore democracy, the role of UN sanctions, and evaluates the results of international intervention. Includes a chronology of U.S. involvement in Haiti from 1991 to 1994.

Durch, William J., ed. *UN Peacekeeping, American Policy, and the Uncivil Wars of the 1990s*. New York: St. Martin's Press, 1996. Comprehensive and intensive analyses by several experts on the widely varying UN missions of the first half of the 1990s. Includes detailed examination of operations in Cambodia, Mozambique, El Salvador, Angola, Somalia, Rwanda, Croatia, and Bosnia.

Feil, Scott R. *Preventing Genocide: How Early Use of Force Might Have Succeeded in Rwanda*. New York: Carnegie Corporation of New York, 1998. A Report to the Carnegie Commission on Preventing Deadly Conflict, April 1998. A report that analyzes the causes of the Rwandan genocide and the regional destabilization that occurred at that time. By discussing the problems that the UN faced in the Great Lakes region, the report attempts to outline what steps could have been taken in order to prevent the genocide.

Feld Werner J., et al., *International Organizations: A Comparative Approach*. Westport, Conn.: Praeger, 1994. Compares the UN and the UN specialized agencies with other international organizations.

Fielding, Lois E. *Maritime Interception and UN Sanctions: Resolving Issues in the Persian Gulf War, The Conflict in the Former Yugoslavia, and the Haiti Crisis*. San Francisco: Austin & Winfield, Publishers, 1997. Studies maritime law and incidents, pays particular attention to the Persian Gulf War, the arms embargo and interceptions in the former Yugoslavia, and U.S. actions to uphold maritime law in the Haiti crisis. Concludes that the end of the Cold War resulted in a changed international climate, where maritime law was upheld to prevent conflict and bolster international agreements.

Fishel, John T., ed. *The Savage Wars of Peace: Toward a New Paradigm of Peace Operations*. Boulder, Colo.: Westview Press, 1999. Perspectives of U.S. military experts on the changing nature of peacekeeping and the future U.S. role.

Findlay, Trevor. *Cambodia: The Legacy and Lessons of UNTAC*. Oxford: Oxford University Press, 1995. An intensive analysis of the UNTAC mission in Cambodia and its various functions.

From Nairobi to Beijing: Second Review and Appraisal of the Implementation of the Nairobi Forward-Looking Strategies for the Advancement of Women. New York: United Nations Department of Public Information, 1995. Evaluation of the UN's Nairobi Forward-Looking Strategies as a guide to prepare for the 1995 Beijing Conference; recognizes the changed economic, social, and political climate for implementation. Identifies the chief issues facing women, such as poverty, barriers to education, health, violence, workplace and economic discrimination. Further identifies the progress that NGOs, governments, and the UN have encountered in addressing these problems.

Gordon, Wendell. *The United Nations at the Crossroads of Reform.* Armonk, New York: M.E. Sharpe, 1994. An overview and history of UN bodies and how the UN has addressed the problems of environment, human rights, humanitarian issues, population, and terrorism. Offers insight into decision-making in the Persian Gulf, Somalia, and Bosnia crises.

Gourevitch, Philip. *We Wish to Inform You That Tomorrow We Will be Killed with Our Families: Stories From Rwanda.* New York: Farrar, Straus, and Giroux, 1998. Tales of the Rwanda genocide and the search for an explanation. Explains how the failures of Somalia and Bosnia gave "Hutu Power" an incentive not to take UN peacekeepers seriously. Criticizes the UN for not bolstering UNAMIR when genocide began.

Gow, James. *Triumph of the Lack of Will: International Diplomacy and the Yugoslav War.* New York: Columbia University Press, 1997. Analyzes the progression of international and diplomatic involvement in the former Yugoslavia, and critiques the roles of the United States, EC/EU, West European Union, OSCE, NATO, and the UN. States that the sheer number of actors complicated crisis management and peace processes, especially because each actor was trying to predominate. Problems with the final settlement are also discussed.

Graham-Brown, Sarah. *Sanctioning Saddam: The Politics of Intervention in Iraq.* London: I.B. Tauris, 1999. Focuses on the humanitarian catastrophe caused by economic sanctions against Iraq and by Saddam Hussein's policies since the Gulf War and on aid programs that have attempted to alleviate Iraqi suffering. Covers a range of issues, including the protection of the Kurds and UNSCOM.

Gregg, Robert W. *About Face? The United Nations and the United States.* Boulder, Colo.: Lynne Rienner, 1993. Analysis of the reversal of U.S. policy toward the UN from hostility in the 1980s to enthusiasm in the early 1990s.

Haass, Richard. *Intervention: The Use of American Military Force in the Post-Cold War World.* Washington, D.C.: The Carnegie Endowment for International Peace, 1994. Analysis by a former national security advisor to President Bush on U.S. intervention, stemming from experiences in policy making during the Gulf War, Somalia, and Bosnia. Urges caution in using U.S. military.

Hall, Margaret and Tom Young. *Confronting Leviathan: Mozambique Since Independence*. London: Hurst & Company, 1997. Analyzes the issues facing Mozambique from independence and the actors in the civil war, Frelimo and Renamo, and their ideologies. Assesses the accomplishment of ONUMOZ as a successful peacekeeping mission following the problems in Angola and Somalia.

Haselkorn, Avigdor. *The Continuing Storm: Iraq, Poisonous Weapons, and Deterrence*. New Haven, Conn.: Yale University Press, 1999. Focuses on Iraqi chemical and biological weapons programs and attempts by UNSCOM to eliminate them.

Hoffmann, Stanley. *The Ethics and Politics of Humanitarian Intervention*. Notre Dame, Ind.: University of Notre Dame Press, 1996. Evaluates the policies that govern interventions for humanitarian reasons, with particular focus on UNRPOFOR in the former Yugoslavia. Appendix includes summaries of peacekeeping operations with humanitarian components that have occurred since 1990.

Holbrooke, Richard. *To End A War*. New York: Random House, 1998. Memoir of the diplomat who was most responsible for brokering the 1995 Dayton Peace Accords. Holbrooke writes critically of the Bush administration for failing to intervene in Bosnia, "the greatest collective security failure of the West since the 1930s," and of the UN under Boutros-Ghali that placed excessively tight constraints on using force. Holbrooke claims that any UN role in the Dayton Accords would have complicated negotiations and concludes that NATO, not the UN, was the appropriate agency to deal with civil war in the former Yugoslavia.

Hume, Cameron. *Ending Mozambique's War: The Role of Mediation and Good Offices*. Washington, D.C.: United States Institute of Peace, 1994. Analysis of peacemaking efforts to end the war in Mozambique, including the crucial role of NGOs.

Jett, Dennis C. *Why Peacekeeping Fails*. New York: St. Martin's Press, 1999. Former U.S. ambassador to Mozambique uses his personal experiences at peacemaking and peacekeeping to explain why certain missions, such as ONUMOZ in Mozambique, succeed, while others, including UNAVEM II and III in Angola, fail. The political will of the United States and other Security Council members is the most important determinant.

Keane, Fergal. *Seasons of Blood: A Rwandan Journey*. London: Viking, 1995. Uses personal accounts to describe political turmoil and genocide in Rwanda and the failure of the UN. Features a chronology of the genocide.

Kressel, Neil Jeffery. *Mass Hate: The Global Rise of Genocide and Terror*. New York: Plenum Press, 1996. Focuses on socio-political factors behind genocide, with chapters on Bosnia and Rwanda, analyzing the psychosocial causes and consequences of the conflicts in these states. Historical references and personal accounts track the emergence of conflicts in Bosnia and Rwanda.

Kumar, Chetan. *Building Peace in Haiti*. Boulder, Colo.: Lynne Rienner, 1998. Focuses on peace building schemes by the UN and other organizations in Haiti after the restoration of President Aristide in 1994 and explains their difficulties in terms of the country's history and appalling poverty.

Levy, Peter B. *Encyclopedia of the Reagan-Bush Years*. Westport, Conn.: Greenwood Press, 1996. Includes description of Bush administration decisions regarding the Gulf War, Bosnia, and Somalia.

Makinda, Samuel. *Seeking Peace from Chaos*. Boulder, Colo.: Lynne Rienner, 1993, 63. Analysis of peacemaking and humanitarian intervention to resolve the Somalia crisis.

Mayall, James, ed. *The New Interventionism 1991-1994: United Nations Experience in Cambodia, Former Yugoslavia, and Somalia*. Cambridge, U.K.: Cambridge University Press, 1996. Challenges the idea that peacekeeping is accomplished with fewer complications after the Cold War. Cases of Cambodia, Yugoslavia, and Somalia are used to illustrate how each potential peacekeeping operation addressed different causes that required a variety of solutions that hampered cooperation and implementation.

McConnell, Fiona. *The Biodiversity Convention: A Negotiating History*. London: Kluwer Law International, 1996. Documents the negotiations that led up to the 1992 "Earth Summit" in Rio. Later chapters discuss how the Rio Plan has been implemented. Annexes include UNEP documents and the text of the UN Convention on Biodiversity.

Mestrovic, Stjepan G. (editor). *Genocide After Emotion: The Post-emotional Balkan War*. London: Routledge, 1996. Chapters on the conflicts in the Balkans, 1991-1995, which analyze the causes and players in the conflicts, the failure of the international system to prevent tragedy, and suggestions for ways that the conflict could have been resolved. Chapters are critical of UNPROFOR and Western governments for their inaction during the fighting and of the UN as a negotiator.

Mingst, Karen A. and Margaret P. Karns. *The United Nations in the Post-Cold War Era*. Second Edition. Boulder, Colo.: Westview Press, 2000. Tracks the evolution of the UN and the trends in international cooperation in the post-Cold War era. Analyzes the changed role of state and non-state actors in the UN system, the changed dynamics of peacekeeping, the UN's progress on sustainable development issues (the Rio, Beijing, and Cairo conferences), to reforms of the UN institutions (Secretariat, Security Council, General Assembly, specialized agencies and NGOs).

Muldoon, James P., et al., eds. *Multilateral Diplomacy and the United Nations Today*. Boulder, Colo.: Westview Press, 1999. Covers a wide range of issues that the UN faces and the various diplomatic approaches in addressing them.

Osborn, Derek and Tom Bigg. *Earth Summit II: Outcomes and Analysis*. London: Earthscan, 1998. Analyzes the progress that had been made from the 1992 Rio Earth Summit to the 1997 review conference in New York, Earth Summit II.

Pavkovic, Aleksandar. *The Fragmentation of Yugoslavia: Nationalism in a Multinational State*. New York: St. Martin's Press, 1997. Traces the origin of national identities in Yugoslavia and subsequent state disintegration. Details the involvement of foreign powers and the UN in the Balkan Wars of the 1990s. The author criticizes the role of "outsiders" and remains pessimistic about prospects for peace.

Peck, Connie. *The United Nations as a Dispute Settlement System: Improving Mechanisms for the Prevention and Resolution of Conflict*. The Hague: Kluwer Law International, 1996. Studies various aspects of preventive diplomacy by the UN and examines the UN's struggle to carry out interventions in an era of greater need for such interventions, in spite of a lack of member support or independent resources. Proposals include an expanded UN Secretariat, expanded jurisdiction for the ICJ, and increased monetary resources for the UN.

Powell, Colin. *My American Journey*. New York: Random House, 1995. Includes an account of Bush administration decision making before the 1992 U.S. intervention in Somalia.

Ramet, Sabrina P. *Balkan Babel: The Disintegration of Yugoslavia for the Death of Tito to Ethnic War*. Boulder, Colo.: Westview Press, 1996. Addresses the problems of different ethnic groups and political practices in Eastern Europe in the post-Cold War period and their relation to issues that have created conflict in the region throughout this century. Economics, security, sovereignty, and the peripheries of war are analyzed. Discusses the intervention of UNPROFOR and other peacekeeping forces from 1992 to 1995.

Ramsbotham, Oliver and Tom Woodhouse. *Humanitarian Intervention in Contemporary Conflict.* Cambridge, Mass.: Polity Press, 1996. Discusses the nature of humanitarian interventions, and the evolution of the UN's role in carrying out these interventions. Examines Cold War norms concerning interventions, the recapitulation and re-conceptualization of these norms in the post-Cold War era, and how these norms were applied in Iraq, Bosnia, and Somalia. Concludes that, in the post-Cold War era, there is a wide range of options to explore concerning interventions and the degree of intervention to be adopted.

Ratner, Steven R. *The New UN Peacekeeping: Building Peace in Lands of Conflict after the Cold War.* New York: St. Martin's Press, 1996. Intensively describes UNTAC mission in Cambodia and analyzes UN operations in the first half of the 1990s.

Ridgeway, James, ed. *The Haiti Files: Decoding the Crisis.* Washington, D.C.: Essential Books/Azul Editions, 1994. Chapters and documents about the uniqueness of Haiti, its history, and institutions of power. The chapter on the crisis details the restoration of Aristide by the United States, UN, and OAS. The book is highly critical of U.S. reluctance to intervene in Haiti to restore President Aristide. Contains a chronology from October 5, 1990, to May 11, 1994.

Righter, Rosemary. *Utopia Lost: The United Nations and the World Order.* New York: Twentieth Century Fund Press, 1995. A constructively critical and comprehensive analysis of the UN since 1945, with a special focus on the post-Cold War era. Argues that the UN must adapt to extra-national and sub-national movements that have become central to contemporary international politics. Criticizes UN specialized agencies but acknowledges their potential to deal with complex international problems.

Ritter, Scott. *Endgame: Solving the Iraq Problem.* New York: Simon and Schuster, 1999. Idiosyncratic account by an insider of UNSCOM's efforts to end Iraq's weapons of mass destruction programs. Reveals UNSCOM's reliance on Israeli and U.S. intelligence sources.

Roht-Arriaza, Naomi, ed. *Impunity and Human Rights in International Law and Practice.* New York: Oxford University Press, 1995. Evaluates the degree to which human rights violations are pursued once stability and democracy take hold in a given country. Concludes that action by new governments can take a variety of courses in dealing with the abusers in the previous regime. Some degree of recognition of the past is necessary to heal those wounds and create a legitimate/stable new government. The cases of South Africa, Haiti, Cambodia are evaluated, as well as UN involvement.

Rotberg, Robert I., ed. *Vigilance and Vengeance: NGOs Preventing Ethnic Conflict in Divided Societies.* Washington, D.C.: Brookings Institution Press, 1996. Case studies of human rights NGOs providing early warning of ethnic conflicts and their role in resolving conflicts. Cases include Rwanda, Burundi, and the former Yugoslavia.

Sahnoun, Mohamed. *Somalia: The Missed Opportunities.* Washington, D.C.: U.S. Institute for Peace, 1994. The Special Representative of the Secretary-General to Somalia in 1992 describes his efforts to negotiate an end to the Somalia civil war and his struggles with Boutros-Ghali that led to his dismissal.

Sellers, Mortimer, ed. *The New World Order: Sovereignty, Human Rights, and the Self-Determination of Peoples.* Oxford: Berg, 1996. Examines the conflicting principles of sovereignty and self-determination that the UN has had to contend with, especially since the end of the Cold War. Chapters seek to identify a model of international cooperation that would allow the UN to function effectively, while protecting these two conflicting, yet important ideals.

Silber, Laura and Allan Little. *Yugoslavia: Death of a Nation.* New York: Penguin Books, 1997. Examines the disintegration of Yugoslavia from a multi-ethnic state to a war zone and analyzes the rise of Slobodan Milosevic and his exploitation of Serb nationalism. Analysis of Bosnia from 1992 to 1994 looks at NATO and UNPROFOR interventions and their shortcomings. The author blames the EU, NATO, and the UN for the bungled ending of the Bosnian conflict in 1995 before the Dayton Peace Accords.

Simons, Geoff. *The Scourging of Iraq: Sanctions, Law and Natural Justice.* 2nd ed. New York: St. Martin's Press, 1998. A critical view of U.S. support for UN sanctions against Iraq based on the high humanitarian costs. Provides a chronology of the various sanctions placed on Iraq. Examines the results of the Gulf War, the effect of the sanctions on Iraqis and an overall evaluation of sanctions as a weapon against regimes. Appendices include Security Council resolutions on Iraq and other related documents.

Singer, Max and Aaron Wildavsky. *The Real World Order: Zones of Peace, Zones of Turmoil.* 2nd ed. Chatham, N.J.: Chatham House Publishers, 1996. A theoretical view of the post-Cold War world, including the UN, which identifies crucial issues such as democratization, nuclear weapons, the future of the former Soviet Union, and the threat of regionalization. Examines the policies of world powers towards democracy and peace and the results of these policies.

Synge, Richard. *Mozambique: UN Peacekeeping in Action, 1992-1994.* Washington, D.C.: United States Institute of Peace, 1997. An intensive analysis of the success scored by ONUMOZ in Mozambique in demobilizing the warring parties and supervising the transition to multiparty democracy.

Stotzky, Irwin P. *Silencing the Guns in Haiti: The Promise of Deliberate Democracy.* Chicago: University of Chicago Press, 1997. Historical analysis of Haiti's government since the Duvalier period, focusing on the period in the 1990s when Aristide was ousted by a coup and restored to power by the UN. Takes both a theoretical and "bottom-up" view of the restoration of democracy.

Stremlau, John. *People in Peril: Human Rights, Humanitarian Action, and Preventing Deadly Conflict.* Washington, D.C.: A Report to the Carnegie Commission on Preventing Deadly Conflict, May 1998. Addresses how the rise of civil conflicts challenges the traditional diplomatic routes to peace. Increasing humanitarian emergencies affect the international system because of refugee problems, humanitarian concerns, and regional instability. The report focuses on the internal factors, such as lack of development, democracy, and human rights, which trigger internal conflicts. The external factors such as refugee management, international cooperation in interventions, and challenges to humanitarian assistance are also discussed in the case studies of Iraq, Rwanda, Bosnia, and Somalia.

Trevan, Tim. *Saddam's Secrets: The Hunt for Iraq's Hidden Weapons.* London: HarperCollins Publishers, 1999. Former advisor to and spokesman for UNSCOM, 1992-95, focuses on the search for and discovery of Iraq's highly secret biological weapons program.

———. *Sharpening International Sanctions: Toward A Stronger Role for the United Nations.* Washington, D.C.: A Report to the Carnegie Commission on Preventing Deadly Conflict, November 1996. Concerned with the changing nature and proliferation of sanctions by the United Nations, especially in the period of 1990 to 1994. By examining the increased use of sanctions, expanded reasons for imposing sanctions, and an evaluation of the effectiveness of sanctions, the report concludes that the UN should reform its sanctions regime.

Tomuschat, Christian, ed. *The United Nations at Age Fifty: A Legal Perspective.* The Hague: Kluwer Law International, 1995. Chapters present the perspective of scholars from all parts of the world on the future of the UN. Peace and security issues (NPT, peacekeeping operations), human rights (Vienna Conference), international law and agreements (Rio Conference), and international economy (UNCTAD, UNESCO, WTO, and ECOSOC) are addressed.

The United Nations and . . . (UN Blue Book Series). New York: United Nations: Department of Public Information. The Blue Book Series reviews crucial issues and events, which involved the UN. Volume I covers the campaign to end apartheid in South Africa through sanctions and public relations and the UN's facilitation of a stable transition to a post-apartheid government. Volume II explains UNTAC's role in resolving Cambodia's protracted conflict. Volume III tracks nuclear non-proliferation efforts, including the promulgation of the Non-Proliferation Treaty and the indefinite extension of the Treaty, secured in 1995. Volume IV covers the role of ONUSAL, from 1991 to 1995, in resolving the long-running conflict in El Salvador. Volume V examines the history of Mozambique's problems, and how UN bodies and UNOMOZ attempted to address them, from 1992 to 1995. Volume VI (revised edition) details the UN's efforts to address women's rights issues at the 1995 Beijing Conference. Volume VII covers the UN's efforts to protect human rights, with documents and analysis from the 1948 Universal Declaration of Human Rights spanning to the Vienna World Conference on Human Rights in 1993. Volume IX focuses on the response of the United Nations and its member states to Iraq's aggression against its neighbors from 1990 to 1996. Each volume has a chronology and contains original UN documents.

Weiss, Thomas G. *Military-Civilian Interventions.* Lanham: Rowman & Littlefield, 1999. Analyzes the interactions between military peacekeepers and civilian officials from NGOs and the UN during the complex operations of the 1990s.

Weiss, Thomas G. and David P. Forsythe and Roger A. Coate. *The United Nations and Changing World Politics.* 2nd ed. Boulder, Colo.: Westview Press, 1997 Analysis of the UN's history, international law, and power relationships which determine the UN's role in the post-Cold War era. Chapters on UN peacekeeping, human rights, humanitarian intervention, sustainable development programs, and proposals for reforming these programs.

Weiss, Thomas G. and Leon Gordenker, eds. *NGOs, The UN, and Global Governance.* Boulder, Colo.: Lynne Rienner Publishers, 1996. Chapters on the 1995 UN Beijing Women's Conference, the 1992 UN Rio Conference, and the 1993 UN Vienna Conference. Analyzes UN and NGO efforts to address conference issues and to emerge with plans of action and stresses the dependence of NGO's on the UN and member states to implement NGO policies.

Xhudo, Gazmen. *Diplomacy and Crisis Management in the Balkans: A U.S. Foreign Policy Perspective.* New York: St. Martin's Press, 1996. Analysis of U.S. interests and actions in the Balkans, focuses on the failure of the United States and the UN to create a coherent policy to prevent, contain, and resolve Balkan conflicts in the early 1990s.

Zartman, I. William, ed. *Collapsed States: The Disintegration and Restoration of Legitimate Authority.* Boulder, Colo.: Lynne Rienner Publishers, 1995. Chapters describe interventions to prevent state collapses, including the UN's role in Somalia and the eventual failure of UNOSOM II. Chapter on Liberia demonstrates how the UN was willing to accede to a regional organization's intervention, especially after Somalia, and questions the UN's role in rebuilding the country. State reconstruction chapter suggests that the UN should only become involved in conflicts if they have pure motives and only after attempts by local actors fail.

————, ed. *Elusive Peace: Negotiating an End to Civil Wars.* Washington, D.C.: Brookings Institution, 1995. Chapters on negotiations which included the UN and that ended conflicts in Angola and Mozambique. Concludes that internal conflicts are complicated matters, and only through a desire by both sides to negotiate and proper handling of the negotiations can lasting solutions be found.

Periodical Articles

Annan, Kofi. "From the Secretary-General: Let Us Embark on a Time of Healing." *UN Chronicle* Vol. 33, Issue 3, 1996, 1-3. Annan's appeal for unity after his election as secretary-general.

Barnes, Fred. "Last Call," *New Republic.* December 28, 1992, 10-12. Account of the inner workings of the Bush administration in deciding to act to stop famine in Somalia and launch Operation Restore Hope.

Boutros-Ghali, Boutros. "Global Leadership after the Cold War." *Foreign Affairs.* 75, 2, March/April 1996, 86-98. Boutros-Ghali's vision for his proposed second term as secretary-general.

Boyer, Peter J. "Scott Ritter's Private War." *The New Yorker.* November 9, 1998. A biographical sketch of the former chief weapons inspector of UNSCOM, details Ritter's contention that Iraq moved weapons of mass destruction from site to site in "a brilliantly executed game of hide-and-seek."

Burkhalter, Holly. "A Preventable Horror?" *Africa Report.* November-December 1994, 18-20. Details the various actions that could have been taken to stop genocide in Rwanda.

Des Forges, Allison. "Burundi: Failed Coup or Creeping Coup?" *Current History.* May 1994, 206-7. Written by an expert on genocide in Burundi and Rwanda, describes the role of the Burundian military in deposing the elected government and in mass killings.

Eban, Abba. "The UN Idea Revisited." *Foreign Affairs.* 74. September/October 1995. Prominent Israeli statesman criticizes the UN for not providing collective security or contributing any "additional technique to the repertoire of diplomacy." Contends that the P-5 veto means that no action can be taken against a major power. Argues that many diplomatic breakthroughs have occurred without the UN, including the Israelis and Palestinians and in Northern Ireland. Claims that UN peacekeeping has been tarnished by failures in Somalia and Bosnia.

Helms, Jesse. "Boutros Boutros-Ghali Dreams of UN Sovereignty," *Human Events.* March 15, 1996, 14. Helms' rejoinder to Boutros-Ghali's 1996 *Foreign Affairs* article, calling for alternative sources of funding for the UN.

Helms, Jesse. "Saving the UN" *Foreign Affairs* 75. September/October 1996. Senator Helms justifies his "hard line" towards the UN and argues that the UN failed under Boutros-Ghali because it expanded its scope in peacekeeping missions and had a "bloated bureaucracy". He argues that the UN should only be involved in peacekeeping to enforce settlements. Helms believes that it is absurd for the UN to play an active role in meeting "the needs of 5.5 billion people"; instead state and local governments should bear responsibility. He presents a radical plan to reform the UN and replace it with a "league of democracies."

"Highest Ranking U.S. Official at the UN Resigns." *Africa Report.* March/April 1994, 10-11. Account of Melissa Wells' efforts to reform the UN bureaucracy and her conflict with Boutros-Ghali.

Ignatieff, Michael. "Alone With the Secretary-General." *The New Yorker.* August 14, 1995. A journalist's account of travels with Boutros-Ghali in Africa. The secretary-general contends that the situation in Africa, the former Yugoslavia and elsewhere would be far worse without the UN. After a period of considerable bloodshed in the former Yugoslavia, including the Srebenica massacre, Ignatieff is critical of Boutros-Ghali for remaining neutral in conflicts with clear aggressors and victims and for being uncaring.

Lind, Michael. "Albatross." *The New Republic.* June 28, 1993. A critical look at Boutros-Ghali's first year-and-a-half as secretary-general, argues that the UN had suffered one embarrassment after another. Lind criticizes Boutros-Ghali for remaining neutral during conflicts, especially the ethnic cleansing in Bosnia, which helped provide legitimacy to violent authoritarian leaders. Lind rejects Boutros-Ghali's desire to expand the powers of secretary-general to include a "commander-in-chief" role.

Malone, David. "Haiti and the International Community: A Case Study." *Survival.* Vol. 39, No. 2 (Summer 1997), 126-46. Analysis of the slowly developing struggle by the OAS, UN, and United States to help President Aristide to restore democracy to Haiti.

Picco, Giandomenico. "The UN and the Use of Force: Leaving the Secretary-General Out of It." *Foreign Affairs.* 73. September/ October 1993. A former Special Representative of Secretary-General Pérez de Cuéllar argues that the secretary-general should remain an important figure in UN-led diplomacy but should be limited in authorizing the use of force. The success of the UN, led by the United States and the Security Council, in ousting Iraq from Kuwait is cited as a model for the use of force.

Rieff, David. "The Bill Clinton of the UN." *The New Republic.* August 5, 1996. Written shortly after President Clinton announced the U.S. intention to veto Boutros-Ghali's second term, argues that the decision resulted from Boutros-Ghali's efforts to please every permanent member (P-5) on the Security Council, including Russia and China. Rieff likens Boutros-Ghali to Clinton, because both were willing to compromise core beliefs in exchange for consensus. In response to the Rwandan genocide, Boutros-Ghali wanted to do the minimum because of disagreement among the P-5. Rieff concluded that Boutros-Ghali remained reluctant to take any blame for UN failures and believed that the "system" let the UN down, not vice versa.

"The Scapegoat." *Economist.* November 23, 1996, 47. Describes the Clinton administration's campaign to remove Boutros-Ghali as secretary-general after Clinton's reelection.

Williams, Ian. "Boutros-Ghali Bites Back." *Nation.* June 14, 1999, 63. A review of Boutros-Ghali's *Unvanquished* and his case against the Clinton administration from 1993-96.

Newspaper Articles

Booth, William. "Aristide at Meeting, Renews Appeal for Haitian

Democracy." *Washington Post.* January 16, 1994, A20.

Branigin, William. "UN: 50 Years Fending off WWIII." *Washington Post.* June 25, 1995, A1.

"Clinton Gives Annan 'Credit' for Iraqi Deal: UN Chief Presses U.S. to Pay $1.2 Billion in Dues it Owes." *Washington Post.* March 12, 1998, A23.

Crossette, Barbara. "UN Chief Chides Security Council on Military Missions." *New York Times.* January 6, 1995, 3.

William Drodziak. "Rich, Poor Meet at Summit, and then Go Their Separate Ways," *Washington Post.* March 12, 1995.

"Finding a New UN Chief." *New York Times.* June 23, 1996, A30.

"Foreign Policy Coup." *Washington Post.* May 24, 1995, A24.

Gordon, Michael R. "Somali Aid Plan is Called Most Ambitious Option." *New York Times.* November 28, 1992, A6.

Goshko, John M. "UN's Normal Decorous Diplomatic Discourse Takes Beating in Dispute." *Washington Post.* December 16, 1995, A30.

Grier, Peter. "U.S. Feud with UN Runs Deep." *Christian Science Monitor.* November 21, 1996, 1.

Hall, Brian. "World's Cops, Kicked Around." *New York Times.* January 2, 1994, Section 6, 23-24.

Kamen, Al. "Resurrection." *Washington Post.* September 6, 1995, A19.

Kenworthy, Tom. "Treaty on Biological Diversity Offers Possibility of Breakthrough." *Washington Post.* June 1, 1992, A15.

Lancaster, John. "Population conference Tests Egypt's Rulers: Mubarak Seeks to Show Country's Stability, But Islamic Groups Threaten Protests, Attacks." *Washington Post.* September 3, 1994, A13.

Lancaster, John. "Vatican Supports Abortion Wording: Population Debate Moves Ahead, But Issue Could Resurface." *Washington Post.* September 10, 1994, A16.

Lippman, Thomas W. "UN Decision Cuts 2 Ways for Clinton: Boutros-Ghali Retains Much Support Abroad." *Washington Post.* June 21, 1996, A25.

Mufson, Steven. "Vatican Will Not Contest Language on Abortion." *Washington Post.* September 8, 1995, A28.

Ottaway, David B. "Universality of Rights Defended by U.S.: Protest over Dalai Lama Mars Vienna Talks." *Washington Post.* June 15, 1993, A15.

Ottaway, David B. "Rights Assembly Demands Action on Bosnia 'Genocide.'" *Washington Post.* June 25, 1993, A31.

"Remembering Rwanda." *Christian Science Monitor.* May 12, 1998, 12.

Rensberger, Boyce and John Lancaster. "Vatican Abortion Stance Riles

Many at Forum." *Washington Post.* September 8, 1994, A30.

Sciolino, Elaine. "Madeline Albright's Audition." *The New York Times Magazine.* September 22, 1996, 44-47.

Traub, James. "Kofi Annan's Next Test." *New York Times Magazine.* March 29, 1998, 46-49, 74.

Weisskopf, Michael. "Climate Treaty Offers View of President's Role in Complex Policy." *Washington Post.* October 31, 1992, A01.

Documents

The 1997 State of the Union Address of President William J. Clinton, February 4, 1997. The University of Oklahoma Law Center, <http://www.law. ou.edu/hist/state97.html>.

Herman J. Cohen, "Update on Operation Restore Hope." U.S. Department of State Dispatch, December 21, 1992.

Decision 7 taken by the Governing Council of the United Nations Compensation Commission: Criteria for additional categories of claims. S/AC.26/1991/7/Rev.1, March 17, 1992.

Gorbachev, Mikhail. "The Realities and Guarantees of a Security World." (New York: USSR Mission to the United Nations Press Release No. 119, September 17, 1987).

"A Note on the Financial Crisis." <www.un.org/Depts/dpko/dpko/intro/finance.htm> United Nations Website.

Report of the Panel on United Nations Peace Operations. UN Document A/55/305, S/2000/89, August 17, 2000.

Report of the Secretary-General on Mozambique. S/1994/511, April 28, 1994.

Report of the Secretary-General on the Return of Kuwaiti Property Seized by Iraq. S/1994/243, March 2, 1994.

Report of the Secretary-General on the United Nations Assistance Mission for Rwanda. S/1994/470, April 20, 1994.

Reports of the Secretary-General on the United Nations Observer Mission to El Salvador. S/1994/179, February 16, 1994, S/1994/304, March 16, 1994, S/1994/375, March 31, 1994.

"The September 1992 Elections." in *History of Angola: Virtual Tour.* <http://www.angola.org/> Angolan Government Web site.

Statement by the President of the Security Council concerning Iraq's compliance with the relevant council resolutions. S/24839, November 24, 1992.

Statement by the President of the Security Council concerning the Iraq-Kuwait Boundary Demarcation Commission. S/26006, June 28, 1993.

Statement by the President of the Security Council concerning the murder of a member of the United Nations Guards Contingent in Iraq on July 16. S/24309, July 17, 1992

Statement by the President of the Security Council concerning the sanctions regime imposed against Iraq and humanitarian conditions of the civilian population in Iraq. S/23305, December 20, 1991.

Statement by the President of the Security Council concerning UNSCOM's special mission to Baghdad, February 21-24, 1992, and Iraq's compliance with relevant Security Council Resolutions. S/23663, February 28, 1992.

"Supplement to An Agenda for Peace: Position Paper of the Secretary-General on the Occasion of the Fiftieth Anniversary of the United Nations." A/50/60, S/1995/1.

Third Report of the Executive Chairman of UNSCOM. S/24108, June 16, 1992.

UN Security Council Resolution 479, September 28, 1980. (Iraq-Iran)
UN Security Council Resolution 660, August 2, 1990. (Iraq-Kuwait)
UN Security Council Resolution 661, August 6, 1990. (Iraq-Kuwait)
UN Security Council Resolution 662, August 9, 1990. (Iraq-Kuwait)
UN Security Council Resolution 665, August 25, 1990. (Iraq-Kuwait)
UN Security Council Resolution 678, November 29, 1990. (Iraq-Kuwait)
UN Security Council Resolution 687, April 3, 1991. (Iraq)
UN Security Council Resolution 688, April 5, 1991. (Iraq)
UN Security Council Resolution 693, May 20, 1991. (El Salvador)
UN Security Council Resolution 696, May 30, 1991. (Angola)
UN Security Council Resolution 713, September 25, 1991. (Yugoslavia)
UN Security Council Resolution 715, October 11, 1991. (Iraq)
UN Security Council Resolution 729, January 14, 1992. (El Salvador)
UN Security Council Resolution 733, January 23, 1992. (Somalia)
UN Security Council Resolution 745, February 28, 1992. (Cambodia)
UN Security Council Resolution 747, March 24, 1992. (Angola)
UN Security Council Resolution 767, July 24, 1992. (Somalia)
UN Security Council Resolution 770, August 13, 1992. (Bosnia)
UN Security Council Resolution 776, September 14, 1992. (Bosnia)
UN Security Council Resolution 780, October 6, 1992 (war crimes tribunal for the former Yugoslavia)
UN Security Council Resolution 781, October 9, 1992. (Bosnia)
UN Security Council Resolution 783, October 13, 1992. (Cambodia)
UN Security Council Resolution 797, December 16, 1992. (Mozambique)
UN Security Council Resolution 808, February 22, 1993. (Bosnia)
UN Security Council Resolution 806, February 5, 1993. (Iraq)

UN Security Council Resolution 814, March 26, 1993. (Somalia)
UN Security Council Resolution 810, March 8, 1993. (Cambodia)
UN Security Council Resolution 819, April 16, 1993. (Bosnia)
UN Security Council Resolution 827, May 25, 1993. (Bosnia and war crimes tribunal for the former Yugoslavia)
UN Security Council Resolution 832, May 27, 1993. (El Salvador)
UN Security Council Resolution 833, May 27, 1993. (Iraq)
UN Security Council Resolution 837, June 6, 1993. (Somalia)
UN Security Council Resolution 863, September 13, 1993. (Mozambique)
UN Security Council Resolution 875, October 16, 1993. (Haiti)
UN Security Council Resolution 882, November 5, 1993. (Mozambique)
UN Security Council Resolution 885, November 16, 1993. (Somalia)
UN Security Council Resolution 899, March 4, 1994. (Iraq)
UN Security Council Resolution 912, April 21, 1994. (Rwanda)
UN Security Council Resolution 916, May 5, 1994. (Mozambique)
UN Security Council Resolution 917, May 6, 1994. (Haiti)
UN Security Council Resolution 918, May 17, 1994. (Rwanda)
UN Security Council Resolution 920, May 26, 1994. (El Salvador)
UN Security Council Resolution 929, June 22, 1994. (Rwanda)
UN Security Council Resolution 940, July 31, 1994. (Haiti)
UN Security Council Resolution 949, October 15, 1994. (Iraq)
UN Security Council Resolution 955, November 8, 1994. (war crimes tribunal for Rwanda)
UN Security Council Resolution 961, November 23, 1994. (El Salvador)
UN Security Council Resolution 976, February 8, 1995. (Angola)
UN Security Council Resolution 986, April 14, 1995. (Iraq)
UN Security Council Resolution 1063, June 28, 1996. (Haiti)
UN Security Council Resolution 1075, October 11, 1996. (Angola)
UN Security Council Resolution 1078, November 9, 1996. (Zaire)
UN Security Council Resolution 1118, June 30, 1997. (Angola)
UN Security Council Resolution 1123, July 30, 1997. (Haiti)

Index

Abkhazia, 28
Afghanistan, 192n
Africa, 2, 7, 107, 170, 179-80, 208
African National Congress of South Africa (ANC), 28
African Great Lakes, 110, 113
African states, 187-89
Alianza Republica Nacionalista (ARENA), 45
An Agenda for Development, 14-16, 59, 142
An Agenda for Democratization, 190
An Agenda for Peace, xvi, 2, 4, 8-12, 14, 16, 55, 71, 76, 142, 178, 183-84, 196-97, 199-200
Agenda 21, 145-50, 158
Aideed, Mohamed Farah, 68, 74-75, 77, 179
Ajello, Aldo, 31, 36
Akashi, Yasushi, 13, 22-26, 28, 36, 94-95
Albright, Madeleine, 106, 179, 183, 185-86, 188-89, 191, 207-8
Amnesty International, 15, 152
Angola, xvi, 4-5, 28, 31-32, 60-67, 77, 81, 110; and Portugal, 61

Annan, Kofi, 100-101, 106, 110, 135, 137-38, 180, 185-86, 189-91, 201, 204-9
Anstee, Margaret Joan, 63
Arab League, 187
Arab states, 7
Argentina, 50, 54, 192n
Aristide, Jean-Bertrand, 48-55
arms control, xvii, 117, 139
arms embargo, 50-51, 68, 85, 93-94, 182
Asia, 2, 166, 208
Asian values, 151
Association of Southeast Asian Nations (ASEAN), 21, 24
assertive multilateralism, 13, 17, 73-74, 76, 114, 174, 176-77, 181, 184, 188, 197-99, 203
Australia, 21, 25
Austria, 117
Ayala Lasso, Jose, 155

Baker, James, 41
Bangladesh, 31, 103, 163
basic needs, 147, 162
Beijing Women's Conference (1995), xvii-xix, 16, 162, 165-70, 206
Belgium, 70-71; and Rwanda, 97, 102

biological weapons, 117, 119-
22, 125-26, 130-33, 135,
137, 139
Blair, Tony, 205
Bosnia-Herzegovina, xv-xvii,
13-15, 60,73, 77-78, 81-82,
84, 86-97, 112-14, 142, 154,
157, 168, 173, 177-80, 182,
184-85, 188-91, 195, 197-
99, 203, 205, 209
Bosnian Croats, 88, 92-95
Bosnian Serbs, 12-13, 15, 61,
88-97, 112, 178-79, 182-84,
203
Bosnian Muslims, 13, 88-91,
94-96, 153
Boutros-Ghali, Boutros, xv-
xvii, 1, 4, 7-8, 10, 12-14, 16,
20, 55, 59, 62-63, 78, 87,
107, 110, 112, 114, 117,
141-42, 169, 173-74, 177-
92, 195-204, 206, 208-9;
and Bosnia-Herzegovina,
89-90, 178-80; and Cambo-
dia, 22-23, 25-26; and Cairo
Conference, 159; and El
Salvador, 41-45; and former
Yugoslavia, 89-91, 97; and
Guatemala, 47; and Haiti,
50; and Iraq, 122, 124, 127-
28, 131-32, 136-37; and
Mozambique, 14, 30, 32;
and Vienna Conference,
154; and Somalia, 68-72,
74-78, 179; and United
States, 13, 70-72, 74-78,
174, 177-89, 197, 203
Brazil, 31, 144-45, 148
Britain. See United Kingdom
Brundtland Commission Re-
port, 145
Brundtland, Gro Harlem, 144

Burundi, 11, 82, 97, 99-100,
102, 106-8, 113, 156-57,
172n, 205
Bush, George H.W., xv, 6-8,
69-73, 76, 85, 122, 128-29,
142, 145-46, 176-77, 197
Bush, George W., 205
Bush administration (1989-93),
205-6, 208
Bush administration (2001-),
205-6, 208
Butler, Richard, 137-38

Cairo Conference on Population
and Development (1994),
xvii, 141, 158-62, 167-68
Cambodia, xvi, 1, 13, 20-28,
31-32, 36, 39-40, 47, 56, 59,
66, 94, 114, 142, 156-57,
192n, 195, 198
Canada, 10, 14, 51-54, 70-71,
100, 110, 145, 196
Caputo, Dante, 50-51, 53
Carter, Jimmy, 53, 159, 184
Carter administration, 175
Central Africa, 156
Central African Republic, 205
Central America, xvi, 39-40,
47, 114, 192n
Centre for Human Rights (UN),
57, 131
Chapter VII of UN Charter, 6,
10-11, 53, 56, 60, 71-72, 74,
91-92, 103, 105, 111, 114,
199, 205
Chapter VIII of UN Charter, 90
chemical weapons, 117-22,
124-26, 130-31, 133, 137,
139
Chidzero, Bernard, 7

China, 6, 12, 20, 24, 39, 137, 139, 152, 160, 165-66, 175, 184, 188, 192, 199, 205

Chissano, Joaquim, 28-29, 33-35

Christopher, Warren, 93, 183, 186-87

chlorofluorocarbons (CFCs), 144

civil society, 22, 46, 141-42, 145, 168

civil wars, 19, 28, 43, 61, 74, 76, 81, 89, 107, 109, 196

climate change, 146, 148

Clinton, William Jefferson, 50-53, 73-77, 106, 128, 146, 163, 174, 176-77, 183, 186, 188-91, 201, 204, 206-7

Clinton administration, xvii, 13, 17, 50, 52-53, 74-76, 78, 93, 104, 127-28, 174, 177-79, 181, 184-88, 191, 202, 204, 206-7; "lift-and-strike" plan for Bosnia of, 93

coalitions, 4, 6, 35, 118-19, 121, 208

Cold War, 2-3, 7, 9, 11, 17, 19, 28, 39-40, 82, 152-53, 163, 178, 191

collective security, xv, 2, 6, 196-97, 199

Commission on Human Rights (UN), 98, 111, 152, 156-57

Commission for Social Development (UN), 164

Commission on Sustainable Development (UN), 149-50

Commission on the Status of Women (CSW), xviii, 165-66, 169

Comprehensive Nuclear Test Ban Treaty (CTBT), 206

Conference on Security and Cooperation in Europe (CSCE), 83, 90

Congo-Brazzaville, 105

Congo-Kinshasa (DRC), 97, 109-11, 174, 196, 203, 205

Congress (U.S.), 3, 14-15, 19, 75-76, 78, 174, 181, 197, 201

Convention on Biological Diversity, 146

Convention on the Elimination of All forms of Discrimination Against Women (CEDAW), xviii, 153, 165-67, 169

Convention on the Prevention and Punishment of the Crime of Genocide, 81-82, 96, 102, 113

Convention on the Rights of the Child, 143

Croatia, xvii, 13, 15, 82-90, 93-96, 113, 184

Cuba, 5, 28, 39-40, 51, 53, 188

cultural relativism, 168

Cyprus, 59

Dallaire, Romeo A., 100-101, 103

Dayton Peace Accord, 15, 96, 112, 157, 190, 195

debt crisis, 176

democracy, 11, 39-40, 55-56, 107, 151, 190, 195

democratization, 67, 107, 153, 190, 195

development, xvi-xvii, 16, 141, 143, 145, 158-59, 162-64, 167, 171, 174-75, 190, 201-202; assistance, 2-3, 13, 54, 35, 163-64; economic, 143,

153, 162; social, 141, 162, socio-economic, 11, 15, 16, 142, 162; thinking, 145; right to, 149, 153, 155; sustainable, 16, 143-51, 166-67, 201, 209

Dhlakama, Afonso, 30-32, 34-36

diplomacy, 10, 68, 196; preventive, 9, 14, 202

disarmament, 11, 13, 22,

dispute settlement, 28

Division for the Advancement of Women (UN), xviii, 165, 169

Dole, Robert, 182-83, 187-88

dos Santos, Eduardo, 60, 64

Earth Summit. *See* Rio Conference on the Environment and Development

East, 144, 152-153

East Timor, 198, 205, 207

Eastern Europe, 83

Eastern Slavonia, 84-86, 88, 200

Economic and Social Council (ECOSOC), 161, 164-65, 169, 200

Economic Community of West African States (ECOWAS), 184; Cease-fire Monitoring Group (ECOMOG), 184, 199

Egypt, 7-8, 67-68, 76, 79n, 122, 159, 179, 189

Ekeus, Rolf, 120, 123, 125-26, 130, 137

election monitoring, 5, 19, 62-63

El Salvador, 1, 13, 20, 39-47, 56, 195; civil war in, 39-40,

43; FMLN in, 40-47; human rights in, 40-47; land transfer in, 42, 44, 45, 47; peace process in, 40-41, 56; reform of armed forces in, 42; voter registration in, 44-45; Truth Commission in, 41, 43-44, 46

embargoes, 19,

enforcement. *See* peace enforcement

environment, 15-16, 141-49, 157, 159-60, 165, 171, 195, 206; movement for the, 142-44, 158-59; protection of the, 3, 143-46, 159, 164

Ethiopia, 67, 104-5

ethnic cleansing, xvi, 7, 12, 60-61, 81-82, 85, 89-94, 96-97, 111, 113-14, 153, 155, 198, 205

ethnic conflict, 88, 113

Europe, 92-93, 97, 143-44, 157, 178-79

European organizations, 83, 90; states 3, 15, 83, 89, 173-74

Europeans, 7, 90, 97, 178, 198

European Community, 50, 83, 85

European Union, 90, 99, 151, 153, 157, 161, 187

Federal Republic of Yugoslavia, xvii, 6-7, 82-91, 93, 111, 113, 156-57, 172n, 184, 185

Framework Convention on Climate Change, 146, 148

France, 7, 24, 30, 79n, 87, 90, 92, 95, 97, 105, 110, 124, 129, 133, 136-37, 179, 184, 188-89, 198-99, 204-5

Front for an Independent, Neutral, and Cooperative Cambodia, 25-26, 36
Front for the Liberation of Mozambique (FRELIMO), 28-30, 34-35

General Assembly (UN), 2-3, 5, 7, 9-11, 13-16, 47, 50-51, 111, 118, 145, 150, 153, 155, 158, 161, 165-66, 175-76, 188-90, 196, 202, 207-8
Geneva, 92-93, 96, 152, 156; Conventions, 111; Protocol (1925), 118, 121
genocide, xvi, 1, 13-14, 20, 22, 60, 76, 78, 81-82, 96-98, 101-14, 154-55, 157, 163, 168, 180, 197, 199, 205
Georgia, 20, 157
Germany, 13, 82, 87-88, 94, 96, 117, 138-39, 161-62, 177, 200
Ghana, 105, 190
Global Environmental Facility (GEF), 148
globalism, 3, 15, 16-17, 142, 171
globalization, 171
global warming, 15, 143-49, 151, 170
good offices, 4, 10, 47
Gorbachev, Mikhail, 3-4, 61
Gore, Albert, 146, 151
Great Britain. See United Kingdom
Greenpeace, 15, 145
Group of Frontline States (GFLS), 34
Group of 77 (G-77), 2-3, 7, 14-16, 162, 175-76, 188, 196
Guatemala, 39, 47-48

Guatemalan National Revolutionary Unity (URNG), 47-48
Gulf War (1990-91), xv, 5-7, 9, 17, 69, 72, 117, 119, 176, 197

Habyarimana, Juvenal, 97-103, 105, 107
Haiti, xvi, 3, 6, 13, 20, 39, 48-56, 59, 73, 195, 197; coup in, 49-54; Governor's Island Accord and, 50-52; human rights and, 48-49, 51-55
Hammarskjöld, Dag, 202-203
Helms, Jesse, 15, 181-83, 186, 188, 202, 204, 207-8
High Commissioner for Human Rights, 155
Holbrooke, Richard, 95-96, 208
Holocaust, 81
Honduras, 44
Howe, Jonathan, 74-75
human rights, xv-xvii, 2-3, 5, 15-16, 39-40, 48, 66, 98, 101, 108, 124, 131, 136, 141-42, 151-57, 162, 164-66, 170-71, 174-75, 190, 196-96, 201, 206, 209; abuses, 9, 24, 42,-43, 49, 51, 139, 152, 156, 205; of Asian states, 151; monitoring, 22, 24, 40-41, 44-46, 50, 54-55, 156; NGOs, 104, 113, 152-53; women's rights as, 3, 151, 153, 155, 167
Human Rights Watch, 98
Hun Sen, 21-27, 36
Hussein, Saddam, 6-7, 117, 119, 124, 133-39, 195, 204

Hutu, 97-98, 100-11, 113; extremists, 97-98, 100-102, 104, 107, 109, 111-13

India, 79n, 196
indigenous peoples, 145, 147, 155, 172n
Indonesia, 203, 205
International Atomic Energy Agency (IAEA), 120-23, 125-28, 130-37
International Bank for Reconstruction and Development. *See* World Bank.
International Committee of the Red Cross (ICRC), 124
International Conference on Population and Development (ICPD). *See* Cairo Population Conference
International Covenant on Civil and Political Rights, 152
International Covenant on Economic and Social Rights, 152
International Criminal Court, xvii, 157, 206
International Criminal Investigative Training Assistance Program in Haiti (ICITAP), 54
International Criminal Tribunal for the former Yugoslavia, xvii, 111
International Criminal Tribunal for Rwanda, xvii, 111-12
International Decade for Women. *See* UN Decade for Women
International Decade of the World's Indigenous Peoples, 155

International Labor Organization (ILO), 5
international law, 6, 168, 175
International Monetary Fund (IMF), 162
International Research and Training Institute for the Advancement of Women (INSTRAW), 165
interstate conflict, 197
intervention, xv, xvii, 1, 9, 12, 84, 89-90, 104-5, 107, 110, 113, 165, 196, 198
intra-state conflicts, 197
Iran, 4, 7, 117-18, 124, 152
Iran-Iraq War, 4, 117-18, 120, 192n, 203
Iraq, xv, xvii, 4, 6-7, 62, 117-39, 187, 195, 197-99, 204-5, 207; Al Atheer-Al Hateen nuclear facility of, 125; Al Fallujah chemical facility of 130; biological weapons program of, 117, 119-22, 125-26, 130, 133, 135, 139; chemical weapons program of, 117-26, 130, 133, 137-39; and Gulf War, xv, 117, 119; nuclear weapons program of, 134-35, 119-21, 126-27; sanctions against, 6, 118-19, 122, 127-28, 132, 135-38, 199; Tarmiya-Ash Sharqat nuclear facility of, 125
Islam, 89, 94-95
Islamic states, 141, 157, 159, 167
Israel, 5, 8, 119, 122, 176, 186-87
Italy, 31-32, 79n, 83
Izetbegovic, Alija, 88-89, 93

Japan, 13, 22, 24-25, 117, 138-39, 151, 161, 177, 200
Jonah, James, 68

Karadzic, Radovan, 88-89, 112
Kashmir, 59, 196
Kassebaum Amendment, 176
Kenya, 29, 69, 112
Khmer Rouge, 20-27, 31, 35-36, 66, 77
Korea, 170
Kosovo, 11, 84, 87, 97, 114, 157, 199, 205, 207
Krajina, 84-85, 95-96, 174
Kurds, 6, 70, 117-20, 127, 136-37
Kuwait, 6, 62, 90, 117-19, 124, 126, 128-29, 131-33, 135-36, 199
Kyoto Conference on Climate Change, 151, 170, 206, 208

land mines, 22, 34, 62, 64-65, 81
Latin America, 2, 7, 41
least developed countries, 164, 170
Lebanon, 186, 192n
Liberia, 7, 15, 184, 199

Macedonia, Former Yugoslav Republic of, 6, 13, 82, 86, 89, 113, 198
Malaysia, 151
Mandela, Nelson, 28-29, 35, 108, 110, 187
Major, John, 9
Mexico, 42, 158, 165
Middle East, 6, 19, 59, 69, 149, 159, 196, 203
Military Staff Committee, 10

Milosevic, Slobodan, 7, 15, 82, 85-86, 89, 95
Mitterand, Francois, 9
Mladic, Ratko, 85, 112
Mogadishu, 67-68, 72, 75
Mohamed, Mahatir, 151
Mozambique, xvi, 1, 13, 20, 28-36, 39, 42, 46-47, 59-60, 67, 77, 99, 195, 198; Armed Forces for the Defense of (FADM), 45; civil war in, 28-29; election in, 34; General Peace Agreement (1992) in, 30; mine clearance in, 35; Nkomati Accord (1984) in, 28; peace process in, 28-30; and Portugal, 28, 30; troop demobilization in, 33; voter registration in, 32-33
Mozambique National Resistance Movement (RENAMO), 28-36, 61
multilateralism, 177, 192, 202
multinational force, 50, 53, 110

Namibia, 5, 13, 19, 29, 40, 61
New International Economic Order (NIEO), 2, 15, 162, 175
Netherlands, 14, 83, 95, 114,
new world order, xv, 5-7, 12, 17, 69, 71, 73-74, 85, 173, 176-77, 181, 191
New York, 156, 166, 170
Nicaragua, 3, 39-40, 44, 48
Nigeria, 79n, 105
no-fly zones, 92, 117, 120, 127-28, 136-37
Non-governmental organizations (NGOs), xviii, 3, 52, 68, 97-98, 103, 105, 113,

141, 159-60, 163, 170-71, 190; and the environment, 15, 144-47; forums, 16, 141-42, 145-54, 159, 167; and human rights, 15, 97-98, 101, 104, 113, 152-54, 156; and women, 157, 159-60, 166-68
Nordic states, 14
North Atlantic Treaty Organization (NATO), xvii, 11, 14-15; 91-96, 111-12, 114, 179, 184, 198-99, 202, 205; Implementation Force in Bosnia (IFOR), 96, 184-85
North Korea, 7, 23, 207
North-South relations, xvi, 15
Norway, 144
Nuclear Non-Proliferation Treaty (NPT), 121, 129
Nuclear weapons, 119-21, 126-27, 134-35

Oakley, Robert, 74-75
Operation Desert Shield/Storm, 6, 12, 67, 85, 175
Operation Provide Comfort, 6, 70, 119
Operation Restore Hope, xv, 6, 69, 71-73, 77
Operation Turquoise, 105
Organization for Security and Cooperation in Europe (OSCE), 157
Organization of American States (OAS), 40, 48-50; International Civilian Mission to Haiti (MICIVIH), 50, 51, 53-54
Organization of African Unity (OAU), 68, 108, 187-88
Owen, Lord David, 91-93

ozone depletion, 144, 148

Pakistan, 68, 75, 79n
Palestine, 131
Palestinians, 2
peace building, xv, 5, 9, 11-13, 34-35, 55, 65
peace enforcement, 1, 5, 9-10, 12-14, 16-17, 28, 59, 74-77, 103-5, 111, 117, 173, 177, 180, 184, 195-99, 203
peacekeeping, xv-xvi, 4-5, 9-14, 17, 19, 20, 22, 59, 94, 96, 102, 110, 117, 173-74, 182-83, 195-96, 198-99; fatigue, 107; funding of, 4-5, 13, 22, 76, 99, 176-77, 182, 202-204; forces, 10, 22-25, 31-32, 35, 50, 55, 60, 76, 87-90, 93, 99-100, 102-103, 180, 185, 198; multi-dimensional operations, xvi, 5, 13, 28, 55, 142, 198; wider, 94, 114, 198
peacemaking, xvi, 3-4, 8-12, 14, 28, 30, 40, 56, 65, 68, 74, 76, 173-74, 177, 184, 196-97, 202
People's Republic of China. See China
Pérez de Cuéllar, Javier, 4, 7, 14, 22, 40-41, 118, 176, 192n
Pezullo, Lawrence, 50-53
Popular Movement for the Liberation of Angola (MPLA), 60-62, 64, 66
Powell, Colin, 53, 70-71
Presidential Decision Directive 25, 13, 104
preventive deployment, 6, 9, 12, 17, 86, 113, 198

Ranariddh, Prince, 23, 26-27

rapid reaction force, 10, 14, 95, 113, 198-200

Reagan administration, 3, 17, 39, 175-76, 181

regime, xvi-xvii, 15-16, 141, 171; environmental, 141-42, 196, 206; gender equality, 170-71, 201; human rights, 142, 170-71, 196, 201; peace and security, 6, 196-209

regional organizations, 9, 11, 14-15, 90, 114, 184, 187, 197, 199-200, 205

Rio Conference on the Environment and Development, xvi, 143-47, 151, 162, 170

Rio Declaration on the Environment and Development, 146-47, 158

Robinson, Mary, 151, 155

Romania, 158

Rose, Sir Michael, 94

Russia, 6,9, 89-90, 136-37, 184, 186, 192, 198-99, 205

Rwanda, xvi-xvii, 1, 11, 13-14, 60, 76, 78, 81-82, 97-114, 155-57, 168, 172n, 173, 180, 184, 188, 191

Rwandan Patriotic Front (RPF), 8, 97-103, 105-7, 108-9, 112, 116n

Rwandan Patriotic Army (RPA), 109

safe havens, 87, 90, 94-95, 105, 114

Sahnoun, Mohamed, 12, 68-69, 74, 77

Salim, Salim Ahmed, 175

sanctions, 6, 12, 24, 50-53, 66, 91, 94, 105, 108, 114, 118-19, 122, 127-28, 132-33, 135-38, 199, 204-5

Sanderson, John, 25

Sarajevo, 89-96

Saudi Arabia, 90, 119, 124

Savimbi, Jonas, 60, 64, 66-67, 77

Secretariat (UN), xviii, 5, 9, 11, 19, 31, 90, 104, 124, 136, 141-42, 155-56, 165, 169, 183, 191, 196-97

Secretary-General (UN), xv-xvi, 1-16, 20, 22-23, 25-26, 31-35, 41-47, 62, 74, 77, 81, 87, 90-91, 101, 103, 110-11, 114, 122, 129, 131-32, 136, 142, 169, 173-75, 177-78, 180-82, 185-87, 189, 191, 196, 201, 203, 208; election of, 7, 174-75, 185, 189; and Security Council, 31, 33-34, 45; and United States, 69, 71-72, 203

Security Council, xv-xvi, 1-14, 19, 21, 24-25, 28, 31-34, 41-48, 51-56, 60-62, 64-66, 68, 70-71, 74-76, 85, 90-94, 99, 101-5, 107-8, 110-14, 117-19, 121-28, 130, 132-34, 136-39, 173, 175-80, 182, 187, 189, 191, 192, 196-200, 202-5; summit meeting, 8-9, 184

Serbia, 7, 11, 13, 82, 84-85, 87, 89-91, 94, 96-97, 112, 114, 198, 205

Sierra Leone, 184, 198-99, 205, 207

Sihanouk, Prince Norodom, 21, 23, 26-27

Siad Barre, Mohamed, 8, 67-68

Slovenia, 82-84, 86-89

Somalia, xv-xvi, 1, 7-8, 13-14,
    28, 51, 60, 67-78, 81, 90-91,
    97, 100, 104, 107, 114, 128,
    173, 178-80, 182, 187-89,
    191, 195, 197, 199-200, 203,
    205, 209; civil war in, 76;
    famine in, 67-69, 72, 74, 76;
    "Mission Creep in, 74; peace
    process, 67-68, 75; warlords
    and, 67-69, 71, 74, 76-77
South, xvi, 2-3, 5, 9-11, 15-16,
    141-42, 144-45, 147, 152-54,
    158, 163, 174-75
South Africa, 2-3, 20, 28-29, 35,
    61, 110-11, 175, 195
Southern Africa, 192n
Southern African Development
    Coordination Conference
    (SADCC), 29
sovereignty, xvii, 9-10, 20, 27,
    30, 49-50, 56, 93, 96, 109-
    10, 117, 123, 133, 136, 154,
    164, 170, 181, 185, 190
Soviet Union, 2-7, 20-21, 28-29,
    39-41, 61, 69, 82-83, 90, 175
specialized agencies (UN), 35,
    68, 72, 163, 175
states, xv-xvii, 1-4, 7-11, 14-17,
    20-21, 29, 48-49, 64-65, 69,
    81-82, 89, 108, 113-14, 118,
    136, 144-47, 151-54, 158,
    162-63, 167-68, 173, 175,
    177-79, 187-90, 196, 199,
    202, 206; UN member, 11,
    13, 112, 117-18,136, 144-46,
    151-54, 163, 167-68, 180,
    191
Stockholm Conference (1972),
    143-44, 158
Strong, Maurice, 145, 148
structural adjustment, 164

sustainable development. *See*
    development, sustainable

Tajikistan, 20
Tanzania, 98-99, 104, 106, 108,
    110, 112
Third World. *See* South.
Tito, Josip Broz, 82
trade, 149-50
transnational corporations
    (TNCs), 149
Tutsi, 97-98, 100-10, 112

Uganda, 97-99, 106, 109-10
Union for the Total
    Independence of Angola
    (UNITA), 60-61, 64-67, 77,
    110
United Kingdom, 14, 30, 87, 90,
    92, 95 124, 128-29, 132,
    136-38, 146, 161, 179, 180,
    184, 192n, 199, 205
United Nations, xv-xvii, 1-17,
    19-22, 24-25, 27-28, 30-31,
    34-35, 39-44, 47-51, 55-56,
    59-64, 66-72, 75-77, 81-85,
    87-92, 94-107, 113-14, 117,
    122, 128, 133, 135-36, 138-
    39, 141-44, 146, 148, 150-
    53, 156-58, 162-65, 169-71,
    173-86, 188-92, 195-99,
    200-204; budget, 4-5, 22, 99,
    174-77, 182, 200-201;
    Charter, 10-11, 71, 90-91,
    103, 111, 154, 196, 183, 202;
    and election monitoring, 30,
    34, 62; funding of, 174-76,
    182-83, 185-86; reform of,
    177, 181, 185, 201-202;
    system, 155, 161-65, 168-70,
    200-201

UN Advance Mission in Cambodia (UNAMIC), 21

UN Assistance Mission for Rwanda (UNAMIR), 76, 99-103, 105-7, 113, 180, 198

UN Children's Fund (UNICEF), 127

UN Commission on Human Rights (UNCHR). *See* Commission on Human Rights (UN)

UN Conference on the Environment and Development (UNCED). *See* Rio Conference.

UN Conference on Trade and Development, 15

UN Decade for the Advancement of Women, 165

UN Development Programme (UNDP), 113, 127, 148, 164

UN Educational, Scientific and Cultural Organization (UNESCO), 5

UN Environment Programme (UNEP), 144-45, 148

UN Fund for Population Activities (UNFPA), 158, 161, 163

UN High Commission for Refugees (UNHCR), 9, 34, 105-6, 108-9, 113, 127

UN Iraq-Kuwait Observer Mission (UNIKOM), 119, 128-29, 132, 135

UN Mission in Haiti (UNMIH), 51-55

UN Observer Group in Central America (ONUCA), 40

UN Observer Mission in Angola (MONUA), 66

UN Observer Mission in South Africa (UNOMSA), 20

UN Observer Mission in El Salvador (ONUSAL), 40-47

UN Operation in Somalia (UNOSOM I), 12, 59, 68, 71

UN Operation in Somalia (UNOSOM II), 17, 72-78, 197

UN Organization Mission in the Democratic Republic of the Congo (MONUC), 205

UN Peacekeeping Mission, Mozambique (ONUMOZ), 28-36, 99

UN Protection Force in the former Yugoslavia (UNPROFOR), 13, 15, 87, 91-92, 94-96, 113, 184-85, 198

UN Special Commission for the Disarmament of Iraq (UNSCOM), 120-38, 204; Al Muthanna destruction facility of, 123, 125, 127

UN Support Mission in Haiti (UNSMIH), 55

UN Transitional Assistance Authority in Cambodia (UNTAC), 20, 22-28, 31, 35

UN Transitional Assistance Group (UNTAG), 5, 19

UN Verification Mission in Angola I (UNAVEM I), 61-62

UN Verification Mission in Angola II (UNAVEM II), 31, 59-60, 62-64, 67, 77

UN Verification Mission in Angola III (UNAVEM III), 65-67, 77

United States, xv-xvii, 1-8, 12-
15, 17, 21, 29, 35, 39, 61, 67,
85, 117, 121, 124, 128-29,
132, 136-39, 173-79, 180-92,
195-204, 206-8; and Bosnia-
Herzegovina, 82, 89-90, 92-
97, 113-14; foreign policy,
76; and Gulf War, 118-20;
and Haiti, 49-53; leadership
role of, 6, 74;and Rwanda,
99, 104-5, 107, 110, 113-14,
180; and Somalia, 67, 69-74;
and UN debt, 191, 202, 207-
8; UN funding share, 191,
208; and Yugoslavia, 184
Unified Task Force on Somalia
(UNITAF), 71-72, 74, 177
Universal Declaration of Human
Rights, 152
U Thant, 175, 203

Vance, Cyrus, 87, 92-93, 96
Vatican, 141, 157, 167
Vienna Conference on Human
Rights (1993), 149, 151-59,
162, 166, 170
Vietnam, 20-21
Voluntary Fund for the UN
Decade for Women
(UNIFEM), 165-66, 169

Waldheim, Kurt, 175, 203
weapons of mass destruction,
xvii, 3, 117-20, 133-34, 138-
39,

West, 3, 21, 28-29, 61, 69, 143,
151-54, 157, 196
West Africa, 184
West European Union (WEU),
83
women, XVIII, 16, 91, 141, 147,
157-60, 162-70, 198;
movements, 142, 162, 165-
66; NGOs, 153, 166; rights
of, 3, 15, 142, 151, 153, 155,
157, 159-60, 165-68, 170,
172n, 190, 195, 201, 206,
209; violence against, 151,
155, 166
World Bank, 113, 162
World Conference on Human
Rights. *See* Vienna
Conference on Human
Rights,
World Food Programme (WFP),
68
World Health Organization
(WHO), 163
World Trade Organization
(WTO), 150, 170
World War II, xv, 22, 81, 111,
117

Yugoslavia. *See* Federal
Republic of Yugoslavia.

Zambia, 31, 105
Zaire, 8, 105-6, 108-10, 172n
Zimbabwe, 29, 31, 79n, 105

About the Author

Stephen F. Burgess is an assistant professor of International Security, US Air War College. Previously, he has been a faculty member at the University of Zambia, Vanderbilt University, and Hofstra University. He completed his Ph.D. at Michigan State University, was chosen as a Fulbright-Hays Dissertation Research Abroad fellow, and was a Research Associate at the University of Zimbabwe. In 1997, his book, *Smallholders and Political Voice in Zimbabwe,* was published by the University Press of America. Dr. Burgess has published several journal articles, including "African Security in the Twenty-First Century: The Challenges of Indigenization and Multilateralism," *African Studies Review* (September 1998). He has published several book chapters, including "Regional Integration Among Unequal States: The European Union and the Southern African Development Community Compared," in *Regions and Development: Politics, Security and Economics,* edited by Sheila Page and published by Frank Cass for the Overseas Development Institute in 2000. Dr. Burgess is an Associate of the US Air Force Counterproliferation Center (CPC), and, with Helen Purkitt, he has written a monograph, *The Rollback of the South African Chemical and Biological Warfare Program* for the CPC and the Institute of National Security Studies, US Air Force Academy.